HISTORY OF EDUCATION

HISTORY OF EDUCATION

By

P. Annie Amala
M.A. (Litt), M.Ed.
Principal
S.V. College of Education
Payakaraopet
Visakhapatnam Distt., (A.P.)

P. Anupama
M.A., M.L.I.Sc., M.Ed.
Principal
Minerva College of Education
Prathipadu
East Godavari Distt., (A.P.)

General Editor
Dr. Digumarti Bhaskara Rao
M.Sc., M.A., M.A., M.Ed., Ph.D.
Reader & Research Director
R.V.R. College of Education
Guntur–522 006 (A.P.)
&
Member, Board of Studies in Education
Acharya Nagarjuna University
Nagarjuna Nagar–522 510

D P H

DISCOVERY PUBLISHING HOUSE
NEW DELHI-110002

First Published - 2004

Reprinted - 2017

ISBN: 978-81-7141-860-2

History of Education

Published by:

DISCOVERY PUBLISHING HOUSE PVT. LTD.
4383/4B, Ansari Road, Darya Ganj
New Delhi-110 002 (India)
Phone: +91-11-23279245, 43596064-65
Fax: +91-11-23253475
E-mail: discoverypublishinghouse@gmail.com
sales@discoverypublishinggroup.com
web: www.discoverypublishinggroup.com

Printed at:
Infinity Imaging Systems
Delhi

CONTENTS

PREFACE

In India, contrary to many other nations, we have not borrowed education from West. Instead, we have our own traditions and a glorious history in this area, Since, Vedic times, India has been bestowed upon with the blessings of knowledge. In fact, we had a perfect education system in Vedic age and Buddhist period and after the renaissance of the Brahmanism this system was further polished and enriched by Arabs, Turks and Mughals, who arrived in this land as conquerors but settled here for ever. Later, came the British who reformed the traditional system and founded a modern Education System in India. Following independence, the Government of India rectified the faults and promoted the system to new heights. As a result, the existing Education System in India is perfect and can match any system in the developed world.

This work covers the whole Education System in the historical perspective, in order to enlighten the reader on the long journey and various phases, the carvan of education in India has passed through.

Hopefully, this book would suffice the need and be acknowledged by all concerned.

—Author

1

INTRODUCTION

Today, we are independent. But, despite political independence, have we become really independent? And, if we have not, then why? The reason for this is that our educational system has not broken from tradition, its basis is the system employed in the time of our slavery. Besides, we have also had to face numerous problems in the educational sphere. In this period of crumbling belief and faith, not only our country but the entire world has lost all sense of direction. As a result, the older generation wants to tie down the rising generation, breaking completely from tradition, has become filled with anger, and is now bent upon revolution. We are finding it difficult to discover the path of synthesis and harmony. at least apparently, there is no possibility of arriving at a compromise.

Problems of the Objectives of Education. If our education from 1947 till the present is categorised as the aimless education of the aimless, it would be no exaggeration. The reason for this is quite explicit - we do not have before us a proper plan or sketch for building our nation. A nation does not undergo development by the building of dams and construction of factories and mills, but through the process and medium of education. There is a famous Chinese proverb, which says, "If you plan for a year, plant grain; if you plan for ten years, plant trees, if you plan for a hundred years, plant men:" And in our case, the kind of nation that will be built or created is not evident even from the declaration on the national plan for education.

At present, the many problems that are afflicting education have one sole cause at their root which is aimlessness. According to Dr. Radhakrishnan, the objective of education is the discovery, and the development through proper training, of an individual's inborn qualities. Universities should fulfill these two prime duties towards their students.

The significant fact before our country today is that is needs of self-reliance in foodgrains, economic development and more employment, social and national unification, and political development can be fulfilled only through the training of students in character, in profession and practice, and development of literacy, artistic and cultural interests. And these, in reality, are the objectives of education.

Problem of Primary and Compulsory Education. The major problem confronting Indian education is the problem of compulsory primary education because the level of literacy has been very low. This shows that primary education has not expanded to the desired extent. Besides, many political, social, religious, economic and geographical factors are creating obstacles in the path of expanding primary education. This problem has been made even more complex by such contributory factors as the curriculum of primary education, problem of school, wastage and stagnation, and. many administrative difficulties.

The important aspect of the problem in primary education is the failure to fulfil the promise of the Constitution, according to which it is the duty of the state to provide for the education of all children upto the age of 14; this is stated in Article 45 of the

Constitution. States have remained indifferent towards the fulfilment of this promise. In the third Five Year Plan, efforts in this direction were made, but in the fourth, this ideal was assumed to be the cause of educated unemployment. In the fifth plan, it was clearly assumed that the objective of compulsory and universal education could not be fulfilled. It was assumed that only 75 per cent of the children could be provided education.

Problem of Secondary Education. Secondary education is the backbone of the country's development, and it is unfortunate that there is no uniformity at this level in our country. The curriculum is spread over 12 years in some states, over 11 years in others and over 10 in yet others. Besides, problems relating to curricula, administration, training of teachers, financial aid, etc., have combined to create obstacles. Among its numerous problems are those of the objectives of secondary education, its limits, form, curriculum, guidance, administration, substitution, finance, evaluation and examination, and the problem of a proper life for students.

Despite this, there has been considerable progress in secondary education. Between 1951 and 1974, the enrolment went up six times in the case of boys and 13 times for that of girls, though this is an average for the different rates of growth achieved in various states. With reference to the total population, admission of girls at the primary stages has decreased. Besides, secondary schools have also been afflicted with problems relating to resources, teachers and facilities. The central problem at this level is that of qualitative growth, though there is also the problem of education lacking a vocational bias.

Higher Education. Higher education, too, has been facing numerous problems in our country. In the main, it has failed to help students to earn their livelihood, and it has continued to expand despite the absence of employment. Its failure in this regard is the result of many factors. University education is lacking in direction because of political pressures, the sovereignty of universities themselves, the quality of student life, lack of finance and absence of clearly defined objectives. The country lacks any concrete plan for taking advantage of higher eduation, and because of this many contradications have crept in. Higher education is suffering from the problems inevitably linked with expansion. The enrolment in arts, commerce and science has risen from 3.2 million in 1968-69 to 3.5 million in 1974. Besides, since most institutions of higher education are located in cities, its benefit goes mainly to students living in urban areas: In addition, there is need for intellectual development, new curricula for the universities, etc.

Problem of Technical Education. India undoubtf.dly needs technical education for its rapid. development, because, a variety of highly skilled technicians are required for exploring the country's considerable natural resources. But, education in this sphere has suffered mainly from a lack of proper planning. As a consequence, while many individuals received training in one branch of technology, there was a complete absence of trained personnel in other branches. This has led to unemployment. Even today, our technical education is handicapped by lack of proper planning, absence of text-books, absence of teachers, lack of laboratories and other facilities. Its problems can be rooted out in only one way- linking it with employment. It is necessary to plan, for technical education in the light of manpower needs.

Problem of Special Education. The need for social education and adult education is indicative of the illiteracy prevailing in our country, because in proportion to the population, the percentage of literate individuals is very small. Besides, the very concept of social education has always lacked clarity. In this sphere, the main problem lies in not finding suitably devoted workers. Besides the administrative structure has also succeeded in covering this education with a veil of intellectuality, with the result that, instead of being something intimately concerned with the masses, it has become only a subject for intellectual discussion.

This is despite the fact that, in the fifth plan, social education has been linked with continuous education. Because of this, social education is being expanded through such schemes as private candidature in examinations and correspondence education institutions. However, the problem of literacy is at the same level as in 1974. In the Sixth Plan, it has been given national importance.

Problem of Teachers. The problem of teachers also afflicts Indian education. It is the teacher who is the link between education and the student. Teachers have become even more dissatisfied, since the new scales of pay favoured by the Kothari Commission were not implemented. The responsibility for this dissatisfaction rests securely with our popular government which has continued to neglect the builders of the nation in its own selfish interests. Recognising the importance of teachers, the Kothari Commission has said that a concrete programme for the professional training of teacher is essential for bringing about qualitative progress. The money spent upon teacher training can bring forth the maximum dividends, since the money spent is less but its return in the form of a qualitative improvement in the education of lakhs of individuals is enormous. The factors which influence the improvement of education and its contribution to national development are- the qualities, ability and character of the teachers. These are undoubtedly of the greatest importance. Nothing is more important than inducting good teachers into this profession. There should be professional training and the availability of satisfactory working conditions, which can influence them profoundly. The investment in the education of teachers can bring manifold advantages because the financial investment is less, but the advantages gained in the context of general education are comparatively much more.

Student Unrest. The new problem that has arisen because of lack of foresight in education is given the name of student dissatisfaction or student unrest. The violence and destruction indulged in by our students in the entire country over the last 15 years has proved beyond doubt that there is some serious fault in our educational structure. Though the phenomenon emerged somewhat late after independence, the entire world has seen with open eyes the anger of the younger generation and the repressive attitude of the older generation. The students who were used before independence to wave the national flag and make clamorous demands for the country's freedom came to raise the flag against the same leaders who had once inspired them. This came about because of lack of direction. This has come to be called student indiscipline. When its causes were analysed, it was discovered that the students trained by crushed and dissatisfied teachers can never turn to constructive activity. Consequently, the discontentment of teachers also came to the fore in the form of tne teacher's movement. This led to the opening of a new chapter, the arrest of teachers by their own students. Now, the teacher has been compelled to give up the selflessness of Dronacharya and to engage in a struggle for survival. This struggle still continues. From this, it is evident that the dissatisfaction of the students can be eradicated only when the structure of education is completely reshaped.

Administration and Planning. The educational system today is suffering from the problems inherent in a dual administration. The administration imposed by the Centre and the States is obstructing education at the local and individual levels. This system of providing grants is also defective. Besides, officials concerned with administration and inspection are ignorant of th real problems of schools, teachers and students. Hence, their decisions fail to benefit the educational system. If education is to be utilized for national development, there is great need for able and efficient administration and suitable educational planning. Hence, there is an urgent need for a suitable administrative and planning mechanism.

Guidance and Counselling. Education aims at the complete development of the individual. Today, education is based on psychology, and efforts are made to adjust students at a mass level with society, despite their individual differences. In India, the advantages of guidance and counselling services is available only to the privileged and so those lacking in opportunities remain in the condition of deprivation.

Problem of Finance. Indian education has been singularly unfortunate in that, whenever a crisis occurred, the budget of every other department remained unchanged while that of education suffered major reductions. Besides, only 2.3 per cent of the national income is usually spent on it. Other countries spend as much as 7 per cent of the national income on education. In the fifth plan, 2.3 per cent of the national income was kept apart for education, although it was planned to be increased to 4.7 per cent by 1981. The present situation is such that even if more resources are allocated for education but remain linked to traditional techniques, which have been the cause of collosal wastages, even the basic needs of educational reform will not be fulfilled for this, the present stagnation must be brought to an end.

Problem of Moral and Spiritual Values. It is becoming increasingly clear that the main cause of the decline in national character is the absence of growth and development in moral and spiritual values. The Education Commission has paid particular attention to this problem.

Problem of Inequality. The glaring fact before us today is that educational opportunities are being exploited mainly by the privileged, and that is why many brilliant individuals in society fail to develop their capacities, and the nation is deprived of their potential. Almost 20 crore individuals are living far below the ideal level of existence in our country. For children belonging to this class, equality in the opportunities for education are inconceivable as long as special provisions are not made for them. This problem is being tackled to some extent through the policy of reservations, but it is also taking the nation towards a crisis. But, if such reservations are based on income, the result will be the eradication of a caste-based communalism, and also provide equal opportunities to children in the educational sphere.

Problem of Educational Structure. The educational structure is not uniform throughout the country; it is different in different states, and, as a result, we do not find mobility in the educational system. If the educational structure is made uniform, it will be possible to achieve a growth in social unity.

The Kothari Commission reflected on the problems of education, considering every aspect and form of education, with the exception of medical sciences. The Commission has made an effort to come to terms with all kinds of problems inherent in the educational world. However, it was found that the Commission's statement of purpose was riddled by inconsistencies. What happened was that instead of solving existing problems, the Commission became the cause of numerous other problems. It gradually became clear that the crossroads at which education now found itself was the age old crossroads, with which we have been familiar since antiquity.

Qualitative Growth in Education. One important basis of qualitative improvement in education is the pay given to teachers. The pay scales considered adequate by the Commission failed to attract the teachers. This is not surprising, in view of the rising price index. In fact, the pay scales are shameful. Connected with this problem is the obstinacy of State governments, of which the government of Uttar Pradesh has provided an excellent example, Institutions are being compelled to face numerous intractable problems in implementing the new scales of pay. The red-tapism of the Education Department must be held responsible for creating many problems.

The teachers movements give an inkling of the revolution which is brewing. Glancing at this state of affairs, the erstwhile Minister of Education, Dr. V.K.R.V Rao was compelled to observe that he had often become aware of the neglect of Indian teachers, which had been going on for decades. This neglect took two forms—denial of an adequate livelihood, denial of any suitable opportunities for his own professional development. Though some steps had been taken in this direction after independence, they were woefully inadequate. On the other hand, the teacher had adopted the method of revolution. In addition, there was a gradual assimilation of external vested interests in this movement, and consequently, the bright and respected image of the teacher in society was undergoing distortion. Dr. Rao did not deny the fact that a revolution was, in fact, necessary. In certain circumstances, revolutions become inevitable, but when they are organised by teachers, they should be in consonance with dignity of teachers so that the feelings of students, guardians and society towards the teachers should not be poisoned, and the teachers' respected image should not be destroyed.

On the other hand, the government had its own limitations. But, Dr. Rao admitted that it was the duty of administrators, politicians and elected representatives not to close their eyes towards the problems of teachers. If the government could not meet the demands of teachers because of limitations of resources, it could at least listen sympathetically to the teachers and explain to the teachers the reality of the situation. For certain unavoidable needs, available resources could be improved, while for others, steps could be taken to find a solution in the near future.

Dr. Rao's ideas are very far from reality, though he is perfectly aware of reality because of his close contact with education in the past. He is also aware of the problems of education. But the atmosphere of ministership surrounding him compels him to a kind of duplicity. This is nothing new in his case. Every teacher who became a minister soon moulded himself to the atmosphere surrounding ministers. The language of administration is marked by 'should', not by 'this is so'. In brief, what this means is that the problem cannot be solved as long as the distinction between professions and deeds continues. In fact, the commission has left no stone unturned in giving birth to class differences. The pay scales applicable to teachers, from the primary to the university level, give not even a slight indication of the principle of 'equal pay for equal ability.'

Problem of Language. The problem of language has also added to the problem of education. The Kothari Commission is also responsible for highlighting and intensifying this problem, because it raised a storm of controversy over this question. It was perhaps not aware of the truth that Hindi is the language of the nation, and that it was being prevented from taking its rightful place by political machinations and manipulations. Dr. Ramdhari Singh Dinkar has explicated the three-language formula in the following terms: We may suppose that a student of Bengal learns Bengali in (a) and English in (b). This allows him the freedom to fulfil the requirement of (c) by studying either French or Marathi. In the same way, if a student of Bihar studies Hindi in (a) and English in (b), he may learn Urdu or Russian to fulfil the requirement of (c).

This elaboration is based on the Commission's following formula.

(a) Mother tongue

(b) The state language of the Union or any parallel state language

(c) any new Indian or European language different from those under (a) and (b).

Social and National Unity. The Commission laid stress on the generation of national and social unity, but without clarifying how this objective was to be achieved. Besides, the Commission also failed to elaborate the meaning of Indian democracy. Dr. Sampurnanand has commented that no one dares argue that the objective of education in Soviet Russia, the U.S.A., England and

France is not the comprehensive development of the country's citizens but the values which are declared to be the objective of western democratic countries are different from the values enumerated by the proponents of the Soviet Russian ideology. What is called dictatorship or tyranny by one country is called democracy by another. The term 'democracy' is one which should be clearly defined because when national and social unity reaches the hands of a dictator like Hitler, it becomes a most potent vehicle of evil.

Work Experience vs Basic Education. The Commission has sought to introduce practical work experience at every level of education and to make education dynamic and productive. Despite the passage of considerable time since the publication of the Commission's report, no State has summoned up the courage to implement its curriculum. They see it as the productive system of Basic Education. On the contrary, the truth is that the scheme of practical work experience is the death knell of basic education. Our state governments try to imitate others or to delay action-whenever it is a question of accepting any responsibility concerning education. Dr. V.K.R.V Rao is of the view that education should be brought into close relationship with life and production. Nevertheless, before initiating this programme, the pre-existing economic situation should be observed carefully. Only then can there be any hope of success. He favours emphasis upon those schemes which do not involve economic problems, for instance, students should be given holidays during the days when they can work on their farms at home, or cooperate with their parents in other ways. By such means, education can be brought into ever closer contact with life, and it will be able to make progress as an effective instrument of society.

Curriculum and Teacher-training. Dr. Rao has pointed out that the view that teachers nowadays have no interest in their work was gaining currency in society. He feels this to be completely unfounded. He suggests that the same remark applies with equal truth to doctors, administrators, politicians and workers. It is a pervasive fact, a national disease. Then how can teachers remain free from its taint? For this, we need dedication, self-confidence, intimacy, and the creation of human values.

In order to increase the teacher's desire for better scholarship and greater ability, there should be some institutions whose membership should evolve great honour upon its possessor. The rules pertaining to such institutions should be based upon the objectives and activities in the educational sphere favoured by the people as a whole. Dr. Rao experesses the feeling that the honour bestowed by institutions of such a nation will be more inspiring and dignified than the awards distributed by the administrative machinery.

There is frequent mention of the decline in quality and standards in education. Qualitative, improvement presupposes the following three things- (1) Adequate material and physical resources should be available in schools, i.e., such things as libraries, buildings, laboratories, apparatus, materials, etc. (2) Capable teachers should be recruited and there should be provisions for training during employment or period of service, and (3) there should be an environment suitable to studying, and teaching in every institution. Of the three, the last factor is the most important, and it becomes possible only when teachers devote themselves dedicatedly to the task of teaching. Caution is also needed to ensure that the teachers' work is not unduly interfered with by persons not connected with education, the administration or the government. Achieving this is not as simple as it may appear. For this, it is necessary to generate the right awakening in society, it is not something which can be achieved by preparing a curriculum or providing the right text-books. Instead, it will be necessary to organise conferences and meetings at state levels for the organisers and administrators of schools in rural areas so that they are aware of their true responsibilities, and are able to manage schools in the best possible way.

From the viewpoint of education, our country is undoubtedly lagging far behind other countries. It has also faced a number of other complex problems. A solution to these problems was offered in the form of the Kothari Commission. Despite this, she path seems completely unchanged. Though government statistics give some satisfaction, the fact remains that education is in the doldrums. One must ask: why does such a state of affairs exist? The reason lies in the misunderstandings harboured by the government as well as the people as a whole, in the wrong techniques adopted, and in the fact that their basis is private self-interest. The Kothari Commission made a telling point in its observation that education must be given the form of a complete process; teachers must be given the opportunities to maintain their existence; national development should be given the greatest attention to maintain the nation's very existence. It recommended that education in agriculture, industry and other professions should be made a part of the educational structure. It advised that the principle of an education co-extensive with life should be adopted.

Need for an Educational Plan. The great educational plan for the next twenty years is unique. Its characteristic principle is that the development of the nation comprehends the development of the individual and the development of the individual contributes to the development of the nation. Because of this, the plan exhibits a touching faith in antiquity while at the same time, it gives expresssion to an attachment, faith and love for the future based on reason, not superstition.

The Question of Existence. On considering the question of existence, we are faced with certain old convictions which have assumed the form of questions. The Kothari Commission has sought an answer to the problem posed by the late Jawaharlal Nehru - Can we associate scientific and technological progress with the progress of the mind and the progress of the soul? We can never be untrue to science because it puts before us the fundamental truths and facts of life. In spite of this, can we not be assured and confident about the facts which India has additionally honoured and observed? We have to take firm steps toward industrial progress, while remembering that all material thing turn to dust and ashes in the absence of charity, patience and wisdom. (Introductory page of Education Commission, para 22, 1.86).

What is to be Done. We must remember that the aim of education is to build the nation. While many factors influence nation building, in the final analysis, this objective can be achieved only through (1) self-reliance in foodgrains (2) economic development (3) political development (4) social and national unity (S) development of human resources (6) national awakening (7) growth of democratic values. This objective is possible of attainment only through a revolutionary change in education.

Suggestions by the Kothari Commission. On the subject of the complete report of the Kothari Commission and the problems it gave rise to, it can be said that it is a very significant educational plan. Society has to resort to modernisation in order to educate itself. It must make an attempt to bring into existence an educated class comprehending citizens belonging to every class, deeply imbued with the qualities characteristic of India, so that it can raise the educational standard of the average citizen. The present age with its lack of faith and sense of direction has brought aimlessness not only to our country but the whole world, and as a result the old generation wants to shackle the younger generation in its own dogmas, customs and traditions. On the other hand, the new generation is filled with the furious desire for a revolutionary change. It is becoming difficult to find the path of accommodation and adaptation.

1. Generation unrest and gap was observed obviously after independence. Students unrest now become a common regular phenomena having its roots in politics. Political leaders gave wrong direction to the youths under the names of political youth organisations.

2. Teachers were exploited by society of haves. They have followed the path of confrontation against the Government for their jobs, social, economic and cultural security and for the survival of their own-selves.

3. The problem of national language still remains unsolved. Though Hindi is declared as a link language of nation, yet it could not get its right place due to the reasons known to all.

4. There is nothing obvious between the masses and the administration. Multi-tier system of education is found in the country which is ultimately responsible for creating drama on the stage of nation.

Therefore the following points should be kept in mind while planning for the education

1. Development of national consciousness should be the important aim of education. For this we should be aware of : (i) our cultural heritage (ii) its revaluation and (iii) firm faith in future.

2. For the qualitative improvement of education due emphasis be given to teacher education. For this (i) right type of persons should be attracted towards teaching profession (ii) they must possess high character, spiritual and moral values (iii) and must have professional wealth.

Ours is a country known by the name of India; ours is the nationality-Indian; ours is the Constitution which has a common goal of achieving justice- social, economic and political; freedom of expression of thought, of development and availing opportunities, achievement of integration national, social and emotional; attaining the common bonds of fraternity and unity.

Needless to say that all these ideals and goals cannot be achieved until and unless we do not overhaul the entire curriculum, method of teaching, rather the entire system of education with our national objectives in view. It is a bare truth that uniformity at all standards of education to bring out a coordination in the prevailing system which is eventually a state subject is the dire need of the hour.

There is population -explosion and that has left a vacuum in providing the equalization of opportunities in the realm of education. The ratio between the teacher and the taught is inadequate. Dearth of foodgrains, economic development, lack of employment opportunities, wide gap between the privileged, domination of the narrow loyalties under the guise of ideology, religion, language, state, caste, creed, etc., are some of the hurdles which require immediate consideration with a concrete follow up programme if national reconstruction is to be made with sincere efforts so that we may not only be able to solve the gigantic problems our country is facing at present but also raise the status of Bharat.

Education is a powerful tool for social change. Society goes on under a continuous process of change. Emerson was right when he asserted that it is not wealth or high pillars which make a man. Education can build a nation and can lead the entire nation on the path of progress. It is only through education that we can inculcate the feeling of self-sacrifice, patriotism, critical and analytical thinking, character building etc., which may ultimately transform an individual and society as a whole. For that we will have to evolve a national policy on education. History gives an evidence that it is only the educated elite which has brought a change in the world. Education trains the mind and leads an individual towards critical thinking and analogical outlook.

Education is not something which may be discussed in an isolated water-tight compartment; it requires aims, contents, teaching points, students, teacher, time table, vocational efficiency. Keeping in view the needs of society and the national objectives and exploitation of the manpower to raise the status of the country in the international sphere. The national development has its base in economic progress and productivity. If we want to bring out a social change we will have to see the modernization without sacrificing the gems of our rich cultural heritage

Only a handful of elite dominate all walks of life. This control is due to the ignorance of the people. The privileged always rule over unprivileged and the former have been exploiting them like any thing. This tendency has been widening the gap between haves and have-nots. The social unrest caused through this can only be removed if the following programmes are implemented.

— Science as a basic component of education and culture.

— Work experience as an integral part of general education, especially at the secondary school level to meet the needs of industry, agriculture and trade, and improvement of scientific and technological education and research at the university stage with special emphasis on agriculture and allied sciences.

As for the question of the adoption of science along with culture, India has been following the same from times immemorial. It is only ignorance which is giving impetus to the technology based on experience rather than science. Work experience is a system which provides opportunities for self-employment and prepares a man for the job in his future and present. That is why the Kothari Commission visualised for vocationalization of secondary education.

There is a lot of diversity in our country. Language, provincialism, factionalism, regionalism, religion have been disturbing the nation's peace and order. National integration can only be achieved through cultural and moral integration. This needs stability in character. For this the following programme should be implemented.

— Introducing a common school system of public education.

— Making social and national service as an integral part of education at all stages.

— Developing all modern Indian languages and taking necessary steps to enrich Hindi as quickly as possible so that it is able to function effectively as the official language of the Union, and

— Promoting national consciousness.

We can breath in a traditional society but we cannot live the life in it in the sense of the term. In the fast running world, there is always struggle for existence. We can exist only when we go ahead by maintaining the progress of science and technology. "Indian society of today is heir to a great culture. Unfortunately, however, it is not an adequately educated society and unless it becomes one, it will not be able to modernize itself and to respond appropriately to new challenges of national reconstruction or take its rightful place in the comity of nations," the National Commission says. For achievement of six major universities has been recommended.

Modernization does not mean that the social, moral and spiritual values be neglected and not given due importance. It is the age of conflict of culture, materialism and ethical values. It is the conflict between discerning and non-discerning, between values, patterns and concepts and man! He is missing his path.

Now education should be accepted as a powerful means of social revolution. There should be radical changes in education. We need quality but along with action. There should be close coordination of plan and execution. We have to go, rather rush with the world in this race. It is a challenge, but who will accept it, you, he or the legislative members, students, teachers, guardians, government, public, who? Who will decide the fate?

Napoleon once told his soldiers to have faith in God, but also to keep their powder dry, because even God could not make we-gun-powder usable. This remark seems to apply appropriately to the social forces bringing about rapid changes in today's volatile society. Education today is equivalent to Napoleon's powder and politics to God. Our powder-that is, education- has become so wet that it cannot be modified and improved in accord with circumstances. And, though politics is God, it cannot dry this wet powder. It is because of this wetness that the student and the teacher of today are completely helpless in providing society with the necessary sense of direction. The corrupt politics and society of today have completely altered the values of life. Human values now have different, unheard of definitions. National values have been swallowed by selfishness.

The life of every nation receives its truest sustenance from its system of education. A living educational system is the foundation of a life full of vivacity and energy, and it is the educational system which gives impetus to society and the life of the nation. It creates, shapes and moulds the national character. The bases of educational policy are the purposes and aims of the nation, for the fulfilment of which the country's administrative system must be possessed of honesty, dynamism and efficiency. These factors advance a nation's interests and take it towards its objectives through the medium of the educational system, and make it prosperous and contented. The individual and the nation are complementary units. In the event of any imbalance or disharmony between the two, both are destroyed. Adjustment with passing time, adaptation to a changing environment are bitter truths of life. A nation must not loose its sense of direction as time passes and circumstances change.

The history of education in India after independence establishes clearly that changing times have brought aimlessness, loss of a sense of direction. In this period of uncertainty, the life of our country is standing at the crossroads, immobile, lifeless, bewildered. It is seeking in vain for the right direction.

Our Constitution made education a subject to be dealt with by the States, not by the nation, a cruel mistake for which the new generation is paying. The acceptance of invisible responsibilities in the sphere of general and higher education was, for the Centre, no more than an escape, a flight from circumstances. Article 45 of the Constitution is a dead letter, a mere pronouncement. Even the question of achieving its implicit objective does not arise.

The Politics of Education. In theory, the basis of the politics of education is the Constitution, which we ourselves have framed and adopted, but it has completely neglected national character, and it was on the basis of this Constitution that our politicians played cruelly and willfully with the future of the nation. These politicians turned their entire energies to the physical or material development of the country. This led to cracks in dams, silence of generators producing electricity, immobilized wheels of the railways, roads leading to nowhere, and aeroplanes sitting idly on the ground. All this happened because the basis or content of education has been hollow. Our politicians lacked the foresight needed to prepare a blueprint for creating the foundation necessary for nation building.

The educational system and educational process in each state have differed so radically from those in other States that instead of encouraging national and emotional unity, it is disunity and alienation which have been promoted. Granting pensions to those who participated in the anti-Hindi movement in Tamil Nadu is an index of this national degeneration. Today, we have arrived at a stage in which citizens of one region face difficulties in working in or doing trade with other regions. Regional imbalances prove the view that making education a state subject was like subjecting the country to slow poisoning.

Political Alienation. The educational system and the social, political and economic circumstances, and the social and psychological diversity have all helped to evolve educational politics as the politics of alienation. And, today, because of this alienation, there is strong discontent in every individual's mind. Every individual is dissatisfied and anxious. It would have been far better if a single educational current had flowed through and enveloped the entire country. Such an education would have arroused social and national awareness. But narrow political interests ignored this vital national need. The consequences of such narrow-mindness are before us. When a troubled mind whispers the word of revolution into one's ears, one is advised to maintain harmony between enthusiasm and commonsense, but this policy does not apply to these politicians.

Today, education has come to be regarded, in the political field, as a device for catching votes. This has entangled the educational class in political alienation, leading to confusion. One must wonder why no attention is being paid to this. Each one of our political parties raises its voice in favour of farreaching changes in education. But these slogan-mongering parties are devoid of any national awareness, though they include members even of the party in power. In the recent election, students were given misleading and false assurances and the result was that these assurances themselves became a halter for the politicians.

Neglect of Teacher. In this field of educational politics, the present state of the teacher is not merely pitiable, it is worse. The one link that maintains the balance and liaison between bureaucrats, polycrats and students has been eliminated. Chancellors of universities do not think it necessary to take the advice of teachers when they are faced with student problems and student movements. It is the teachers who are asked to organise examinations, but directions are issued by the university administration, which drunk in the glory of its power over teachers, overlooks every important aspect.

The alienation pervading our universities and colleges has further intensified social differences, because of which harmony and balance have become impossible to maintain. Even such basic ideals as equal pay for equal work or equal pay for equal ability have been trampled underfoot. The Kothari Commission was right when it observed that, unfortunately, on the whole, our school system lacks any concrete traditions for the development of national unity and national consciousness. What is needed for developing national consciousness and cultural awareness and evaluation is an inspired devotion. This is completely lacking.

Impact of Active Politics. Now, the sole task of the teacher has degenerated into pointing out some important question and dictating the simplest possible answers to them, thus completing the courses of study. The teacher, today, is no better than an insignificant servant, who, on the one hand, must bow low before superiors, officials or suffer their anger, and on the other hand, suffer the indignities heaped upon him by his students. The general degeneration of social character is evident from numerous incidents every day. Our political parties have organised students unions into destructive forces. This is as true of one as of another student union, irrespective of whether they bear the name of Youth Congress, Vidyarthi Parishad, Yuvjan Sabha, Yuva Janta or any other name. All that students do is to wear the appropriate badge and organise political mass fights. A clear symbol of the crisis in education is the fact that central ministers and members of parliament take the deepest possible interests and give vent to their fiercest political loyalties in the elections to the students union of Delhi University.

Political statements also aggravate the crisis among students. In 1974, one newly elected minister of Uttar Pradesh went so far as to declare that students would be promoted without examinations. As a result, the entire order and timing of examinations has gone haywire. Examinations in most universities are postponed from March to May, and then again to August, when they are actually held. With the result, students suffer the loss of one full academic year.

The express demand of our time and our environment is that students should not be dragged into politics, that their creative energies should be employed to generate 'a national spirit. But, nothing concrete has been done in this direction. Our political leaders have yet to find the key to this problem.

It is a strange anomaly that, at the national political level, the education minister is not a minister of cabinet rank. One wonders why the chief executive authority in the educational sphere, though education is regarded as the foundation for nation building, is not provided with a suitable rank. This fact clearly suggests that our legislators are perpetrating a huge fraud upon the nation. State ministers of education are in an even worse position, since their voice echoes hollowly and ineffectively in the schools owned and managed by industralists and self-styled social workers. Managers of educational institutions reap rich harvests in a period in which the politics of education is riddled with corruption.

If we are to think of education in the context of a national awakening, it is necessary to change our present Constitution. As long as the articles of the present Constitution, relating to education,, stand unchanged, we cannot ever dream of a healthy educational system. Hence our objective should be-one nation, one Constitution and one educational system. In the last analysis, there should be no provision for private enterprise. Otherwise, we will continue to wander and roam, as we have been doing till the present.

The crises in education actually arose as soon as we got independence. In our ignorance, we thanked our fortune for the social structure we had inherited from our period of slavery to a foreign power. We were so deeply obliged for that we accepted it as an invariable part of our life. Before independence, we were staunch opponents of Macaulay's educational system. After independence, ironically enough, the makers of our nation and a few vested interests began regarding Macaulay as a messiah. They recklessly adhered to Macaulay's ideas, with the result that his educational system sowed the seeds of casteism and class conflict in our society and in our educational world. Education of a particular group led to the emergence of a class of bureaucrats and politicians, while on the other hand, a governing class was created in the name of education of the people. It was this class conflict that has led to the crisis in education.

The crisis in education has overwhelmed the whole world, because the rise in population brought forth increasing numbers of students. The opportunities of education did not keep pace with the rise in population. Despite this, the expenditure on education increased at a rapid pace. At the same time, education began to grow in, the form of a local industry or enterprise, and hence the crisis in education is the product of many factors.

Increase in Population. The population has risen rapidly all over the world, while at the same time, the death-rate has registered a dramatic fall. It was only natural that the problem of providing the means of living for this increased number of people should confront the world. Educational opportunities did not increase in the same proportion, and consequently, an educational emergency arose all over the world. It is also true that a nation's educational system is closely linked with the struggle for life. There is inadequacy of money, teachers and classrooms, but there is no paucity of students. The gravity of the educational crisis confronting the world can hardly be delineated through maps.

Differences due to Local Factors. Though the educational crisis is universal, local differences have created much variety in its form and context at different places. However, the model of this crisis is the same in every country, a model which was variously called Change, Adaptation and Disparity. Since 1945, the world has witnessed a remarkable scientific and technological revolution. And, the consequent unregulated changes in educational policies led to educational crisis and conflict.

The major reasons responsible for the universal educational crisis are the following—(1) Increasing desire for education, (2) Lack or inadequacy of the means to education. (3) the internal permanent agency of education, (4) the structure of society. With the development and extension of the field of knowledge and science, the desire for education in the common people has increased, and as a result, the need for expanding education was felt. The change in the prevailing educational values in the traditional system gave rise to the view that national development was possible only through the maximum utilization of the nation's educated manpower.

Education and society must undergo adaptation in order to overcome this crisis, without which the structure of both must necessarily undergo degeneration. In order to face this challenge, the resources of domestic life, as distinct from the resources of national life, have to be adopted. Money is needed, but the allocations made for education in the national budget are not sufficient to provide all the means of education. Consequently, the optimum utilisation of the nation's manpower, should take place with a view to quality, efficiency and productivity. Transformation is possible only through ideas, courage and determination. It is here that the responsibility of the planners of education increases manifold. Each nation needs an educational system suited to its circumstances and resources.

Education is not the panacea for all the ills of society. Education-does not have adequate time to seek and provide a cure for all of society's varied ills. For the same reason, education cannot satisfy and fulfil all of society's ambitions Education is, in fact, a faith, on the basis of which the individual undergoes development for his own benefit and the benefit of society. In providing the means for human development, the wastage that results is not due to education, but due to the circumstances of society. An important question must be asked here: Can a dogmatic faith provide assistance to any specific system in the process of rational analysis? The answer to this dogmatism gradually erodes reason in education and undermines foresight. The system of education seems to combine the teaching of folk songs with that of science and technology, it is a cruel satire on education. At the same time, from the social viewpoint, such means also suffer misuse because these means fail to satisfy the real needs of society.

On the other, it is no less a fact that, even in the absence of means, an educational system for society can be evolved by putting faith in the philosophy of 'Know Thyself.'

Attitude towards the Teaching Profession. With changing circumstances has come a change in the attitude towards teachers and the profession of teaching. With the invention of new methods of teaching and modern teaching aids, the teacher can increase his efficiency. But, the explosion in knowledge, which is also responsible for the educational crisis, has not been able to give the requisite impetus to the teaching profession. Classes are still devoid of new knowledge. Consequently; there has come about an imbalance between the expectations from education and its achievements.

Dogmatism. One cause of the educational crisis is the dogmatism of teachers. There was a time when the dogmatic farmer hesitated in introducing the new methods of farming in his field, but today, the same situation is found with regard to teachers. The position of small schools is similar to that of small and scattered fields. They are lacking in the means for research. One cause of the fragmentation of education is the transference of traditional knowledge from one generation to another, because of the traditions practised in society. Today, education is bearing a heavy load of responsibility, but, in the existing circumstances, the fulfilment of this responsibility is a complex and difficult task. The task of educating the nation is no easier than the task of putting man on the moon. Hence, in the sphere of educational conflict, it is essential to get victory over the dogmatism inherent in this sphere.

INPUT-OUTPUT PROCESS

Input		*Output*
		Creation of stalled persons in the field of
1. Knowledge	1. Educational aims	1. Family
2. Values	2. Contents	2. Trade
3. Goals	3. Students-teachers activity	3. Leadership
4. Population and qualified manpower	4. Finances	4 Cultural
		These are developed by-
5. Economic output and income	5. Physical items	1. Fundamental knowledge
		2. Physical and mental abilities
		3. Value, attitude and motivation
		4. Logical power
		5. Creativity
		6. Cultural praise
		7. Social responsibility
		8. Knowing the modern world

Table given rise to many questions through the use of such terms as management, technology, efficiency, quality; etc. In reality, all these combine to give rise to the educational process as well as the crisis in education.

In his work *'World Educational Crisis'*, Philip H. Coomb has delineated the educational crisis in many countries, of which India is one. This crisis in India has been viewed and analysed from various points of views, such as-policy on admission, inefficient administration, students at the primary level, dropouts, economic growth, economic expenditure, college population, problems of teachers, etc.

The Kothari Commission has reflected on the educational crisis in terms of Input and Out put. the three spheres examined by it are—

1. Transformation of the internal form of the educational method, so that it can be brought into intimate relationship with the life, needs and ambitions of the nation.
2. Qualitative improvement in education so as to make the standards achieved by it adequate, and to ensure that such standards keep on improving with the aim of making them comparable to standards in the international sphere.
3. Expansion of educational facilities according to the needs of the population and stress upon equality of educational opportunities.

The three problems point towards the educational crisis. Hence education has been considered in the context of the problem of national development. Our nation's problems are-self-sufficiency in foodgrains, economic development, universal employment, social and national unification, and political development. Consequently, education must be made to conform to the lives, needs and ambitions of the people. The crisis in education can be rooted out only when education becomes flexible enough to change along with social dynamism and mobility.

Once, during a seminar, an informal discussion on educational objectives brought to light the fact that in India, the determination of educational priorities did not exist. After the analysis of the curricula of many states, it was found that they were incapable of fulfiling any educational purpose. It was felt that educational curricular are formulated merely to bestow priority on the choices indulged in by some Commissions.

Whenever I go to schools, I am overwhelmed by the feeling that we are indulging in a gigantic game in the name of education. After a glance at the results of examinations and marks obtained by my own children, I am compelled to view with alarm the yawning gap between profession and practice. On talking to lady and gentlemen principals of schools, I feel that the whole blame rests squarely on the shoulders of teachers. In talks with teachers themselves or the office bearers of teachers unions, the entire blame shifts to the government, but when I glance helplessly at the predicament of my own children, I feel that the entire fault lies with the parents themselves. The present day analysis of the educational process turns into mutual recrimination and shifting of the responsibility and blame to others. The unfortunate victim of this game of passing the buck is the helpless student.

Books on education have always provided impressive lists of the objectives of education, because they include such things as social, individual, professional, and cultural development, proper utilization of leisure and entertainment, integral development, spiritual development, and external or physical development. Students appearing for examinations learn such lists by rote, though they cannot imbibe them. They win freedom after learning of such objectives in the way best suited to them. I often see and meet many old teachers who never obtained any training anywhere, never studied the elaborate explanation of educational foundations in the context of the philosophy of education, never possessed any practical knowledge of educational psychology, and yet their students are performing their duties devotedly and faithfully in many walks of life. The success with which these untrained teachers have achieved the objectives of education is worthy of imitation.

The teacher of today receives training. In the context of its philosophical, sociological and psychological foundations, the curriculum of training is completed in one or two years. During training, he takes a variety of oaths-that he will be a devoted teacher, adopt the scientific and psychological methods of teaching, etc. But, when he enters the sphere of action his entire training goes overboard. His acquired skill becomes worthless, and like his predecessors, he anxiously waits for the 'pay-day' after making motions of having done his duty. An artificial dissatisfaction enters his life. Possibly, it may be difficult to find a better instance of the projection of reproach.

The questions staring us in the face are- why do such things happen? Have we strayed from our objectives? We are feigning ignorance, and hence, we cannot find an answer to these questions. And so, we come to feel that both our vision and our sense of direction have suffered distortion and mutilation.

Soon after independence, Dr, Radhakrishnan pointed out, on the basis of the suggestions of the Commission, that the objective of education is to discover the innate qualities of the individual and to develop them by training. Universities should fulfil these obligations towards their students. In fact, these obligations should be fulfilled not only by universities but by each and every educational institution. It is obvious that these objectives imply the development of a healthy mind. Personalities themselves lacking in harmony and balance; of which there is no dearth in any sphere of education, have failed to make students balanced and harmonious.

The crucial and challenging question before our country immediately after independence was the question of survival, or of existence. Man's existence is founded on material goods and the nation's existence on thought, awareness and consciousness. These latter elements bear a direct relation to education. Education has its beginnings at the primary level, but the suggestions of the Radhakrishnan Commission were adopted, and once again the Secondary Education Commission was granted the responsibility for determining and achieving the objectives of education. This

Commission made its first attack on educational objectives. It profoundly observed that the political, social and economic circumstance had changed and new problems had emerged. It had become necessary to make a careful examination and re-determine the objectives of education at every level. This statement applies not only to the present situation, but also to the future evolution of education, the future of nature and social system, in which education has to modify itself, and to which education must adapt itself.

Consequently, the foundation for the development of democratic citizenship. professional efficiency, personality and leadership was given the following shape- (1) students should be given training in character so that they may be able to take part in the democratic process, (2) students should be given practical and professional training so that they may contribute to making the country economically prosperous, (3) students should be prepared for literary, artistic and cultural interests, which are essential for man's integral development and expression of self;. in the absence of this, the country's culture will be underminded.

It is clear that the country's educationists had determined the objectives of education in conformity with the potential needs of the new democratic nation. But by the time the year 1964 came, it was felt that the implementation of the objectives of the 1953 Commission had been faulty. Students were taught mob behaviour in the name of democracy, anarchistic behaviour in the name of organisation, ignorance in the name of knowledge, irresponsibility in the guise of devotion and dedication, disbelief in the name of faith, and rights in the name of duties. The outcome was that the three points of the educational wheel-the teacher, the student and the curriculum continued to sink steadily into a quagmire from which there was, for them, no emerging.

The declared purposes of the Commission of 1964 caused an explosion whose echoes can be heard even today. The truth of the matter is that society does, in reality, want to build the nation, but the management of society is in the hands of profiteers and black marketeers who are short-sighted and conscious only of their immediate interests. So, they regard the expenditure on education as no better than the money spent on a charity. The results of such negligence are before us. The student movements and the teacher movements are the result of this exploitation and torture. This has made it painfully evident once again that we have failed to achieve the objectives we ourselves created.

In restructuring educational objectives, we have kept before us the vision of national development. We have reflected on the possible modifications in the prevailing educational system. We have laid stress on determination and patience. Hence, the objectives of education have been determined in the new context, which comprehends such things as self-reliance in foodgrains, economic development and employment, social and national unification, development, etc.

Objectives of education have remained more or less the same in all ages. The main aim has always been-giving direction to society and the individual. But in this context, the dominating pattern has been that of the individual. Individuals have proved lethargic and negligent in honouring educational objectives, irrespective of whether these individuals are managers or legislators, teachers or parents, students or any others. Each one has given priority only to his own convenience. The teacher does not bother about fulfilling the objectives of education but about completing the course, as though that were the sole objective of his effort. The principal's sole objective is a satisfactory result. The management aims solely at grabbing money, by means fair or foul. Parents feel satisfied when they have sent their children to the prison of the school. What all this means is that there is so much variation and instability in the patterns and models of individuals that the aid which a liberal attitude has given them itself prevents them from regaining their balance.

Today, the contexts have altered. The negligence of the last twenty five years may have cheated no one else, but it has certainly cheated theyounger generation. The founders of education, who have indulged in the worst possible exploitation of and injustice towards students, should now beware. For the present, student unrest is only a foreshadow of its real self, but it has indicated that the objectives of education, modes of teaching, behaviour, all must be changed; if they are not changed, students will replace those who was responsible for education.

These questions keep flashing through my mind. I see that the form of education lies entangled in the legislative assembles of states, the chairs of ministers, the files of secretaries and the helpless shortsightedness of our legislators. There is a need for dedication to the nation, for development of the nation, for its cultural development, for religion, morality and character. All its needs are lost sight of in the futile exercises in manpower planning and determination of the objectives of education, and devising suitable plans and schemes for achieving them. It is impossible to forecast when our nation will arise from its long slumber, when it will look at itself and the people with new eyes. What I wonder is whether our people have the necessary courage, dedication and ability?

The following steps will have to be taken to resolve the educational crisis in the country—

1. Educational values must be remoulded and reshaped from the social, moral and spiritual viewpoints.
2. Education must be linked with production. Science, practical experience and professionalisation will be elements in this education.
3. A uniform system of school education must be implemented for social and national unification. A programme for national and social service will have to be

implemented. The language policy will have to be geared to achieve national unity. A national awareness will have to be generated.

4. Education must be linked with modernization.
5. Teachers must be given a position of respect and honour, a high social position.
6. Administration of education must be improved.
7. Stress must be laid on job oriented education.

2

Ancient Times

"Education was regarded as a source of illumination and power which transforms and ennobles over nature by the progressive and harmonious development of our physical, mental, intellectual and spiritual power faculties." Dr. A. S. Altekar has rightly said so about the education of early period of history.

As soon as we glance into the mirror of history, it is our own image, our own reflection, which stands sharply delineated before us. Our acquaintance with reality is sharpened for us by the traces of history. Its pages unfold our glory, telling us about what we were, what we are, and what we will be. Its knowledge helps us to a discovery of the germinal seed out of which our future society takes birth. The term history is variously defined in different dictionaries. For instance, (1) History is that branch of knowledge which relates to man's social and political development; (2) History is the science which makes a Scientific and Chronological study of mankind (3) It is also defined as the systematic study of the events that occur in the life of people; (4) History is also said to be the growth of philosophy, art, institutions, laws, language and human development along with the chain of chronological changes in social development.

In view of these definitions, contemporary education can find the right direction if education is studied from the historical perspective. Whatever aspect of education that we choose to study, our view-point should be objective. And it is the historical perspective that grants objectivity in studying educational problems. A study of the growth, the ancestry and the culture of education opens before us new, horizons of thought. It is with this in view that we here embark upon a study of education in ancient ages.

Early Days

The present has its roots deeply embedded in the past. India's past has been singularly glorious. Its refulgence has not only illuminated the present, but also aroused faith in the future. Her past has been influenced not so much by social, cultural and economic factors as by the spirituality which took birth here. In this land, man's philosophy has been *Sarva Brut Hite Rath*. The culture of our land has dreamt of universal brotherhood and a super humanity. It has sought to give concrete shape to this dream.

In the ancient period, all the political, economic and social currents emanated from spiritualism. Social life was solidly founded upon good conduct, love, non-violence, etc. Cooperation and coexistence formed its spirit. The fundamental unit of society was the individual. And, for the individual, life had a definite objective, certain definite ideals. Material resources were employed solely for the attainment of this objective and these ideals. The principle upon which education in the ancient period was founded can be expressed best in the following words, "Learning in India through the ages had been prized and pursued not for its own sake, if we may so put it, but for the sake, and as a part of religion. It was sought as the means of salvation or self-realization, as the means to the highest end of life, through., 'Mukti' or Emancipation."

Education in India had its beginnings in the need to satisfy man's innate curiosity, while he lived in the lap of nature. It is usually argued that the elements, methodology and organisation of education in India originated during the Vedic period, but the truth is that the highly developed form the Pre-Vedic civilization, i.e., the civilization of Mohen-jo-Daro, or the civilization of the Indus valley, points to the fact that man could not have achieved this degree of development without the growth of education. The Aryan period is regarded as the healthy, peaceful, mature and practical age of education. As Dr. Altekar has put it, "From the Vedic age downwards the central concept of education of the Indians has been that it is a source of illumination, giving us a correct lead in the various spheres of life."

India's educational and cultural traditions are the most ancient in the world's history. All that India is today, is the gift of its cultural and social heritage of the last 5000 years. In ancient India, the traditions of society and the nation were preserved in schools. At that time, means of public communication did not exist, but contacts and relations were strengthened through schools.

Regarding education, Manu has said that the first-born Brahmins, who took birth on this earth, have imparted education of character to all human beings.

The Vedas occupy the first place among ancient texts which provide knowledge about ancient Indian education and society. Dr. Radha Kumud Mukerjee has said that from the very birth of the most ancient Vedic epics we find that Indian literature was profoundly influenced by religion. In ancient days, there were provisions for education in various subjects. Proof of this lies in the Chandogayopanishad which mentions Naradji's advice to Santt Kumar about studying all subjects.

As is the case today, even in past, the home was the child's first school. The family was his primary school. He learnt many things unconsciously as a part of his growth and development.

He acquired the rudiments of social behaviour and the language of society from the home itself. From the viewpoint of education, India's ancient period has been so glorious and rich that foreign scholars have praised it lavishly. Dr. F W. Thomas has stated that education is no new thing for India. No other country in the world has a more ancient or more powerful tradition of the love of knowledge. In those days, the foundation of education lay in religion and religious activities. The main basis of education was Vedic activity. Life in all its aspects was inspired by and infused with religion.

The Significance

Such terms as knowledge, awakening, humility, modesty, etc, are often used to characterise education in the Vedic period. Ancient texts refer to the uneducated person as an ignorant beast. Education is regarded as the source of light. The main features of Vedic education can be briefly enumerated as follows:

Knowledge, the Third Eye: Education is knowledge. It is man's third eye This aphorism means that knowledge opens man's inner eye, flooding him with spiritual and divine light, which forms the provision for man's journey through life. Through education, the development of every aspect of human life becomes possible. Knowledge protects an individual like a mother, inspires him to follow the path of good conduct as a father does, and gives the pleasure that one's wife provides.

Education leads to the development of personality. The word 'Veda' originates from the root 'vid' which bears the meaning of knowledge. Sayana declares that the Veda is a means to the obtaining of the adored, that which is worthy of worship, as well as a means to the banishment of the undesired the evil. Knowledge of the four Vedas (Rigveda; Yajurveda, Samaveda, and Atharvaveda), along with the knowledge of Shruti, Smriti, etc., provided an individual, with new knowledge which broadened his intellectual horizon.

Aims of Education: In the Vedic period, education had an idealistic form, in which the teachers (acharyas) laid stress upon worship of God, religiousness, spirituality, formation of character, development of personality, creation of an aptitude for the development of culture, nation and society. It is in this context that Dr. Altekar said that the objectives of education in ancient India were worship of God, a feeling for religion, formation of character, fulfilment of public and civic duties, an increase in social efficiency or skill, and the protection and propagation of national culture. These objectives and ideals took an individual along the path of spiritual development. In their fundamental form, these objectives and ideals were—

Emphasis upon Knowledge and Experience. The Gurukuls laid emphasis upon knowledge and obtaining of experience. During the Vedic period, the practice of distributing degrees did not exist. Students exhibited the knowledge obtained through discourses and discussions conducted in a concourse of scholars. Dr. R.K. Mukerjee opines that the objective of education was not merely reading, but the subjective assimilation of knowledge and experience.

Sublimation of Instincts. Man is the virtual slave of the instinctive drives embedded in his psyche, and when he is obsessed by his senses, he often adopts the wrong path. The objective of education was to sublimate these instinctive tendencies, to turn the mind away from material knowledge, and centre it upon the spiritual world, thus establishing control over materialistic and base tendencies.

Spirituality. In the Vedic period, Nature was regarded as divine and worshipped. During this period, many hypotheses concerning spirituality took birth. Knowledge came to be seen as the instrument, of salvation. Fire sacrifices, fasting and taking of vows became a part of life. Education was given the objective of inculcating control over these aspects and learning right conduct based on them.

Growth of Character and Personality. The objective of education was the formation of character and personality of children. It was achieved through an appropriate environment, lessons on right conduct, and teachings based on the life, character and ideals of great persons. Education aimed at developing the virtues of self-control, self-respect, love, cooperation, sympathy, etc., in the students.

Fulfillment of Duty. Great importance was attached to developing such qualities as discipline, obedience, performance of hostly duties, rendering help to others, fulfillment of social responsibilities, etc. Through such education social skills were developed in the students. In addition, education was also provided for earning a livelihood, and for this, one or more skills were taught. Dr. Mukerjee says that this education was not exclusively theoretical or literary. It was related to one or the other manual skill.

Preservation of Culture. During the Vedic period, considerable attention was given to the protection and propagation of national culture. Knowledge and skills were transmitted to the succeeding generations through the medium of the schools, known as Gurukuls. In essence, the achievement of the above mentioned objectives implies making the individuals a completed individual. Knowledge leads to man's physical. as well as spiritual development. It is knowledge that leads man to his salvation. This truth lies concealed in the aphorism In ancient times, strenuous efforts were made for the achievement of these objectives of education. Stress was laid on proper conduct. The student was prepared both for knowledge of the self as well as knowledge of the Absolute. Accepting as the foundation, primacy was given to fire sacrifices, rituals, prayers, and religious festivals.

The Method of Education. During the Vedic period, the Gurukul method prevailed, in which the student lived in the house of the Guru, instead of living with his parents. Along with his colleagues, he led a celibate life and obtained education in the house of the Guru. Initially, in the Vedic period, it was the teacher who occupied the primary place, but in the later period, it was the student who occupied the central place in education. The process of education passed through the three stages of comprehension, meditation, memory and nidhi-dhyaasana. The Gurukuls were the centres of education, in which education was imparted only by individuals of character and ability. The student remained with his Guru for 12 years. There were parishads or committees to satisfy the student's thirst for knowledge. Congresses of scholars were also organised from time to time. In these, awards were also given to prominent scholars.

The 'Upnayana' Ritual. The word 'Upnayana' means to take close to, or to bring in touch with. A ceremony called the Upnayana ceremony was performed before the child was taken to his teacher. This ceremony was performed at the ages of 8, 11 and 12 for the Brahmins, Kshatriyas and Vaishyas, respectively. The ceremony signalled the childs's transition from infancy to childhood, and his initiation into educational life. In this context, the term 'Upnayana' means putting the student in touch with his teacher. With the passage of time, the ceremony came to be confined to the Brahmin class only.

Celibacy or Brahmacharya. Every student was required to observe celibacy in his specific path of life. Purity of conduct was regarded as of supreme importance. Only the unmarried could become students in a Gurukul. On entering student life, the student was made to wear a special girdle called a *mekhla*. Its quality depended on the caste of the student. Brahmins wore a girdle of *moonj* grass the Kshatriyas of string *gut-taanta*-and the Vaishyas a girdle made of wool. The clothes worn by them were also accordingly of silk, wool, etc. The students were not allowed to make use of fragrant, cosmetic or intoxicating things.

Service of the Teacher. Every student was required, while residing in the Gurukul, to serve his teacher compulsorily. Any violation of the Guru's instructions was regarded as a sin, and subject to stern punishment. The student's duties included obtaining such daily necessities as water, a twig for brushing the teeth, etc., for his guru. The teachers also ensured that the students should not be distracted from their studies while performing such duties. During the vacations in which the student returned home he was not required to perform any service for the teacher.

The work of teaching began early in the morning. After performing their ablutions, students participated in some religious rituals, such as havans. Subsequently, they were put to the task of studying. In the afternoon, after partaking of lunch, the students returned to their studies. At sunset, some more religious rituals were performed. They denoted the end of the day's routine.

Alms System. The student had to bear the responsibility of feeding both himself and his teacher. This was done through begging for alms, which was not considered bad, since every domestic knew that his own son must be begging for alms in the same way at some other place. The reason behind the introduction of such a practice was that accepting alms induces humility. The student realised that both education and subsequent earning of livelihood were made possible for him only through society's service and its sympathy. For the poor students, begging for alms was compulsory and unavoidable, but even among the prosperous, it was a generally accepted practice.

Practicality. The education of that period encompassed the necessary activities of life. Students were given education about animal-husbandry, agriculture and other professions. In addition education in medicine was also imparted. According to Dr. Altekar, the purpose of education was not to provide general knowledge about a variety of subjects, but to produce specialists of the best kind in various spheres. Because of this, practical education had a very important place in vocational education.

Education for the Individual. In the Vedic period, every teacher devoted himself to the integral development of each student. He aimed at the physical and intellectual development of his wards. The maximum attention was devoted to the individual development of every student, but there was no provision for the education of the incapable and the handicapped, especially those who were lacking in mental and moral qualities or were known for moral turpitude.

Duration of Education. In the house of the teacher, the student was required to obtain education upto the age of 24, after which he was expected to enter domestic life. Students were divided into three categories:

(a) Those obtaining education upto the age of 24-Vasu.

(b) Those obtaining education upto the age of 36-Rudra.

(c) Those obtaining education upto the age of 48-Aaditya.

Curriculum. Although the education of this period was dominated by the study of Vedic literature, historical study, stories of heroic lives and discourses on the Puranas also formed a part of the syllabus. Students had necessarily to obtain knowledge of metrics. Arithmetic was supplemented by a knowledge of geometry. Students were given knowledge of the four Vedas -Rigveda, Yajurveda, Samaveda and Atharvaveda. The syllabus took within its compass such subjects as spiritual as well as materialistic knowledge, Vedas, Vedic grammar, arithmetic, knowledge of gods, knowledge of the absolute, knowledge of ghosts, astronomy, logic, philosophy, ethics, conduct, etc. The richness of the syllabus was responsible for the creation of Brahman literature in this period.

The foundation of the education imparted in this ancient period was inherent tendency or aptitude (*abhivrati*). It is written in the Atharvaveda "O Lord Indra! fill us with that ability which a father imparts to his son:" It is also stated in the Sabra Bhashya, " How a child learns is apparent from the fact that the child of a Brahmin learns the Vedic aphorisms while still at home. The imprint of these aphorisms upon his mind is indelible." Along with education, the performance of certain rituals was also regarded as essential. It was after these rituals that the child embarked upon a study of the subjects of his choice, though he was also required to study some other subjects. In this connection Sanat Kumar inquired of Naarad what he had studied. Naarada replied, "I have read the Rigveda, Yajurveda, Samaveda, Atharvaveda, the fifth Ved, history, the Puranas. I also know the Vedic grammar, the Veda of the Vedas. I am also read in rules pertaining to service of one's father, arithmetic, the science of time, knowledge of gods, the absolute, ghosts, etymology, astronomy, knowledge of snakes and `devas', dance, music, recreation and creation of fragrance."

Method of Teaching. In this period, the educational process was centred round the teacher. Studying was similar to the recitations of folk songs. Emphasis was placed upon-understanding and giving practical implementation to aphorisms. Sanskrit was the medium of education.

The actual process of teaching was as follows- (i) The student memorised the lesson. (ii) The second lesson was taught only when the first had been memorised. (iii) After memorising lessons, the students meditated upon them. (iv) Special emphasis was placed upon correct pronunciation. (v) Discussion also had a place in the method of teaching.

The method of teaching was based upon apprenticeship. While at home with the family, the child learnt the language of the family and its profession. Here, he was also required to practice twelve rituals. From the time of conception to the time of performing the Upnayana ceremony, the child developed ability, sufficient to prepare him for his future life.

In the school, memory was regarded as the basis of knowledge. The Aitreya Brahman throws light upon the various methods of memorisation. In the *nyayasutra* of Gautam, emphasis has been placed upon attention, recall, intuition (*abhigyana*) association of ideas and recollection, as contributors to memorisation. In the Yagyavalakya Smriti, the concept of the 'Smriti Mana' is based on these ideas. Importance was attached to accuracy and purity in memorisation and recollection.

Sanat Kumar had laid greater emphasis upon the formula of proceeding from the simple to the complex in the educational process. Subjects were clarified with the help of examples (*drashtanta*). Memorising without first understanding a subject was adversely criticised. Nighantu and Nirukta, too, have declared that a person does not become a scholar by performing common deeds and memorising blindly. In order to become wise, students should understand the meaning of the Vedas. Kautilya attached importance to the development of skill. The student's power of reasoning was developed and sharpened through the question-answer technique.

Relations Between Student and Teacher. Dr. Altekar has said that the relation between a student and teacher was a direct one. It did not function through an institution. Students went to receive their education only from those gurus who had won fame by their scholarship. In this period, students served their gurus to the greatest extent. Their respective duties were described thus:

Duties of the Student. Begging for alms, collecting firewood, looking after animals, obtaining water, obeying the teacher, etc. If students criticised their teachers, they were punished.

Duties of the Teacher. Teaching, making arrangements for the boarding and lodging of the students, medical treatment, taking care of the students, etc. The teachers encouraged their able students, and some went to the extent of offering their own daughters in marriage to these students.

The basis of this mutual relationship between ability and skill in behaviour. The teacher's ability was measured in terms of his universality and his humility. Gargeya sermoned to king Ajaatshatru. At the end of the sermon, the latter enquire if that is all. The teacher says that it is. The king objects and says that through such knowledge God cannot be known. Upon this the teacher himself requests the king to make him his disciple. What this incident implies is that a real teacher was he whose ambition it was to know the absolute and who was perennially engaged in the search for it. Similarly the person who possessed both materialistic and spiritualistic knowledge was regarded as a real teacher. He had to possess knowledge of etymology, grammar, metrics, astrology and nirukta. Manu has stated that the teacher's prime task and moral duty was to discharge his obligations towards his students. He must not only treat the student as his own child, he must also impart to him true and complete knowledge, without concealing any knowledge from him.

Women's Education. In any community, the education of women is a more complex task than the education of men. On this subject, a vast variety of views have been expounded. Man's ego has generally adopted a biased view of the education of women. The Vedic period consistently believed that despite the differences in physiology, woman is in no way intellectually inferior to man. She possesses excellent memory, intelligence, and other mental powers, and hence she has the capacity to obtain any kind of education.

A woman's fulfilment lies in womanhood and the latter's in motherhood. It is because of this that the nature of feminine education differs from that of masculine education. She should be skilled in household duties. Consequently, girls were educated at home, despite which the names of such women as Vishwavara, Jooha, Apalla, Ghosha, Romsa, Lopamudra, Saraswati and others are mentioned in ancient texts, as examples of women who composed commentaries on the Vedas. Yagyavalkya has mentioned the names of Maitreyi, Kaushitiki, while Brahman has mentioned the name of Gandhrava Grahita, as instances of women who obtained the highest education.

Manu has gone so far as to say that it is the duty of parents to give their daughters an integral education. They should also be given education in the various arts.

Vocational Education. Education in the Vedic period was not limited to spiritual education alone. Because of the caste and ashrama systems in society, vocational education, too, had been given a definite form. Brahamans, Rishis or sages and Purohits performed the task of teaching.

It was compulsory for the Kshatriyas to study logic and the Vedas. Education and training in the various aspects of military science was also imparted. Princes were educated in Samkhya yoga, public administration, diplomacy, agriculture; animal husbandry, and trade and commerce. Vaishyas were educated in agriculture, trade and animal husbandry. The Students were taught about agriculture, cow care, animal husbandry, manufacture of weapons, construction, sculpture, drawing and painting, and other material subjects. Among other professions education was also imparted in the science of medicine, i.e., ayurveda.

Analysis of Vedic Education. An analysis of the achievements of education in this ancient period indicates that the aim of education was to make the individual a useful and productive member of society. The educational achievements of this age were as follows:

1. Education emphasised the development of spirituality. The ashram system was adopted for paying of the individual's debts towards the gods, his forefathers, his teacher and society.

2. The minds of the parents were first prepared to instill in them a desire for the education of their children. It has

been said that those parents are the enemy of the child who do not teach their children.

3. Great attention was paid to the development of the child's character. Teachers laid stress on the integral development of the individual's personality.
4. Social skill was evolved through training in the fulfillment of duties.
5. Efforts were made for the preservation and propagation of the national culture.
6. Education was free. Its expenses were borne by the society and the king.
7. While living in the Gurukul, the child imbibed education in a favourable environment.
8. A student was compelled to obey the ideals of the Gurukul. He had to shoulder the burden of existence through begging for alms. This practice developed humility and tolerance in the student.
9. In developing the student's character, attention was paid to his nature, early experiences and impression, upbringing and circumstances.
10. Self-study (*swaadhyaya*) was considered more important.
11. The medium of education was divine pronouncement, and the period of education, according to caste, was 48, 36, 24 and 12 years.
12. The examination was oral one. The student was required to give oral answers in a congregation of scholars. If he satisfied them, he was given a degree or title. the consensus of the scholars' opinions was essential for obtaining such a title.

13. During this period, vocational education was also in vogue. Military science, agriculture, animal husbandry, veterinary science, medicine, etc., were among the subjects taught. Chemistry was also taught. Arts and handicrafts were highly respected. Education in commerce was very popular.

Dr. A.S. Altekar says—Infusion of piety and religiousness, formation of character, development of personality, inculcation of civic and social duties, promotion of social efficiency and preservation and spread of national culture may be described as the main aims and ideals of ancient Indian education. The basic tenet of the ancient educational tradition was the paying of. the social debt. Teachers took up this profession to pay off their debt to society. They enjoyed the highest social status. Examples from the educational sphere in this period can be useful for us in organising our educational system in the contemporary world.

Teachers should imitate their ancient forerunners, the gurus of old. They should treat their students as their own children and pay attention to their development. They should also maintain the highest standards in their own conduct because students are profoundly influenced by their teachers' conduct. Undoubtedly, education has undergone various changes because of changed priorities and beliefs. Now, we have the university system of education in which the hours of teaching are fixed and students are required to pay fees. But students' hostels remind us of the Gurukuls of ancient days. However, it is not these differences but the fact that the teacher of today is no longer respected, which catches our attention. In the past, the teacher was placed on a pedestal and revered. Hence, now just as the teachers should mould their own conduct, the students, too, should respect their teachers as they respect their own parents.

Thus, the propagation and spread of education should be in accordance with the individual's abilities. It is only then that the real form of education will actually blossom forth and demonstrate its real potential. Dr. Altekar has argued that from the Vedic period to the present age, the basic tenet of Indian education has been the view that education is light. It is that source which gives us the truest guidance in the various spheres of life.

Age of Vedas

The educational structure in the Brahmanic Age was, to a very great extent, only a refined and developed form of Vedic education. However, during this age, various forms began to emerge in the institutions of education. Various institutions, such as *shakha, charana, parishad, kul* and *gotra*, began to emerge at the various levels of education. Besides the Uppishads, Aaranyaka, Brahman and other classical texts were created in this period. Famous ashramas or monastries came to be established in the forests. It was in this period that the Sutra literature was created, along with the development of the six systems of Indian philosophical thought - Samkhya, Yoga, Nyaya, Vaisheshika, Karma or Purva Mimamsa, and Vedanta or Uttara Mimamsa. A significant characteristic of this period is the determination of the syllabus according to the Caste and Ashrama system. However, the education of the Shudras and women suffered a decline.

The best mirror of any country or society is the literature, it produces. From the Vedic to the Brahman period, literature and additional literature continued to be created. Even in the Brahman period, education continued to be looked upon as the means to knowledge. It has the same objectives that Vedic education had. However, with the passage of time and a change in the needs of society, the importance attached to them underwent a change. In this period, the following objectives were ascribed to education.

1. Self-control
2. Development of character
3. Generation of sociability or social awareness

4. Integral development of personality
5. Propagation of purity
6. Preservation of knowledge and culture.

Education in this age continued to proceed on the foundations given to it during the Vedic period, but a certain rigidity and narrowness now marked its implementation. Education now aimed at equipping the student for the struggle for existence. After the Upnayana or introduction ceremony, teachers imparted education to their students according to the latter's interests, tendencies and nature. Celibacy was rigidly observed. Teachers paid full attention to the psychological make-up of their students while teaching. Corporal or physical punishment was regarded as the last resort of administration and discipline. It has been stated in the *Manusmriti*- (4-164). In the same way, Yagyavalkya has declared- (1-115).

Students lived in close contact with their teacher or guru in the Gurukul. But, restrictions had now been placed upon the receiving of education by Shudras. for social reasons, they were not considered fit to receive education. After Vedic education, there was a gradual increase in ritualism. The result was that Shudras and women began to lose their place in the educational sphere. But, on the other hand, education became more comprehensive in this period, as it was closely associated with every aspect of life. Some of its general characteristics are—

Dominance of Religion. As in the Vedic period, education in the Brahman period also was dominated by religion. Students were given knowledge of religious activities. Numerous religious and cultural activities were organised so as to acquaint students with them.

Worldly and Other-Worldly or Spiritual and Materialistic Education. During this period, education paid equal attention to spiritual as well as materialistic or worldly matters. Education comprehended the materialism of life.

Individualism. Because of the absence of collective education, the emphasis was upon the individual. Teachers paid attention to the personal development of individual students.

Celibacy (Brahmacharya). Like the education in the Vedic period, education in this period also laid great emphasis upon celibacy. Students were expected to obey their teachers and indulge only in moral conduct.

Physical Punishment. In the Brahman age, the practice of giving physical punishment to students was not prevalent. Such famous acharyas as Manu, Gautam, Vishnu opposed physical punishment because they considered it inhuman.

Method of Education. In the Vedic period, education was primarily oral. Students were made to memorise aphorisms and then elaborate them. But, by the advent of the Brahaman age, the art of writing had developed, and so both oral and written education came into practice, though the emphasis was upon oral education. Bhojpatra, the bark of a tree, was used for writing. Teachers gave importance to purity in pronunciation. Education was conducted through discussion, answering of questions, removal of doubts, etc. Students were given continuous practice in the art of writing and for this they were required to copy manuscripts. Practical work was emphasized in such subjects as grammar, astrology, nyaya, medicine, etc. The students as well as the teachers themselves obtained informal education through the concourse of famed scholars.

Curriculum. In this age, too, primacy was given to the study of the Vedas. Among the subjects taught were grammer, arithmetic, geometry, astrology, economics, history, politics, agriculture, military science, nyaya philosophy, etc. A special feature of this period is that, as time progressed, two kinds of syllabi came to be prepared one for the short-term and another for the long-term. In addition, clear and correct pronunciation of consonants and vowels was stressed. Students were also given knowledge of metrics and figures of speech. It was on this basis that learned commentaries on the Vedas came to be composed. The Pingal Shastra was composed for the teaching of matrics. Surgery had also developed by this time.

Student Teacher Relationship. The relationship between the teacher and the student was that of father. and son. Students lived in the teacher's household as members of his family. They performed such duties as serving the teacher, performing household duties, begging for alms, etc. When the student's education came to an end, the teacher blessed him with the principle of following religion, self-study and truth.

In this age, when the student came to his teacher, he offered the (*samidha*) to the latter. This samidha was transformed into the light of knowledge. When education came to an end, the student offered *guru dakshina* to his teacher in return for the service which the teacher had performed for him.

Indian culture has developed through its system of education. This system was especially fruitful in propagating the ideas of love, truth, non-violence, religion, peace and world brotherhood. It also pointed out the path to salvation. It was also responsible for the creation and preservation of literature. FE. Keay has expressed wonder at the fact that though divine texts were composed such a long time ago, and that though it seemed impossible to preserve them intact, this was done, and is still being done today. The education of this period possessed the following features.

1. It paid the greatest attention to the child's physical and mental development.

2. It was conscious of the development of the child's character.

3. The gurukuls were situated at a distance from inhabited areas so as to prevent excessive contact between students and society.

4. In the teacher's house, there was an abundance of family feeling. Students did not suffer from the lack of any familial necessity.

5. The teachers imparted education without any discrimination.

However, during the Brahman age, education came to be bound with the chains of formality. As Dr. RE. Kaey has pointed out, "Not only did the Brahman educators develop a system of education, which survived the crumbling of empires and the changes of society, but they also, through all these thousand years, kept aglow the torch by higher learning."

During this period, education as a process was controlled by such rituals as *vidhyaarambha* (initiation into education), *upnayana* (taking the student to the teacher), and samaavartana (completeness of education). Buildings for teaching purposes also began to be constructed, but intimate contact with nature was regarded as an essential condition of education. The gurukul system, began to grow and develop into numerous institutions of higher learning and specialised education. The educational calendar had its beginning in the full moon of Shraavana, and it concluded at the time of the full moon of Paush. Holidays, too, were granted to the students.

In the Brahman age, education was free and universal. Among the methods of education, the methods of listening, contemplation, comprehension, self study and recall were adopted. New teachers were brought into existence through the method of appointing class monitors. On the whole, the education of this period was free from external control and restraint. In the opinion of Dr. PN. Prabhu, education in ancient India was free from such external controls as the influence of the state, the administration, or political parties. Consequently, it gave rise to powerful personalities with highly developed mental powers and a pure and active love of knowledge.

Certain demerits had crept into the educational system of the Brahmanic age. They were—-

Dominance of Religion. Since education was dominated by religion, less importance was attached to material or worldly development. This dominance also led to an increase in an anarchic attitude towards religion among the students and prevented the growth of rational thought.

Emphasis upon Philosophy. Education during this period laid excessive stress upon the study of philosophy, since the purpose was to put the student onto the path to salvation through a study of philosophy. The result was the growth of an escapist attitude towards life.

Deprivation of the Shudras right to Education. During this period, the right to education became confined to the Brahmans, Kshatriyas and Vaishyas, because of the emergence of aristocracy. The Shudras were deprived of the right to education.

Faith in the Vedas. In this period, people came to have blind faith in the Vedas. They were convinced that only the Vedas were true. Consequently, the tendency towards logical and rational thought was hampered.

Women Education. There is some evidence of education of women during the Vedic period, but during the Brahman age, this was neglected. In addition, women became the victims of many restraints.

Lack of Handicrafts. During this age, the caste system became characterised by rigidity and narrow mindedness. Those engaged in handicrafts came to be regarded as inferior. The consequence to this was that handicrafts gradually vanished from educational curriculum.

Absence of Synthesis. The education of this period was taking in synthesis. Instead, it laid emphasis upon profound scholarship in any one subject.

Thus, the ideals and methods of education in the Brahman and Vedic ages did not differ substantially from each other. The only major difference was the neglect and outlawing of the education of women and Shudras in the former. Many subjects underwent development, but there was absence of synthesis between them. These shortcomings are indicative of the growth of individualism in education. Religion was the basis of the entire educational process. Each activity was performed through religious rituals. Even science, economics, political science and arithmetic could not overcome the influence of religion, Instead, they continued to progress on their path with the help of religion. During this period, the excessive emphasis upon intellectual elements led to the neglect of handicrafts. Those skilled in handicrafts were regarded as inferior and mean, and as time progressed, the Varna system was transformed into the rigid caste system. The various arts came to be regarded as suitable only for women and the Shudras, not for members of the higher castes. Sanskrit was the language of common converse, but special attention was given to it in education. The language of the common people was growing and changing, and so it failed to become the medium of instruction.

Age of Buddha

R.K. Mukerjee said, Buddhist education and learning centred round monasteries. The Buddhist world did not offer any educational opportunities apart from or independently of its monasteries. All education, sacred as well as secular, was in the hands of the monks. In the words of R.E. Kaey. - For over fifteen hundred years Buddhist education was in vogue and developed a system of education which was a rival of the Brahamanic system though in many ways similar to it.

Education of the Brahman period came to be allied with the national and social life. Ritualism had increased, and the people were profoundly troubled. A sense of aimlessness prevailed in society. In such circumstances, Buddhism emerged as a reaction to Vedic ritualism. Buddhists began to establish educational monastries in competition to the Vedic system of education. Initially, these Buddhist monastries provided education only to Buddhists, but gradually they came to impart education to all classes. Dr. R. K. Mukerjee says that, properly considered, Buddhist education is only one of the ancient Hindu or Brahmanic systems of education.

Buddhist education came into existence in the 5th century B.C. Brahmans deprived the common people of their right to education, and hence the emergence of Buddhism granted the people the freedom to obtain education and to practice their religion themselves. Lord Buddha imparted to life a perfectly practicable form. Consequently, a practicable religion and a practical educational system became a variable to the common people.

It is undoubtedly true that though Buddhist education had an individual character, it was, in essence, based upon the educational system of the Vedic period. The Buddhists imparted education in Sanghas or collective groups. R.K. Mukerjee has pointed out that the Buddhist educational method is the method of Buddhist congregations (Sanghas). Just as the rituals of fire sacrifice (*yajnas*) were the centres of culture in the Vedic period, the congregations of the Buddhist period were the centres of education and knowledge. In the Buddhist world, there was no opportunity for the individual to obtain education independently, away from his Sangha or congregation. Every kind of religious as well as worldly education was in the hands of Buddhist monks.

During the Buddhist period, education had two levels- primary and higher levels.

Primary Level. The Jatakas stories indicate that during the Buddhist period, primary education took the form of worldly or materialistic education. Fa-Hien has also mentioned the existence of a system of general education. Children of six were admitted to this level of education.

Higher Level. Dr. Altekar opines that the Buddhists raised India's international stature considerably by the high level of education in their monastries since students from as far as Korea, Tibet, Java and other distant countries were attracted to them.

Centres of Learning

During this period, some prominent centres of education sprang up. Their characteristics were their collective nature and their association with Buddhist Viharas or monastries. There was no discrimination between students on any. basis. Some of these centres possessed an international reputation, proved by the fact that Chinese, Japanese, Tibetan and other students came there to receive education.

As already pointed out, there were many universities in India during the Buddhist period. It was a time when democratic feelings were evolving, and hence many famous educational centres came into existence. Wherever Buddhist monastries or Viharas were established, educational centres too emerged. Among the most notable universities to develop during this period were the universities at Taxila, Nalanda, Ballabhi, Vikramshila, Odantpuri, Nadia, Jagdalla.

Taxila. Taxila was an important centre of education during the Buddhist period. It was then the capital of Gandhar. It had been founded by King Bharata after the name of his son Taxa. Being situated on the borders of this subcontinent, the kingdom was subject to frequent external aggressions. Because of this, the university in this kingdom developed on the basis of the family. Students started their education at the age of 16. The university provided education in numerous subjects, such as the three Vedas, Vedanta, Grammar, Ayurveda, the eighteen Sippas, military science, astrology, agriculture, commerce, treatment of snake-bite, (*Sarpa-dansha chikitsa*), magical charms (*Tantra Vidya*) etc.

Nalanda. The Nalanda university was situated in the state of Bihar, 40 miles south west of Patna and 7 miles north of Rajgraha. It was an internationally famed Buddhist centre of education. It became famous because it was the birth place of Sariputra the disciple of Lord Buddha. Emperor Ashok had a monastry constructed here. By the 4th century B.C. it had become a famous centre of education, and by the 7th century it became the foremost centre of education.

Kings of the Gupta dynasty took interest in the growth of the university. Buddhist monastries were constructed here by Kumar Gupta, Narsingh Gupta, Baladitya, Buddha, Gupta, Vajra, and Harsha. Because of these monastries, the university continued to grow and expand. Its land was surrounded by a rampart at the entrance to which lived a profound scholar who administered an entrance test to the students desirous of joining the university. The university had eight large assembly halls and 300 rooms for study. It had been stated in *Epigraphic India* that the highest point of Viharavali kissed the clouds. The buildings of the university are a fine example of the engineering skill existing in that age. The remains of these buildings are sufficient to prove that the art of construction had reached a peak during this period. In addition to the buildings, the university had beautiful lakes, numbering 10, according to It-Sing. The university also had a massive, nine-storeyed library which was divided into three parts, called Ratna Sagar, Ratnodadhi and Ratna Ranjaka. As books of all religion were obtainable in this library, it was given the name of Dharma Ganja, or the meeting place of religions.

Thirteen of its many monastries served as hostels for the students. In each room there were stone seats, space for keeping books and other facilities. the university possessed huge kitchens. 10,000 students lived and received free education at this institution. The university fulfilled all their needs of food, clothing, medical treatment, education, etc. 200 villages had been gifted to Nalanda. Apart from the income derived from them, the university also received sizable donations from the king and the people, who thus contributed their mite to education.

It-Sing studied at Nalanda for 10 years. According to him, Nalanda was a centre of Mahayana, a branch of Buddhism, but it also provided education in Himayana, and Vedic and Jain religions. In addition, the Vedas, Vedanga, philosophy, the Puranas, medicine, etc., were also taught here. The method of teaching was discussion and question-answer.

In Bihar, the Buddhist monks, teachers and students led a balanced, regulated and spiritualistic life, far removed from leisure and luxury. Students of this university earned great respect in many foreign countries. Students came from Java; Sumatra, Japan, China, Ceylon and other countries to receive education here. The staff of the university consisted of 1500 teachers. Huen Tsang, in his travelogues, mentions the names of such renowned teachers as Chandrapal, Dharampal, Gunamati, Sthirmati, Prabhamitra, Gyanchandra, Sheelbhadra, etc.

Nalanda continued to serve, preserve and propagate Indian culture for 800 years. It was in the 12th century that this brilliant source of light was quenched by Bakhtiar Khilji.

Ballabhi. From 475 A.D. to 775 A.D., Ballabhi, in Kathiavar, was a famous centre of Buddhist education. Heun Tsang visited Ballabhi also in his travels. At that time, there were a hundred Sangarama here., This university imparted education in politics, diplomacy, medicine and various other disciplines apart from religious education. Its students obtained senior positions in the courts of kings after completing their education. This university, too became the unfortunate victim of foreign invasion in the 12th century.

Vikramshila. Vikramshila was located on the banks of the Ganga in Magadha, Bihar. It was surrounded by a strong rampart. The teachers of this university were among the finest scholars of the day. Many important religious texts were translated into the

Tibetan language at this university. Its administration was in the hands of a committee. Students were granted admission only after a test was administered to them at the gates. Among the famous scholars of that time who administered this test were Ratankar Shanti, Baghiswara Kirti, Naroha, Pargyakamanti, Ratna Vajra, and Gyana Srimitra. The university provided education in grammar,. logic, philosophy, tantra, etc. It, too, was destroyed in the 12th century by Bakhtiar Khilji.

Odantpuri. Odantpuri had evolved as an educational centre before the Pal dynasty came into existence. The kings of this dynasty further developed this university. Its library was internationally known. 1000 monks received education here.

Mithila. Mithila had been a centre of Brahman education in ancient times, and when the Buddhist period came, it became an important centre of Buddhist education. It was here that a scholar named Jagdwara composed his renowned commentaries on such famous compositions as the *Gita, Devi Mahatamaya, Meghdoot, Gita Govinda, Malati Madhava,* etc. Vidyapati was born here. Apart from other subjects, Nyaya philosophy also was taught here. A student was deemed to heave passed only after he had taken a difficult examination in Nyaya and Logic.

Nadia. Nadia was established at the junction of the Bhaghirathi and Jalangi rivers in the 11th century by the Sen kings of Bengal. Jayadeva's Gita Govinda and Shoolapani's Smriti-viveka were composed here. It was a centre of teaching in Nyaya and Logic. It retained its reputation even during the middle ages.

Jagdalla. Rampal had the town of Ramvati established on the banks of the Ganges in Bengal in the 11th century. He also had a monastry named Jagdalla established here. This soon emerged as a centre of Buddhist education.

Vibhutichandra, Dansheela, Shubhkara, and Mokshakara were some of the famous teachers of this university.

This period gave birth to distinctions of class and Varna in the sphere of education, and it was in reaction to this that the Buddhist and Jain religions came into existence. Their system of education changed from the method of teaching by gurus to an institutional method.

Buddhist education had many notable features, the most significant of which were the following—

Abilities of the Student. In the Buddhist period, every class in society, except the Chandals, had the right to receive education. It was denied only to the ill, the handicapped, the dishonoured and those punished for crimes. Education began at the age of 8. Till the age of 12, the student remained in a state of Sharamana. After attaining the age of 20, he was qualified to became a monk. Education was imparted through the medium of Pali.

Pababja Ritual. Before a student could enter a monastry for receiving education, he had to perform the Pababja ritual. In which, according to the 'Vinaypataka', the student had his head shaved of all hair, dressed himself in yellow clothes, placed his forehead at the feet of the monks living in the monsatry, and then sat cross-legged on the floor to repeat the following words thrice-

I take Refuge to Buddha.
I take Refuge to Dharma.
I take Refuge to Sangh

He was then ordained to obey ten rules, which included abstaining from theft, killing of any living being, impure conduct, partaking of food at prohibited times, use of intoxicating things, use of cosmetics, taking things without being offered, accepting objects of gold and silver in alms; watching dances or listening to music, etc. After the performing of this ritual, the student was called a 'shramana' or 'samner'.

Upsampada Ritual. After attaining the age of twenty years, the student had to adopt 'Upsampada': On this occasion, the presence of ten monks was essential. After this ritual, the male monks were called 'Bhikshu' and the female monks 'Bhikshuni'. Even at this stage, monks were required to observe such rules as living under a tree, eating food obtained in their begging bowls, wearing clothes begged from others, and drinking the wine of a cow as a medicine, etc.

Duration of Education. The total period of education was 22 years, composed of 12 years as *pababja*, and 10 years as *upsampadaa*.

Students-teacher Relationship. Students were required to serve their teachers, beg for alms; eat food thrice a day, wear three items of clothing, bathe themselves with pure water, and live in discipline. According to Dr. Altekar, a teacher's relations with his new students was akin to the father-son or paternal relationship. They were linked to each other in mutual respect, faith and love. During this period, equality was the foundation of this relationship in which both students and teachers fulfilled their respective obligations and duties.

Feminine Education. In the Buddhist period, women occupied a position inferior to men. Initially, they were prohibited from joining a Sangha or congregation. Later on, they were granted admission to such congregations and it was then that feminine education progressed. Dr. Altekar points out that the permission for women to enter congregations gave great encouragement to feminine education, particularly to the education of women belonging to the noble and trading classes. There is considerable evidence to prove that feminine education prevailed during this period. Separate monastries were established for women. Among the women who attained fame were Sheel

Bhattarika, Vijayanka, Prabhudevi, etc. A lady named Sanghmitra went to Ceylon to propagate the Buddhist faith.

Vocational Education. The syllabus of education during this period was comprehensive. It comprehended education in writing, agriculture, commerce, cottage industries, animal husbandry, elephant lore, archery, magic, knowledge of reviving the dead, knowledge of animal cries and sounds, prophesy, control over sensuous activities, bodily gestures, medicine, etc. Dr. R.K. Mukerjee, explains that the demand for the knowledge of Sippa or professional and scientific education was no less than the demand for general education or for religious studies.

Syllabus. During the Buddhist period education was imparted in art, handicrafts, military science, the science of taming and training animals, archery, geology, etc., along with education in script writing, arithmetic and religious discussion. The educational syllabus was divided into the religious and the material or worldly.

Education was conducted in this period according to two kinds of syllabus- the religious and the material. The former comprehended the teaching of Vedas and Buddhist literature, since it was a time when both these kinds of literature were studied liberally.

The material or worldly syllabus paid attention to the material or physical needs of society. It included training in such subjects as writing, arithmetic, argumentation, spinning and weaving, printing, dyeing, knitting, stitching, sculpture, art, music, agriculture, animal husbandry, etc.

In this period, too, as in the preceding Vedic and Brahmanic periods, the relations between students and teachers were cordial. It was the duty of the student to obey and to serve his teacher. In addition, there was provision for penance in the event of crime.

Education in the Buddhist and Vedic periods, can be compared thus—

	Vedic Education		*Buddhist Education*
1.	Education was conducted in the gurukul or teacher's house.	1.	Education was imparted in schools or universities
2.	Students lived as members of a family.	2.	Education was institutionalized.
3.	The emphasis was upon the study of the Vedas. subjects.	3.	Emphasis was upon propagation of religion and study of general
4.	Sanskrit was the medium of education.	4.	Praakrit was the medium.
5.	Brahmans were the teachers	5.	Teachers were chosen from among the monks
6.	Education was not available to every class of society	6.	Education was universal.
7.	The student's life was rigorous.	7.	It was convenient, lacking in rigour.
8.	Education was free.	8.	A fee was payable-in some form or the other.
9.	Sanskrit was taught.	9.	Pali and other languages were taught.

In the sphere of education, the Buddhist period has its own contribution. According to Dr. F.E. Kaey, the Buddhist religion played a very significant role by putting an end to the monopoly of Brahamaṇic schools and providing opportunities for education for men and women of every caste. It thus gave rise to a general desire for education among all people. It encouraged this demand, and as a result, the concept of public primary schools evolved.

Initially, Buddhist education was free from defects. Like Vedic education, it was dominated by religion. However, the teaching of physical skills came to be denigrated during this period. Besides, the monastries soon became places for lecherous indulgence among monks and nuns. Besides, the excessive emphasis upon non-violence led to the enfeeblement of the nation. The education of women also came to be neglected. It also became one-sided and partial because of its primary emphasis upon religion. Dr. R E. Kaey has pointed out that Buddhism presented an ideal of life in which there was hatred for this transient world. Consequently, the education based on such a philosophy prepared the individual for the other world, not for this world.

The education imparted during the Buddhist period was in reality, a reaction to the education of the preceding post Vedic period and the Brahman period. During this period, educational institutions for general education were established. They made provisions for imparting primary as well as higher education. An important contribution of this period is the imparting of education in various practical subjects, a tradition which has come down to the present day. It was in this period that the method of collective teaching and the presence of numerous teachers in a single institution was evolved. Educational institutions were formally organised and established in this period. The organisation of the Nalanda and the Ballabhi universities was so advanced that it continues to influence the organisation and structuring of universities till the present day. The system of determining a minimum age for higher education, providing a set of rules and taking a test for admission are even today guiding the educational structure.

However, the Buddhist age too, like the Vedic age, did not remain without blemish. In the beginning, in this period too, equal respect was given to manual and intellectual skills but with the passage of time, the former came to be regarded as a pre-requisite the higher class of society. A religion which evolved as an institution led to the development of an institutional system of education, but then this itself became the cause of its downfall.

However, it is no less true that the educational method of the Buddhist period provided new standards in the sphere of morality and discipline. The accounts provided by Huen Tsang, Fa Hein and It Sing throw light on the contributions of this age to education.

3

MEDIEVAL TIMES

Islamic education was a foreign system which was transplanted to India and grew up in its new soil with very little connection with Brahmanic education. —*Dr. F.E. Kaey*

Era of Change

With the emergence of Islam, the attention of Muslim kings turned towards India. Time was kind to them. It allowed them to settle themselves firmly in this country. After the Gulam, Khilji, Tuglak, Sayyed and Lodhi dynasties, Mogul kings established many educational institutions in India. This education, too, had its roots in religion. During this period, Indian art and culture came under the influence of Arab culture and civilization. It was only natural that the same political influence should also have made itself felt. In consequence, education too came under this influence. Islam had its origin between 570 A.D. and 632 A.D. Hazrat Mohammed collected his messages in the Holy Quran, and this text came to be an instrument of social direction for the Muslim kings. During this period, these kings made arrangements for education in order to serve their own interests. Mohammed Gauri started his aggressions on India, but at the same time, he also had mosques and schools constructed in Ajmer to make arrangements for education in Islam and Muslim law. His successor Qutubuddin also followed in his footsteps. The other rulers of his dynasty, Altamesh, Razia Begum, Nasiruddin Balban and others also had mosques, maktabs and schools established with government aid.

According to Hazrat Mohammed, of all the gifts that parents can give to their children, the best is the gift of a liberal education. The ink in the pens of students is purer and noble than even the blood of martyrs.

In the same manner, Ferozshah Tuglak of the Tuglak dynasty made efforts for the propagation of education. One of the schools established by him in Delhi has been described as follows. The school was located in a large ground and a big building with massive towers. It was situated in a garden in which human skill harmonized with nature, thus creating an environment most suitable for contemplation and thought. Near the school was a lake, whose water shone like silver. The grand building of the school was reflected in its waters. It was an enchanting sight to see hundreds of students crossing the polished and smooth floors and congregating round their teachers. According to N.N. Law there were provisions for governmental aid and scholarships in these schools.

During the reign of Sikander Lodi (1489-1519), Indians, too, had begun to learn Persian (Pharsi). Aftet obtaining knowledge of this language, they began to work in governmental departments. The Muslim rulers themselves felt the need for Hindu workers in the administrative sphere, and hence they made arrangements for the study of Indian languages. And, as a result of the contact between the Hindus and Muslims, Urdu, which was the spoken form of Persian mixed with Hindi, was evolved.

The Mughal rulers who followed the earlier Muslim rulers had relatively greater interest in education, and hence it was in this later period that education developed more adequately. Akbar authorised the translation of many important Indian texts, including the *Mahabharata,* the *Ramayana, Atharvaveda* and *Lilawati*, into Persian. Akbar's deep interest in education is highlighted by Abul Fazal's comments in his famous work Aiene Akbari to the effect that in every country, and especially in India, boys were kept in school for years where they were taught about consonants and vowels. Since they had to read numerous books, a large part of the boys' time was wasted. Emperor Akbar declared that each student should be taught to write the alphabet in various ways. Each student was required to learn the name of every letter (varna) within two days. Emphasis was laid upon imparting education in moral values, arithmetic, political arithmetic, agriculture, medicine, logic, and physical, mathematical and divine philosophy to every student.

Jehangir went so far as to enact a law that the property and wealth of any person dying without an heir would be utilized for the repair of schools and religious buildings. Shahjahan had a university established near the Jama Masjid. Aurangzeb did propagate Muslim education, but at the same time he destroyed Hindu schools and temples. He granted excessive facilities for Muslim students, but he accorded a low status to teachers.

After the collapse of the Mughal Empire, schools suffered a severe blow. Many such institutions closed down due to anarchy and lack of finances. According to Vakil and Natrajan - "It must be noted that while mosques, maktabs and madrassas sprang up with the spread of Mohammadan power and provided facilities for Islamic learning in different parts of the country, the Hindu system of education continued to prevail in *pathashalas, maths* and temples except where their work was disturbed or dislocated by Mohammadan inroads or invasions." One finds a lack of organisation in Muslim education.

In the Muslim period, education was founded on community basis. Hence, it is illogical to claim that the Muslim ruler sought to propagate education liberally. Whatever the extent to which they propagated education, it was motivated by their own objectives, selfish interests and ambitions.

Bernier, the famous French traveller who visited India during this period, observed that during the period which he had described, it was only natural to find deep and universal ignorance. Was it possible to establish suitably financially aided schools and colleges or other centres of education in India? Where would the organisers be found? And, even if they were found, from where would the students be obtained? He also observed the absence of individuals whose wealth was adequate for providing suitable aid to colleges. And, even if such individuals existed, he felt that no one had the courage to compel them to bring out their wealth for such an investment. He felt that even some individual did venture on such a foolish act, there was an absence of religious places, enterprises and offices with employment potential which could utilize the ability and science imparted to students, and thus serve as an inspiration for youth to be hopeful and to compete for future success.

The Significance

During the Muslim period, education developed so slowly that no notable characteristic of it ever emerged. Minor rulers had educational institutions established for the satisfaction of their interests. However, the following features can be noted

Encouragement by the State. Muslim rulers took an interest in education, and so they provided aid to maktabs and madrassas. There were granted jagirs or landed property. Scholars were given places of eminence in the courts of kings. The rulers started giving aid to madrassas and maktabs being run in or along with mosques. Hence, their propagation of education was communal.

Arabic and Persian. During this period, special stress was laid on the teaching of Arabic and Persian, which were made the media of education by Muslim rulers. Knowledge of these two languages was essential for securing employment in government offices. Consequently, Hindus too began to learn Arabic and Persian.

Religious Influence. The education of this period was profoundly influenced by Islam. Every Muslim sought education for the purpose of searching for knowledge and for religious purposes. There is direct evidence of the influence of Islam on the education of this period. Students were required to memorise the Koran. Importance was attached to study of Islam. This religious influence upon education was positive proof of the communal attitude of Muslim rulers.

Materialism. Muslim education sought the spread of education only from the practical and materialistic viewpoints. Education in manual skills, sculpture, agriculture, medicine, etc., is proof of this. In addition to religious education, teachers tried to ensure that after receiving education, the child should become capable of earning his livelihood. Consequently, knowledge of military science, painting, sculpture, housing construction, manufacture of weapons, etc., was also imparted. Knowledge of such subjects was given to students directly and individually by experts through a system of apprenticeship.

Development of History-writing. By initiating the writing of the history of their period. Muslim rulers helped to develop the art of writing history. Both Mughal and Muslim rulers commissioned the writing of the histories of their period or reigns. Among the most famous of these are *Babar nama, Akbar nama*, etc.

Emergence of Urdu. The evolution of the new language 'Urdu' which emerged from the inter-mixing of Arabic and Persian, is the greatest contribution of the Mughal period. The importance that this language enjoys today is due entirely to the Muslim period.

Aims of Education

The education imparted in the Muslim period had numerous objectives. Its prime objective was to create able employees for the political and administrative system. However, the objectives of education underwent modifications as the attitudes of successive rulers changed. The objectives of education during Akbar's reign were completely different from its objectives during Aurangzeb's rule. In general, Muslim education had the following objectives-

Propagation of Knowledge. Religious knowledge could have been propagated among the Muslims who had come to India or those who had been converted to Islam only through education. Hazrat Mohammad had said that knowledge is divine and without it salvation is not possible. He taught people the difference between duty and wrong actions, religious and irreligious deeds, and laid stress on the need for knowledge through education.

Propagation of Religion. Religion was the basis of education, and hence the purpose of education was propagation of religion. Maktabs were established along with mosques. It was generally held that the propagation of Islam was synonymous with the propagation of religion and he who engaged in this became- a martyr. It was for this reason that knowledge of Koran was imparted in the maktabs. Hazrat Mohammad had also declared that a proper and liberal education was the finest of gifts that parents could bestow on their children.

Propagation of Religious Laws. Education also aimed at propagating the major laws of Islam and the shariyats of the holy Koran. Islamic religion had evolved very specific moral criteria, and it was the purpose of education to propagate them. All these elements contributed to the achievement of Islam's social and political objectives and the strengthening of its laws and customs in this period.

Wordly Progress. According to Jafar, the state encouraged the educated, people in every conceivable way. The posts of

Kazis (preachers) and wazirs (ministers) were reserved for the educated. Besides, Muslim education also aimed at preparing the individual for future life. Many Hindus received the highest Muslim education and rose to high positions.

Strengthening the Administration. Another objective of Muslim education was to strengthen the administration. Muslim rulers believed that their administration could not be firmly entrenched in the absence of education, and hence they wanted to utilize the educational system for strengthening their own political position.

Centres of Learning

The political organisation of the Muslim rulers was decentralised. The Mansabdars, kings, zamindars or landlords, etc., became dependent rulers of their individual areas after paying the requisite tax to the royal treasury. These rulers had mosques constructed, and soon the mosques changed into maktabs and madrassas. During the Muslim period, Agra, Delhi, Jaunpur, Lahore, Ajmer, Bidar, Lucknow, Ferozabad, Jullundur, Multan, Bijapur, etc., became important centres of education.

Agra. Agra was founded by Sikandar Lodi. He had the town established as a centre of Islamic education, and it soon took the form of a university. Hundreds of madrassas in this town provided education in literature, mathematics, philosophy, medicine, etc. Later on, Akbar, Jehangir and Shahjahan also contributed to the development of education in this town.

Delhi. Delhi was renowned far and wide as a centre of Muslim education. Nasiruddin established the Nasaria Madrassa here. The Gulam dynasty also helped the spread of education in Delhi. During the reign of Alauddin Khilji, 34 famous scholars of Islam lived in Delhi. Feroz Tuglak had 30 madrassas established. Humayun opened madrassas for imparting knowledge of astrology and geography. Akbar, Jehangir, Shahjahan and Aurangzeb also established various madrassas for imparting knowledge of various specific fields.

Jaunpur. During the reign of Feroz, Jaunpur was a prominent centre of Muslim education. It had many schools imparting education in the arts, literature and other spheres of knowledge. The Sharkias made valuable contributions to the development of education. Sher Shah Suri himself was a student here.

Bidar. Bidar, too, was an important educational centre. Mahmood Gawan had a huge madrassa and a library established here. Later, Alauddin Ahmed contributed to the development of education.

In addition to the above centres, there were at least one maktab and one madrassa in every village of Bijapur, Golkunda, Malwa, Khandesh, Multan, Gujarat, Lucknow, Sialkot and Bengal.

The Infrastructure

During the Muslim period, the system of education was organised in the following manner—

Bismillah. Education began with the performance of the ritual known as 'Bismillah', which was performed at the age of 4 years, 4 months and 4 days. It was similar to the Upnayan ceremony of the Vedic period and the Pabbaja ritual of the Buddhist period. On this day, the child was adorned with a new crown anti sent to his teacher, the Maulvi, where the latter inaugurated the child's education with a recitation from the Koran. Affluent people had this ritual performed at home.

Maktab. Education began in the maktab, i.e., a primary school. The teachers called Maulvis taught the alphabet along with verses from the Koran. The child's primary education took place in these schools. Generally, most such maktabs were appendages of mosques. The child was taught writing, the Koran, namaz or prayer, azaan, arithmetic, drafting, conversation, letter-writing, etc.

Madrassa. Madrassas provided higher education to the students. They were aided by the government. Here higher education was imparted through lectures. There were arrangements for hostels in the madrassas. They were owned privately as well as by the state.

Syllabus. The syllabus of education in the Muslim period included such subjects as the holy Koran, the biography of Hazrat Mohammed Sahib, the history and the laws of Islam, Arabic and Persian, grammar, literature, logic, philosophy, law, astrology, history, geography, agriculture, Unani system of medicine, etc. There were provisions for teaching Sanskrit to Hindu children. Madrassas provided both religious and material or worldly education. Subjects of religious education included Quran, Islamic laws, history and Sufi philosophy, while worldly or material education consisted of grammar, language, literature, etc. There were some specialized centres for education in particular subjects.

Method of Teaching. Emphasis was placed on memorisation in addition to reading, writing and arithmetic. The most prevalent method was the oral. Individual attention was paid to students. The monitor system had been used in maktabs and madrasssas.

Student-teacher Relationship. During this period, relations between students and teachers were not marked by intimacy, but there were no doubts about sincerity and purity. Though teachers received a low salary, they had an important place in society. People respected them and bestowed faith on them. The teacher had a paternal attitude towards his wards. It was believed that the students who served their teachers made God happy. Despite this, there was nothing notable in this relationship. Aurangzeb is known to have insulted his teacher Mulla Shah Saleh.

Reward and Punishment. There was a system of severe punishment to maintain order and discipline, but brilliant scholars were also rewarded.

Medium of Education. During the Muslim period, Arabic and Persian were the media of education. However, after the growth of Urdu, education began to be imparted through this language.

Examination System

The stream of Muslim education continued to flow in India for a period of almost 500 years. Its system passed through the hands and reign of many rulers. This process inevitably left an indelible mark of Indian life. The shortcomings and virtues of this method of education can be enumerated as follows.

According to Mrs. Sarojini Naidu, "The impact of the Muslims and the Hindu has evolved the present Indian culture. We cannot, even if we are foolish enough to try, untwist this closely interwisted and inter-twined unity of culture that makes modern India."

1. In this period, there began a synthesis between worldly or materialistic and religious education, and consequently, a tendency towards professionalization or vocationalization emerged. Only high educated individuals were given employment in state services.
2. Education had achieved objectivity. Education was not merely for the propagation of knowledge. Its practical use fulness was another essential condition. Aurangzeb laid great stress on making the education of princes highly practical.
3. Education was compulsory for Muslim children. Hazrat Mohammad had declared that receiving education was akin to achieving God. He who obtains education obtains God.
4. During this period, great attention was paid to the growth of history and the art of writing history. In fact, the tradition of writing history had its roots in this period. The various forms of literature also underwent significant growth.
5. The relations between students and teachers were generally good, but during Aurangzeb's reign, teachers lost their high status in society.

6. During this period, Agra, Delhi, Jaunpur, Bidar, Ajmer, Bijapur, Golkunda, Hyderabad, Malwa, Khandesh, Gujarat, Lucknow, Sialkot, and Bengal emerged as important centres of Muslim education.

Though education underwent considerable propagation during this period, it was not free from shortcomings. It also became lax when the Mughal empire began to decline. The invasions of Nadir and Ahmed Shah Abdali also had a detrimental effect. Its defects were the following—

1. During this period, excessive stress was laid on the material aspect of education. Though religious education was a part of the curriculum, more attention was given to the material aspect of life.
2. Madrassas and maktabs had a short life during-periods of anarchy. Political instability undermined their economic strength.
3. Durring this period, Arabic and Persian education had great influence. Akbar did make attempts to popularise and spread Hindi, but they proved futile. In the end, it was Urdu that emerged.
4. During this period, only the affluent received education. There was no arrangement for public education. Besides, education was limited to towns, since there were almost no educational facilities in village.
5. The education of women was completely neglected during this period. special provisions were however made for ladies belonging to the royal families. Besides, since a sense of insecurity prevailed almost everywhere, no attention was paid to the education of women.
6. In this educational system, the emphasis was not upon integral development; it was almost exclusively upon reading and writing.

7. Not much importance was attached to self-study, and students were often found enjoying their comfort instead of studying. Most students and teachers remained involved in useless controversies.

The history of Muslim education has been the history of a system of government and a social system extending over 700 years. As a result of numerous political and social factors, Muslim education could not touch the heart of public life, and ultimately, not even governmental protection could prolong its life.

4

Modern Times

Changing Pattern

British and other foreign education had its beginning in India with the activities of Christian missionaries. The first of the missionaries to come to India belonged to the Roman Catholic sect. Escaping from the changing circumstances in Europe, these missionaries set foot in countries outside Europe with the intention of establishing a new religious empire. In their search for new territories in which to propagate their religion, these missionaries discovered India, Africa, the America and Australia, which, till then, were unknown to the Europeans.

As soon as the Portugese found their feet in India, Franciscan, Dominican, Jesuit and other Roman Catholic sects began their work of spreading their religion among the country's tribals. They also began to set up educational institutions for this purpose. These sects established four kinds of institutions—

1. Portugese and Latin language primary schools attached to churches and missionary institutions.

2. Schools providing vocational and agricultural education along with traditional education, to the orphan children in India.

3. Jesuit Colleges for higher education.

4. Theological training centres for training padres and missionaries.

The first Christian priest (padre) to take upon his shoulders the task of propagating both religion and education in India was St. Francis Xavier. He collaborated with St. Ignatius Loyola in the establishment of a Jesus society. St. Xavier made a practice of roaming from village to village with a book in one hand and a bell in the other. He ordered his brother Mansila to establish a school in every village to make it possible for children to go to school every day. The St. Anne College was established at Bandra, Bombay in 1555, while in 1580 a Jesuit College was opened at Chaul in Goa.

Robert Nobili worked at Madura (Madras) from 1605 to 1656. He was shrewd enough to make contact not only with the shudras but even the higher castes, including Brahmins. He declared himself to be a brahmin belonging to the European world and the bearer of the lost Veda. He wore saffron clothes and lived like the sanyasis, (those who have renounced the world) of India. It was he who originated the process of religious conversion.

Like the Portugese in south India, the Dutch were carrying on the work of religious conversion and education in Bengal. The French established educational institutions at Mahe, Yeman, Chandranagar, Karkil and Pondicherry. In these, French was taught along with other subjects. The Danish traders set up their trading companies at Tanjore and Srirampur, and along with their trading activities, carried, on religious conversion and education, in cooperation with the British. In 1719, the Danish people set up a Christian Mission Society to further their goals.

Company's Role

The East India Company was established by a few Englishmen in 1599 for the purpose of trading with India. In 1660, it obtained the permission of Queen Elizabeth to trade with eastern countries, and for the purpose of implementing this design, It set up its trading centre at Masaulipattam. Soon, its trade began to expand rapidly; its financial position became strong. The East India Company had made spread of religion its goal, in addition to its trading ambitions. For this purpose and for the spread of education, the company sent a few Indians to England in 1614. In addition, a department of Arabic was set up at Oxford University for training missionaries.

In 1673, Pringle established a secondary school at Madras, in which teaching was done by the Company's employees. The Company also issued instructions for the setting up of schools in every cantonment and fort. In keeping with the charter of 1698, the Company opened schools in Madras, Bombay and Calcutta between 1715 and 1731, while financially aided schools were set up at Tanjore and Kanpur. In all such institutions followers of the Protestant sect were given priority. Some of the following causes were responsible for the East India Company's efforts at spreading education-

The Company's Educational Policy (1765-1813). The ambitions of the Company grew with its victories in the battles of Plassey (1757) and Buxar (1765). It now began to dream of setting up an empire. In order to fulfill this dream, it now began to follow the policy of appeasement. In the educational sphere, this meant adopting the policy of religious indifference, in pursuance of which it stopped giving aid to schools.

Policy of Appeasement. In order to please the Muslims, Warren Hastings set up the Calcutta Madrassa in 1781, in which, through the medium of Arabic, the Quran, law, mathematics, logic and grammar were taught. In 1791 Jonathan Duncan established the Benaras Sanskrit College, and in 1800, Lord Wellesely established the Fort William College at Calcutta.

Individual Efforts in the Educational Field. Mrs. Campbell set up an orphanage for girls at Madras in 1786. Dr. Enduebell set up an orphanage in 1787. In 1788, Brown set up a school for imparting English education to Indians. Mrs. Pitt, Loshan, Copland and others set up numerous schools.

Missionary Efforts. The Anglican missionaries started an aided school in Calcutta, besides which a 'free' school was also established. The Baptist Mission also did commendable work in the spread of education. In 1800, a printing press was set up at Srirampur for the printing of books. In religious controversies books printed here began to abuse the Hindu and Muslim religions as well as religious persons belonging to these religions. Consequently, Lord Minto confiscated the press. Despite this, the missionaries continued their activities.

Role of the British Parliament. Charles Grant (1767-1780) remained an employee of the company for some time, but he subsequently became its Chairman and also a member of the British Parliament. He propagated the view that Hindus were ignorant and hence championed the cause of their education. He stressed the view that they should be given western education.

The Charter of 1793. Influenced by the views of Charles Grant, William Wilberforce suggested the following amendment in the Company's charter. He said that it was the special and inalienable duty of the British Parliament (*dhara sabha*) to employ all proper and rational means for the security and prosperity of the British interest in India. For the achievement of these objectives, it must adopt means by which the level of Indians in knowledge, religion and morality could be raised. Opposing the proposal, Sharp argued that the religious tendency and morality of Indians was not, inferior to those of other persons, and hence any attempt at converting them from their religious beliefs or giving them more knowledge would be insane?

The Charter of 1813. Despite the rejection of the educational proposal of 1793, Christian missionaries continued their efforts. The Company's charter was due for renewal in 1813. In view of this, the following proposal was put forward at this opportunity. It was proposed that since education was gradually deteriorating in India, the administration of the Company should take upon itself the responsibility of educating Indians, and for this purpose substantial investments should be made. This proposal was accepted. Lord Minto made arrangements for aid to the extent of ten thousand pounds per year for education. This charter is a unique link in the history of Indian education. In the. opinion of Narulla and Nayak, this charter laid the foundation for a state policy of education in India. It also marks the turning point in the history of modern education in India, a point at which the first period ended and a new one began.

West vs East

In India, during the British period, education was founded on an individualistic base: One hundred thousand schools were operating in Bengal alone. But, despite this, the Christian missionaries who came to India during the East India Company's reign began to propagate education in their own way. Gradually, their stray endeavours took the concrete shape of formal schools, colleges and universities. The main controversy raging at the time was whether Indians should be given English education or education in Indian languages and subjects. This is referred to as the East-West controversy.

The Charter of 1813 had made the state responsible for education. It had made provisions for the expenditure of ten thousand pounds (the equivalent of one lakh rupees), but in the absence of proper distribution, the amount could not be utilized even in ten years. Till 1833, the Company remained quite indifferent towards education, and hence this period of twenty years remained, essentially, a period of uncertainty. The East-West controversy continued to rage during these twenty years.

In 1831, a General Committee on Public Instruction was constituted. It laid stress on useful or utilitarian knowledge. The main questions the committee faced were the purposes, objectives, media and means of education. These problems led to the emergence of three classes in the educational sphere. (1) One class consisted of those who wished to teach Indian and other sciences to Indians through the medium of Sanskrit, Arabic and Persian. This group supported the policy of appeasement of the different linguistic communities. (2) The second group favoured English as the medium of education. Among its supporters were Charles Hunt and Raja Rammohun Roy. (3) The third group was in favour of education through the language of the masses, i.e., regional languages. All the three groups were composed of the employees of the company.

This was a period of uncertainly, controversy and lack of clarity. The company itself wanted to evade the burden of education, and as a result of this controversy, the Charter of 1813 could not be implemented. In 1814, the Directors of the Company issued a directive, clarifying the educational policy. In it, they laid emphasis upon financial aid, distribution of titles of honour, preservation of ancient literature, and acceptance of the Hindu system of education. However, this directive as well as clause 43 of the Charter remained futile.

The declaration of the charter remained buried in the company's files till 1823, since the company wanted to concentrate all its energies upon trading activity. Warren Hastings was in charge of the company's affairs from 1813 to 1823, a period in which the company engaged in wars with the Gurkhas, Pindaras, Marathas and Pathans, and concentrated upon strengthening its administration. Consequently, it made only the- weakest efforts on the educational front.

By 1824, however, the Directors of the Company in India had developed a political awareness. In 1824, the British government sent a directive to the Company's Governor-General in which it was said that the government was extremely anxious for the progress and improvement of the educational system for the people of India. It wanted the company to be fully aware of this interest and zest. For the fulfillment of this purpose, the government was prepared to make extensive sacrifices, if it could be told about the resources required. Consequently, the Public Instruction Committee became active. It took the following steps—(1) reorganisation of the Calcutta madrassa and the Benaras Sanskrit College; (2) establishment of oriental studies colleges at Calcutta, Agra, Delhi and Murshidabad; (3) setting up of the Calcutta Educational Press, (4) translation of European texts.

Indians opposed the policy suggested by the Committee. Their opposition was put succinctly into words by Sharp. As he viewed it, the Indians argued that the government of the country wanted to keep them narrowminded through education in' oriental sciences only. They wanted the administration to abandon its thoughts of setting up a sanskrit college at Calcutta, and instead to encourage a more liberal and rational system of education which should encompass the inculcation of such subject as mathematics, natural sciences, biology, chemistry and other practical sciences. As a consequence, arrangements were made for providing education in English at Calcutta, Benaras, Agra and other places.

In 1819, Elphinstone spent a part of the allocation for the spread of education upon establishing the Poona Sanskrit College. He also formulated a scheme for the spread of public education, but it was opposed by Warden, one of the members of the committee. Warden supported the principle of Downward Filtration of Education, arguing that education reached the common man through filtration from above. It was argued that "Education was to permeate the masses from above. Drop by drop from the Himalyas of the Indian Life, useful information was to trickle downwards, forming, in time, a broad and stately stream to irrigate the thirsty plains." Accepting this principle, the Company rejected Elphinstone's proposals who, being disappointed, returned to England in 1829. Munro, the then Governor of Madras, was conscious of the administration's neglect of public education, and hence he laid stress upon the establishment of vernacular schools in every district or tehsil, but he did not succeed in his objective.

Christian missionaries opened schools along with their centres of religious propagation in Bengal, Bombay, Madras, Agra, Meerut, Benares, Jaunpur, Mathura, Ludhiana, Burdwan, Ajmer and other places. In these schools knowledge of the Bible was imparted along with education in other subjects through the medium of the regional languages. Among the many who propagated the cause of education through their individual efforts were Raja Rammohun Roy, David Heyer, Edward Hide East, Radhakant Dave, etc.

In 1833, the Company's Charter came up for consideration. The British government expressed its dissatisfaction with the educational activities of the Company's employees. As a result, in, the new Charter of 1833, provisions were made for giving facilities to missionaries, an annual grant of ten lakh rupees, appointment of a Law member, basing the government's policy upon the power of the Governor General, etc. This charter brought about an increase in the posibilities of educational development among Indians. Lord Macaulay was sent as the Law member to India.

European Style

On June 10,1834, Lord Macaulay, who was a great scholar of English, came to India as the Law Member of the company. He supported the views of Charles Grant, and believed that Eastern education was inferior. On his arrival in India, Lord Bentick made him the chief of the Public Instruction Committee also. His advice was sought regarding section 43 of the Charter of 1813 as well as about the expenditure of one lakh rupees. Macaulay was waiting for just such an opportunity. On February 8, 1835, he presented his historical 'Minutes' in which he made a bitter attack upon Indian literature and culture and vilified it.

Theory of Macaulay

(a) In his elaboration of Section 43, Macaulay included English literature along with Sanskrit and Arabic literature, and along with the Indian scholars of Sanskrit and Arabic, he also enumerated English scholars. He also gave complete authority to the Company for spending the grant.

(b) A supporter of western literature, he had this to say for Indian literature- "A single shelf of a good European library was worth the whole native literature of India and Arabia." (Macaulay's Minutes). From the same viewpoint, he also praised the English language, arguing that it was the most flourishing and useful of all European languages. He, who knew this language, could easily obtain that vast treasure of knowledge which had been created by the most intelligent races of the world. English was the language of India's rulers, and hence, the higher classes living in the capitals also spoke it. It is perfectly possible that English may become the language of the trade on Eastern seas. (Macaulay's Minutes).

(c) Macaulay attached importance to the education of the higher classes and thus emphasised the theory of Downward Filtration.

(d) In education, Macaulay laid stress on religious objectivity. As he put it, it was the duty of England to teach Indians what was good for their health, and not what was suited to their tastes. He implemented the theory of Downward Filtration. He opined that the English rulers should create a class which could mediate between the English and the millions over whom they ruled. He wanted them to be Indians by colour and blood, but English by interest, morality and intellect. But, because of this principle, the objective of an education in consonance with Indian society could not be achieved.

Lord Macaulay was very typical, sincere to his country. He always thought about the propagation of English language and culture. His ideas for India were full of prejudices. Some of them are given here.

1. A single shelf of a good European library was worth the whole native literature of India and Arabia.
2. It is possible through English education to bring about a class of persons, Indian in blood and colour, but English in tastes, in opinions, in morals and in intellect.
3. English stands prominent even among the languages of the west. Who ever knows the English language has ready access to all the vast intellectual wealth which all the wisest nations of the earth have created.

Macaulay's resolution was put into the hands of the leader of the Orientalists in the Public Instruction Committee, Mr. Princep who was the leader of the opposition, he reduced it to shreds with his arguments. Despite this, Lord Bentick, who was prejudiced against eastern systems of thought, supported Macaulay's educational views and declared an educational policy founded on it. This policy gave primacy to the propagation of European literature and science, suspension of scholarships for students, neglect of publication of Eastern literature, and the propagation of English literature.

Lord Bentick's acceptance of the educational policy enunciated by Lord Macaulay gave stability to the English educational policy. This was the first genuine educational policy adopted by the contemporary government. Different people held different views on Macaulay's policy, but, in general, he is accepted as the inspiration behind the new educational policy. At least, he removed the element of doubt in this sphere and helped the government overcome its uncertainty.

It is beyond question that Macaulay said many prejudiced and bitter things about India, but his arguments had a definite force, and as a result, English came to be the language of government usage. Macaulay's dream of giving rise to a race which was Indian in colour and blood but English in dress conversation, ideas and thoughts, came true.

Policy of Auckland

Lord Auckland succeeded Lord Bentick as India's Governor General. Supporters of eastern education presented him with a representation opposing Macaulay's declaration. Lord Auckland agreed that the financial restraints upon oriental education were excessive. Consequently, he increased the educational grant for the orientalists, gave primacy to oriental studies, increased the number of scholarships for these studies, and made arrangements for printing and publication of oriental works. However, he also permitted the spending of more than one lakh rupees for the spread of English education.

During Lord Auckland's reign, Adam, who had been appointed by Lord Bentick to prepare a report on Indian education, had published his resort. It was a comprehensive document, containing some valuable suggestions for bringing about a Renaissance in India. Unfortunately, nothing was done to implement his ideas.

Declaration of Hardinge

In 1844, the then Governor-General, Lord Hardinge declared that priority in employment in the Company's organisation would be given to those who had received English education. As a result, the demand for English education increased, and education came to be directly linked with livelihood. At the same time, employment became more important than domestic crafts, which came to be neglected. Between 1833 and 1853, Bengal, Bombay, Madras, the Frontier areas, Uttar Pradesh, and Punjab witnessed the kind of growth in education which had not taken place in many previous years. Professional or vocational institutions providing education in medicine, engineering, law and other professions were established. However, at the same time, dissatisfaction with the Company's working was also being expressed. These improvements in the educational sphere were no more than a drop in the ocean.. Hence, in 1854, Wood's Despatch was enunciated.

In 1853, when the Company's Charter again came up for consideration and renewal, the need for a permanent and comprehensive educational policy was felt. The British Parliament asked the Select Committee to consider this question. After deliberation, the committee declared that the spread of education in India was not detrimental to the Company's interests. At that time, the president of the Company's Board of Control was Charles Wood, who published his declaration regarding education on 19th July, 1854. It is referred to as Wood's Despatch.

Letters by Wood

The Company's Charter was reviewed and modified after every twenty years. After modifications in 1773, 1813 and 1833, it was again to be modified in 1853, and hence a one-member committee evaluated the progress of Indian education. It said clearly that education in India could not be neglected. Consequently, a new declaration in the name of Charles Wood was published. It proved to be a monumental declaration, since it heralded a new era in the educational sphere.

By 1853, education in India had come to suffer from numerous problems. Consequently, a survey was organised. Its conclusions are contained in a declaration known as Wood's Despatch. On the basis of its recommendations, new educational policies were framed, under which a public Instruction Department, a post of Director Public Instruction, and universities which conducted examinations came to be established. These universities began to organise secondary and higher education. The notable features of this declaration were the following

1. Providing education was the government's duty.
2. The purpose of education, in addition to intellectual and moral development, was the creation of individuals capable of contributing to the government machinery.
3. The study of western language and literature, along with the study of oriental literature, was made a part of the curriculum.
4. Both English and Indian languages were accepted as the medium of instruction.

According to this declaration, new educational policies were framed and implemented. These policies included—(1) establishment of a department of education (2) establishment of universities (3) setting up of hierarchically linked educational institutions-primary, middle, high schools, colleges, universities (4) spread of public education (5) a system for giving aid (6) training of teachers (7) education of women (8) professional of vocational education (9) granting of priority in government services (10) authorship and publication in Indian languages and (11) education of Muslims.

Concerning this declaration, Paranjape's view is than its objectives were the following—education should evolve leadership in Indian students, industrial development should take place in India, education should make efforts for the protection of the motherland, education should aim at a self disciplined government. Thus while in 1854 it may have been a declaration, but to refer to it as such today would be ridiculous. Similar views have been expressed by Nurullah and Nayak. It does not appear rational or logical to refer to Wood's Despatch as the Magna Carta of Indian education.

Wood's Despatch contained the following main recommendations :

1. An educational department should be set up in each province and its highest official should be a Director of Public Instruction.
2. Universities should be set up at Calcutta, Madras and Bombay. These universities should have Chancellors, Vice-Chancellors and Fellows.
3. Emphasis should be laid upon the spread of public education.
4. A system of granting aid should be adopted.
5. Special institutions for training teachers should be set up.
6. Importance should be given to the education of women.

While on the one hand, this declaration was being published, on the other, the spark of independence was slowly glowing in the country. In 1857, the first bloody revolution for the country's independence took place, and it put an end, for ever, to the administration of the Company. The reins of India's administration passed into the hands of the British Parliament.

Control of Empress

The revolution of 1857 was responsible for farreaching changes in Indian education. The British Parliament now took over the reins of administration in India. Besides, Wood's Despatch had also put an end to the monopoly of missionaries over education. Thus, under the influence of this despatch, the British government established a General Council of Education of India in England. When Lord Rippon became the Viceroy, this institution asked him to carry out a survey of education in India. On reaching India, Lord Rippon appointed an Indian Education Commission on February 3, 1882. Its Indian members were Anand Mohan Bose, Sayyad Mahmood, Bhudev Mukerjee, T.K. Tailang, P Ranganand Mudaliar, Maharaja Jitendra Mohan Thakur and Haji Gulam. Its member secretary was B.L. Rice.

Hunter Commission

The chairman of this Commission was William Hunter. Of its 21 members, seven were Indians and of even these seven, three were nominated by the government.

Jurisdiction. The jurisdiction of the committee was put into the following words- "It will be the duty of the commission to enquire particularly into the manner in which effect has been given to the principles of the Despatch of 1854; and to suggest such measures as it may think desirable in order to further the carrying out of the policy therein laid down." (Resolution : Appointing the Commission, 1882). According to this declaration, the Commission was expected to reflect upon the possibilities for the spread of primary, secondary and higher education, and also to consider the state of grants.

Primary Education. Concerning primary education the Commission said that it should be regarded as public education. Its curriculum should be in accord with life. Its medium should be the regional language. It should get protection from the government. Local bodies should be converted into school-districts, and after considering the propriety, of school boards, budget and, aid, plans should be made for construction and repair of buildings.

Syllabus. Arithmetic, account of income and expenditure, local methods of mensuration, introduction to natural and physical science, agriculture, health and industrial arts.

Training. An adequate number of Normal Schools for the training of teachers should be established.

Financial Management. The local budget should invest in education and the provincial government should give one third or one half as aid to the local government. A part of the local budget should be collected through school fees, local bodies and other sources.

Secondary Education. The Commission put forward the following suggestions for removing the shortcomings of secondary education:

(i) Secondary education should be propagated through local bodies.
(ii) A system of providing aid should be introduced.
(iii) The government should establish schools wherever needed.
(iv) There should be one secondary school in every district.

The Commission remained silent on the question of removing the drawbacks of secondary education. It was faced with finding a solution to the problem of medium of education, training of teachers, and vocational education. All that it suggested was that there should be an emphasis upon the principle and practice of teaching in training colleges.

Higher Education. For the development of higher education, the Commission suggested that while giving aid, the following factors should be kept in mind; number of teachers, expenses, abilities of teachers, local needs, construction of building-furniture, and buildings, the grant of special aid for libraries and other teaching aids, giving priority to individuals trained in Western universities, provisions for optional subjects, preparation of ideal text books, lecture series on civic duties, granting limited rights of collecting fees to non-governmental colleges, providing free education to a fixed number of students, provision of scholarships for studying abroad, etc.

Religious Education. The Commission stressed that religious education should be in accordance with each student's own religion. It made no provision for religious education in governmental colleges. It allowed non-governmental institutions to make arrangements for such education, if they so wished.

Education of Women. For education of women, the Commission laid stress on free education and separate curriculum. It suggested that schools for girls should be opened wherever there was need or demand for such institutions.

In addition, the Commission also made provisions for the education of Muslims, Harijans and backward classes, tribals, people of hilly regions, and members of royal families. The Commission stressed the view that aid should be given to Indian or local institutions to encourage them. It suggested that there should be provisions for scholarships for students studying in them, that their administration should be taken over by local municipal boards or local bodies, and that they should have independence in framing their syllabi. The result of this attitude was that individual efforts at the spread of education benefitted profoundly and private institutions began to spring up. On the whole, the Commission's suggestions benefitted secondary and higher education. Missionaries opposed this effort, but the Commission argued that the burden and responsibility for the higher education of such a large country as India, with a wide diversity of local needs, could not be put into the hands of any one group, and especially the missionaries, who, despite their honesty and liberality, could never win the confidence of the Indian people. In addition, the Commission felt constrained to note, in complete unanimity, that the removal of direct responsibility of the educational department did not mean that it should be put into the hands of the missionaries.

In order to overcome the other defects in the Education Department, the Hunter Commission made useful suggestions for making grants systematic and regular. Students were given complete freedom of religious education, but the system of grants had no connection with this form of education. However, the Commission also gave due recognition to the education of women

Commission on Indian Universities

The recommendations of the Hunter Commission did lead to the growth of higher education, but Indian Universities continued to lack uniformity. The period of 1882 to 1902 was one of astonishing progress in various spheres. The system of grants made praiseworthy contribution to the spread of education.

In 1899, Lord Curzon became India's Viceroy. He is regarded as the most able and also the most hated administrator. In 1901, Curzon called a 'secret education commission' consisting of 15 members in Simla. There was not a single Indian on this commission. It put forward 150 resolutions, the main aim of which was to crush the nationalistic upsurge. Hence, Lord Curzon declared the setting up of a Commission on January 20, 1902, whose terms of reference were stated thus-"To enquire into conditions and prospects of the universities established in British India, to consider and report upon any proposals which have been, or may be made for improving their constitution and working, and to recommend to the Governor-General in- Council such measures as may tend to elevate the standard of University teaching, and to promote the advancement of learning". (Report of the Indian Universities Commission, 1902).

This Commission, stressing the need for reorganisation of universities, rejected the idea of setting up new universities. It also suggested the fixing of a limit for each university. It recommended that the standard of matric and higher education should be improved. It gave importance to the study of classical languages and arrangements for the best possible teaching of English. Its main recommendations were as follows-

1. New universities should not be established.
2. The constitutions of universities should be changed to make provisions for teaching in the universities.

3. Under-graduate and post-graduate curricula should be introduced.
4. Conditions for recognising colleges should be stern.
5. The Syndicates should have from 9 to 15 members.
6. The standard of the matric examination should be improved.

The Indian Universities Act (1904) was formulated on the basis of these recommendations. As a result, the standard of universities rose. They got the authority to conduct examinations, research and to make appointments. Their Senates now had from 50 to 100 members, appointed for five years.

For the Calcutta, Bombay and Madras universities, the number of elected members was fixed at 20 and for others at 15. The Governor-General was given the authority to determine the regional limits of universities. This Act granted a systematic form or structure to higher education in the country.

However, Indians soon became suspicious of Lord Curzon's educational policy, and it came in for criticism, though this did not cause Curzon even a moment of anxiety. In this connection, he went so far as to declare, in a lecture, that he felt no repentance at this opposition because he was confident that his policy had granted new life to Indian education. Expressing his views on Lord Curzon, A.N. Jha said that now, when the memory of innumerable clashes and conflicts was growing faint, every Indian was grateful for the statesmanship of this great Viceroy, Lord Curzon, who made such great endeavours to raise the portals of education in our country and also to protect our valued ancient monuments. He was still remembered for these great achievements, and he would always be praised for them by each succeeding generation of Indians. Nurullah and Nayak express the view that while on the one hand all government sources claimed this Act to be a panacea for all the evils of higher education in India, on the other hand, Indians loathed it as a retrograde legislative step. However, it was neither the first, nor the second. Undoubtedly, the Universities Act 1904 did not benefit higher education materially, but the fact remains that the credit for initiating a university improvement campaign must go to Lord Curzon. This campaign was moving slowly but steadily towards its well defined objectives.

Movement of Liberation

Curzon's policy of Divide and Rule and the consequent impetus to the National Struggle for Independence gave birth to the realization that our country needed a nationalistic education. At the Calcutta Conference of the Congress in 1906, Annie Besant declared that throughout the country a national education should be organised. This education should have the potential for satisfying the country's needs and making possible the achievement of its national objective. The national movement emphasized the following elements for a national education.

1. The educational system should be under Indian control.
2. It should arouse love for the motherland.
3. Imitation of the west and slavery to it should come to an end.
4. Western knowledge and science should be studied.
5. The dominance of the British should be brought to an end.
6. Vocational education should be developed.

This current of thought inspired the establishment of national schools. Such institutions as the Arya Samaj, Brahmo Samaj, Prarthana Samaj, etc., set up schools which provided education for creating a national character. The result was the emergence of such institutions as Shanti Niketan, Gurukul Kangi, Jamia Milia Islamia, Gujarat Vidyapeeth, Kashi Vidyapith, the Women's

University SNDT, etc. These institutions had a distinctly national character.

In 1910, Gopal Krishna Gokhale put forward a proposal for free and compulsory education, but he withdrew it when the government assured that such a scheme would be implemented. After this, the government put forward its own proposal regarding educational policy, and in it, were a number of resolutions regarding primary, secondary, higher and Women education:

In 1912, the government announced its educational policy. In this, it was proposed that, at the primary level, subjects such as writing, reading, arithmetic, drawing, making plans of a village, observation of nature and physical health should be taught. Arrangements were made for improving good primary schools and raising them to the level of upper primary schools. Provisions were made for replacing government-aided institutions by new institutions managed by local bodies, Arrangements were also made for providing trained teachers, fixing an upper limit of 50 students to a class, constructing good school houses, providing practical education to girls, and freeing universities of the responsibility of the matric examination. As a result of this policy, the field of school education was clearly separated from that of higher education.

Calcutta University

The first world war (1914) had a detrimental impact upon education. After its conclusion, the government appointed the Calcutta University Commission (1917-19).

This commission was appointed on September 14, 1917, under the Chairmanship of Dr. M.E. Sadler, the Vice Chancellor of Leeds University. It had six other members. The main purpose of the Commission was to study the circumstances which arose after the world war Its report consists of 13 parts. The Commission studied the circumstances of other universities also, in addition to those of Calcutta University.

Jurisdiction. -The jurisdiction of the Commission was stated thus- "To enquire into the conditions and prospects of the University of Calcutta and to consider the question of a constructive policy in relation to the question it presents."

This Commission converted secondary education into an intermediate link between primary and university education, and laid stress upon eradicating the problems of Calcutta University. It recommended that secondary classes should be removed from the purview of university education and the establishment of independent board of higher secondary education. It also recommended the restructuring of other Indian universities. It provided for pass courses as well as honours courses. It suggested that the Vice Chancellor's post should be a full-time one, with proper salary. Its views were that universities should be freed from governmental control. It stressed the setting up of academic councils in universities. It suggested that such subjects as art, engineering, medicine, law, agriculture, commerce, teachers training, etc., should fall within the sphere of higher education. It also attached importance to the creation of residential universities. It also gave greater importance than hitherto education of women, training of teachers, professional and vocational education.

The report of the Sadler Commission was influenced by the Halden report on the London University, and on its basis, arrangements for constituent colleges, incorporated colleges, professors, readers, court, academic councils, etc., were made in Indian universities also. Though the report was intended primarily for the Calcutta university, it came to influence the structure of the universities of Mysore, Patna, Benares, Aligarh, Dacca, Lucknow and Hyderabad as well.

Hertog Committee

A committee was set up under the chairmanship of Sir Philip Hertog in 1929. It took the view that the matric examination of the universities had influenced secondary education. It opined that students opting for other professions should be stopped at the middle level and taught according to a different curriculum. It wanted that the larger number of boys should be turned towards the industrial and commercial sphere from the middle level itself. They should be sent to institutions providing education in these professions. It attached great importance to the extravagance in the sphere of primary education and the obstacles existing there. It suggested that the causes of these phenomena should be identified and removed. It also paid heed to the professionalisation of education at the secondary level. It also emphasised the enrichment of libraries.

In its report, the Committee had reviewed the progress in education during the decade 1917-1927. It was the decade in which education had come to be seen as a medium for the building up of a nation. It was said in the report that education was now being seen as an important instrument of nation building. Interest in education had spread to the common people with the education department coming under the control of an Education Minister belonging to their own tribe. Even the backward classes were realising the importance of education and the demand for a right to education was becoming stronger.

The Hertog Committee also turned its attention towards extravagance and the problem of stagnation in the sphere of primary education. It pointed out that this problem arose from ignorance, lack of education, poverty, absence of means of transportation, seasonal diseases, and religious and caste prejudices. It stressed that, in order to overcome these obstacles, education should be organised on a firm and strengthened basis. It set down the age of 4 as the minimum limit for admission to the primary level, and pointed out the need for training to teachers, a liberal and useful curriculum, attention to local needs and problems, and giving national importance to primary education.

In the field of secondary education, the Hertog Committee pointed to the problem of failing candidates. In view of this, it suggested that the standards of earlier classes should be improved and the less capable students should be diverted to professional and commercial classes having their own separate curriculum. And, in order to ensure that only the most capable students reached the university, the Committee suggested that the entrance test should be a strict one.

The Committee also considered the unsatisfactory situation of feminine education, and made certain recommendations. It recommended that an Education Commission should be organised at the centre.

The report became the government's guide in the formulation of an education policy, and government employees and officials began to obstruct the spread of education under its cover.

Sapru Committee

The Sapru Committee was appointed in 1934 to study the problem of widespread unemployment in Uttar Pradesh. The committee expressed the view that in such circumstances, the solution lay in introducing a variety of curriculum at the secondary level which should be complete or comprehensive in themselves and be capable of meeting the vocational requirements of the students. Curricula preparing the student for university education should be parallel to these and there should also be technological, commercial, industrial and professional subjects.

Recommendations by Wood

In 1936-37, the Indian government invited Messrs Wood and Abbot. They recommended to the government that the act pertaining to professional and industrial educational institutions should be independent, and their status should be similar to that of other traditional schools. In consequence of this recommendation, polytechnic institutions emerged in the country. At the same time, general curricula, pertaining to professional studies, commercial subjects and agriculture were initiated in high schools. The recommendation also laid stress on infant education, education of women; and education according to the child's interest and inclination.

Basic Education

The independence movement naturally encouraged awareness of the need for self-government. It was because of this that, by the India Act 1935, local self-government came to be established in the provinces. At this time, Mahatma Gandhi conducted an experiment which he called Basic Education, for the purpose of developing a national education.

On October 2, 1937, Mahatma Gandhi published an article in the 'Harijan' in which he pointed out the inadequacy of British education, provided the alternative of a national education, and suggested the introduction of a seven year primary education and industry-centred education. He gave a call for a meeting at Wardha to consider his views.

At the Wardha meeting, Gandhiji's plan for education was examined in detail. Dr. Zakir Hussain was made the chairman of a committee with nine members. This committee put forward its recommendation at the 1938 Haripura Congress meeting, and these were accepted since they were considered of national importance. The scheme was immediately implemented in all those provinces which had a local government. However, in 1939, when the local governments resigned, the British officers dubbed it impractical and abandoned it.

This policy of education had industry as its focal point. Its characteristics were developing qualities of good citizenship, self-reliance, the imparting of education with the child as the focal point, treating knowledge as a single, complete unit, freedom of action, introduction of socially useful curricula, etc.

This system of education began to develop with the organisation of Hindustani Talimi Sangh, and it was supported by the Kher Committee at Bombay. However, despite its being a complete system of education, the concept of Basic Education has not escaped criticism and censure.

Suggestions by Sargent

The Central Education Advisory Council organised a survey headed by Sir John Sargent, the Advisor to the Indian government, in order to examine and evaluate the educational system in India in the light of post-war circumstances, created by the World War II. Its report said that children between the ages of 6 and 14 should be given free primary education. It suggested that after 11 years of age, at the middle level, there should be different kinds of syllabi for a period of five years. In character, these syllabi should be cultural, but at the same time, they should help the student both in entering a university and also securing a suitable profession and livelihood. In its opinion, there should be two kinds of high schools- (1) academic (2) technical. Both should aim at developing and imparting integral education. In its twelve parts the report reflected on every aspect of education, from primary to the university level, and produced a plan on which Rs. 312.60 crores were to be spent.

Sargent was fully aware of the fact that the real regulator in complete education is the teacher, while the administration only provides assistance. Hence, his report suggested that suitable scales of pay should be introduced to attract talented person to the educational profession.

The report also reflected upon the existing shortcomings of education. Because of this, it stressed that the syllabus should be made more practical. He formulated an educational plan for teachers covering 40 years, of which the first 5 were reserved for preparation, and remaining 35 for loyal and dedicated service.

On the basis of this report, a polytechnic college was established in Delhi. A University Grants Committee was also set up. A 16 year plan had also been suggested within the framework of this plan.

The Examination

An evaluation of the educational policy and its implementation over the entire British period leads us to the conclusion that it both benefitted as well as harmed our country. However, the historical cycle was moving forward in such a manner that this could not possibly be prevented or ignored. It had the following virtues and defects.

The Significance

1. It brought Indians into touch with western knowledge and science.
2. This system created social and political awareness in the country.
3. It led to scientific development. Ramanujam, Jagdish Chandra Bose and C. V Raman were famous scientists of this period. In later years, the number of scientists has been increasing.
4. New means for the spread of education were evolved.
5. It led to the development of Indian arts.
6. It inspired the development of literary and cultural consciousness.
7. Popular political and social institutions were established.
8. It developed nationalistic feelings.

The view of M.R. Paranjape is that this educational system was a foreign plant which could not take root suitably in Indian soil. Hence, it developed in an unsystematic manner. It was also an attempt to destroy the national characteristics of India so that the people of this country, despite being Indians, should become British in their thought and conduct, and Christianity should be worshipped instead of Indian religions. The various drawbacks of British education in Indian can be enumerated thus—

1. This education was contrary to the atmosphere of the country.
2. It sought to destroy the national character and qualities.
3. Its objectives were vague and undefined.
4. It lacked a clear plan for education.
5. It was based on and guided by colonialism.
6. The nation's innate talent could not develop because English was the medium of instruction.
7. Local educational institutions were neglected.
8. The principle of downward filtration was followed.
9. It encouraged secularism.
10. It stimulated communal passions.
11. Education became dependent upon the government.
12. The government paid scant attention to education as well as educational institutions.

All of us Indians have been compelled to suffer the advantages and disadvantages of British Education. As a consequence of it, materialism has become the dominant ingredient of the attitude of Indians.

5

CHANGING TIMES

It is assumed that freedom struggle had been started since 1857. This struggle was fought between kings of states, Nawabs, Jamindars, Samants and Britishers of East India Company, who were ruling over this country. Because of several selfish policies adopted by East India Company, the existence of Indian rulers was in danger. To save themselves, Indian rulers took the help of Indian masses to fight against English people.

After conquering over the struggle for freedom by the Indians, East India Company was dissolved and since 1858, the Crown had started ruling over India. Sir A. O. Hume, a reformist Britisher, had founded Indian National Congress. The main objective of this Congress was to establish mutual relationship, creating faith between the crown government. Hume was not in the know that this Congrees would have been the cause for removing the British rule from India.

To unite India, as a nation, the concept of Bharat Mata had emerged. To save Bharat Mata, it was obvious that the British should have to quit. Under British rule during 18th and 19th century, Indians had come in contact with British Education.

Since then, they have evolved a free sovereign concept for India. There was a spirit being developed for nation's safety and even a common man had started to think over nationalism and nation's safety. Britain tried to win over France but nationalism had been emerging in France in shape of John of Arc. In Europe, nationalism had been spreading after the division of Poland, French revolution and fight against imperialism of Napolian Bonapart, National Freedom movement had been started in Italy, Hangery and Germany. There was Unification in Italy and Germany, Sarkia, Montenegro, Rumania and Bulgaria got freedom. This current of freedom movement was being spread over Finland, Ireland, Cheekoslowakia, Poland, Egypt and India. Slowly and gradually all these nations had become free and emerged in form of independent sovereign. This nationalism and national spirit is the contribution of 18th century.

Before we discuss about the concept of education in free India, we must be acquainted with the concept of nation. Dr. Tara Chand stated- The struggle for independence was not narrowly limited for political emancipation. It was broadly an endeavour to reconstruct an old, static, collective society and to establish in its place a modern dynamic; organization for the promotion of such value as Liberty, Justice, Individualism, Humanism and Seculairsm. Rabindra nath Tagor says- Hindu and Muslims constitute the two major communities of India. We must be prepared to show the sacrifice, the patience, the care and the self-restraint that are needed to unite them into a common political organisation.

The renaissance in India played an important role in developing nation system of education. It was the outcome of the ideas of political thinkers. Zacharia says- Renaissance movement produced striking religious and social reforms long before it issued in a movement for political emancipation.

Indian Nationalism was the outcome of the suppression by the Britishers. Indians wanted to be free from the clutches of British Government. Many struggles for independence movements were launched. Peoples and leaders made several sacrifices. Thousands of the people had been hanged to death, lacs of people were imprisoned.

Raja Ram Mohun Rai, Devendre Nath Thakur, Swami Vivekanand, Swami Dayanand, Lokmanya, B. G. Tilak, G. K. Gokhale, M. K. Gandhi, J. L. Nehru, M. N. Rai, J. P Narain and many others had launched movements for the spreading of national feelings. It was understood that only education could be helpful to inculcate the feelings of nationalism and patriotism in the country. Therefore, in northern India the Arya Samaj, founded by Swami Dayanand had started to establish DAV schools and colleges, Arya Pathshalas, girls schools all over Panjab and United Province (Now Haryana and Punjab, Uttar Pradesh). Similarly Swami Vivekanand spread the feelings of nationalism and humanity over the country.

Lokmanya Tilak gave a slogan- Swarajya is my birth right and I will take it. This slogan gave an impetus to the national movement, use of Indian articles and ignoring the foreign material and the national feeling emerged. National Education Institutions had been established. During First World War, Indian leaders gave help to Britishers with the hope that they might give us freedom. 1919 Two Houses were established- House of Commons and House of Lords, to satisfy Indians; but this was not an end.

Movement of Freedom

In South Africa, Mohan Das Karam Chand Gandhi, commonly known as Bapu or Father of Nation, had been emerging as a national leader. He came to India and established himself as national leader through his new ideas of Satya and Ahimsa. He started non-cooperation movement but he failed in his mission. He did not loose his temperament. In 1928, again, M. K. Gandhi regained leadership in Congress and a resolution for complete autonomy was passed. In 1930, the Civil Disobedience Movement was started. British government had been compelled before Indians and she had agreed to have talks with the leaders of the freedom movement. Gandhi-Irwin pact was the outcome of this movement.

During the World War Second, it was cleared that sooner or later British rule would have been ended. In 1942, Quit India movement had forced Britishers to leave India. But it was a bad luck for India that it was divided into two- India and Pakistan, but both were complete sovereign. India got freedom on 15th of August 1947 and this was the end of 200 years old British rule over India.

Movement of Education

The concept of national education had been evolved through the freedom movement launched from time to time. The pioneers of India were of the opinion that until the masses of India would have been educated there would not be any socio-political consciousness among them. Swami Vivekanand, Swami Dayanand, M. K. Gandhi, Aurobindo Ghosh and R. N. Tagore established various types of educational institutions for the development of national feeling among the children.

There was the need for the eradication of mass illiteracy from India. Therefore literacy movements were launched. Even ministers had to go to the villages along with role up boards, chalk and duster to teach the villagers.

M. K. Gandhi indicated the drawbacks of education run by Britishers-

(i) Education is related with the injust government.
(ii) This education is based on foreign culture. There is no place for Indian culture in it.
(iii) The education, run by British Govt. stressed on the mental development. It does not give emphasis on hand and heart.
(iv) The medium of education is English, therefore reality is lost.

Considering the above defects of British education, M. K. Gandhi stated the following objectives of national movement:-

(i) The gain of Sovereignty.
(ii) Use of Indigenous things.
(iii) Avoidance of British Goods.
(iv) Demand of National Education.

Even Mrs. Annie Besant had opposed the English shape of education and felt the need of national education. She said, nothing can more surely emasculate national life, nothing can more surely weaken national character, than allowing the education of the young to be controlled by foreign ideals.

The Institutionalisation

There was huge demand for national education and many institutions had been established to meet this demand and to achieve the following objectives.

Indian Control. In the words of Annie Besant—Indian education should be formulated, controlled and run by the Indians. Indian leaders had stressed on the education which should be free from the clutches of Britishers.

Love for Motherland. Annie Besant had rightly said that Indian education should stress on patriotism, sacrifice and love for motherland. It develops love, sympathy, sincerity and enhance the real feelings of nationalism.

Ideals for Education. Indian education should stress over spiritual, national, social development which gives energy to national freedom movement.

Development of National Character. Education must develop the national character, Annie Besant was of the opinion that there was no place for national education in British system of education.

Opposition of British Ideals. There was a coconscious among Indian leaders that the objectives of British education may be good for Britain but they were not good for India, therefore these objectives must be opposed.

Emphasis on Indian Languages. The education, given through the English medium, is incomplete, only education given through the medium of mother tongue achieves real objectives.

Vocational Education. To eradicate the unemployment from the country, some sort of vocational education must be provided to the student. For this, the use of indigenous things had been stressed.

Western Knowledge. It was also emphasised that proper knowledge of western thought, system, literature, science was given to Indians to keep pace with the world.

Indian education was the reaction against the rule of East India Company and the Crown. It got momentum after 1858. Even then George V expressed his views- It is my earnest desire that there must be a web of schools and colleges in India, from where the pioneers in the field of agriculture, industry and professions of life and loyal persons should come out. Therefore, British Govt. established many universities, colleges, technical institutes and inspired private sector to establish the various types of institutions.

As far as the achievements are concerned, done by Indians, Gurudass Banerjee organised a society for the expansion of National education which opened 51 High Schools in Bengal. In North India, Arya Samaj started to establish DAV institutions, Arya School. Similarly Ramkrishna Mission had also established several educational institutions. Movement for Buniyadi Education, run by M. K. Gandhi, gave birth to Sabarmati Ashram, Sewagram, Gujarat Vidyapeeth, Kashi Vidyapeeth, Hindu University, Gurukul Kangri, Shanti Niketan, Jamia-Millia and Bihar Vidyapeeth, etc. Thus parallel to British Govt. new nation systems had come into existence.

6

Post-independence Period

The movement of education in India took a significant turn from the fateful night of August 15, 1947. Slaves had finally won independence and in the free air of independence, attention turned towards changes in education, formulation of an educational policy, and the needs of the country. In the early days of independence, India's educationists felt that it was not possible to find the right path without altering the structure of education.

In order to educate itself, society, has to resort to modernisation. It must make an effort to create a class of educated individuals, drawn from every part of society, whose beliefs and ambitions bear the deep imprint of Indianism. Such persons are needed to raise the educational level of the average citizen. In a democracy, the end is the individual himself. The major purpose of education is to grant the individual the maximum possible opportunities for the fullest development of his capabilities. Today, it can be said that India's destiny is being shaped in its classroom In this world of ours, founded upon science and technology, it is education alone which determines the level of prosperity, well-being and security of individuals. The success we achieve in the task of national reconstruction depends directly upon the qualities of our students emerging from our colleges and universities. Awakening a national consciousness should be an important objective of our school education. We must endeavour to achieve these objectives by bringing about a growth in knowledge based upon our cultural heritage, by indulging in its constant revaluation and by instilling the deepest faith in its future progress. Today, education has undergone multifaceted growth and progress. In consequence, literacy has increased, but at the same time, the rapidly increasing population has also increased the problems of education. In the various spheres of education, many problems have assumed gigantic and frightening proportions. Although the Five-Year plans have made some progress in this direction, education has, on the whole, failed to satisfy the individual's needs.

Guaranteed by Constitution

From one viewpoint, it is appropriate to treat the declarations of the Constitution as the starting point of education in free India. The Constitution states explicitly that education is a State subject. This has been made clear in entries 63, 64, 65 and 66 of Schedule 1, and the 25th entry of the Third Schedule.

The ideas expressed in the Constitution concerning education in free India are the following :

Free and Compulsory Education. Articles 45 of Constitution states, "The state shall endeavour to provide within a period of ten years from the commencement of this Constitution for the free and compulsory education of all the children until they complete the age of 14 years."

In this statement, the term 'State' refers to the States subordinate to the Union government.

Education of Women. According to Articles 15 (3) of the Constitution the State cannot be absolved of the responsibility of framing special scheme for the education of women and children. This section does not restrain the State in any way in making special provisions for women and children.

Religious Education. Article 28 (1) of the Constitution lays down that religious education of any kind will not be imparted in any educational institution financed from the national treasury. However, according to Article 28 (2), any institution established by a trust or a religious body can impart religious education, eves though such an institution may be aided by the government.

It has also been made clear that, in such educational institutions, children cannot be forced to imbibe a religious education which runs counter to their own religion, without the permission of the parents. In this context, the Kothari Commission has also pointed out that in the new generation, social and moral conflicts are coming to the fore. Western thinkers have come round to the view that there should be a balance between knowledge and skill, science and technology should be linked with morality and religion, research into knowledge of oneself should be encouraged, the meaning of life should be understood, the real truth should stand revealed and there should be an understanding of human relations. (Education Commission, p.19, para 14.7).

Union and State Lists. In the Constitution, educational activities have been divided in the following manner- (1) According to the 62nd entry of the schedule- national libraries, national museums, the Imperial War Museum, Victoria Memorial, and historical places of national importance will be under the charge of the Union. (2) According to entry 63, Benaras, Aligarh and Delhi universities will be under the control of the Union government. (3) The 64th entry of the Schedule points out that scientific and technical institutions of national importance, so declared by Parliament, will remain under the charge of the Union. (4) According to entries 65 and 66, the union government will have the responsibility for professional and technological institutions, research institutions, institutions for research into crime eradication, etc., as well as determining the standards of higher education and research. In the same way, Article 239 gives the Union the responsibility for education in all Union Territories.

A total of 66 subjects relating to education have been placed within the jurisdiction of the States. The 12th entry in this regard classifies that- the States will be responsible for libraries, museums, archeological institutions and memorials of national importance.

In addition to the above, the Constitution also contains a Concurrent list, which lists the following subjects- (1) economic and social planning, (2) professional and technological training, (3) scientific research, (4) technological education, (5) the development and propagation of Hindi, (6) preservation of national art and culture, (7) preservation of Sanskrit literature, (8) education of disabled persons, (9) development of educational research, (10) protection of the cultural interests of minorities, (11) educational development of the scheduled castes; regions and classes, (12) national and emotional integration, (13) provision of scholarships to brilliant students, (14) continuous professional training, (15) establishment of central institutions and agencies, and (16) free and compulsory education for children upto the age of 14 years.

Commissions on Education

Consulting Body. In 1948, the Central Advisory Board held its 14th meeting, in which it reflected upon secondary education. It put forth the suggestion for the appointment of a Commission, whose main functions would be to (1) evaluate the existing secondary education in the country, and (2) give suggestions for the problems relating to it.

This suggestion was implemented when a committee was appointed under the Chairmanship of the then Advisor on educational matters, Dr. Tara Chand. Its report was considered in the 15th meeting of the Advisory Board, and in consequence, the government of India was requested to appoint a commission for determining the objectives and purposes, and suggesting solutions for the problems of basic, secondary and university education. This requirement was then reiterated in 1951.

Commission on University Education

A University Education Commission was appointed in 1948 under the Chairmanship of Dr. Radhakrishnan. This Commission came forward with numerous significant suggestions for the improvement of education at the university level, and in consequence the following changes occurred : (1) emphasis was placed upon teacher education and training, (2) the curriculum was made comprehensive and diverse to accommodate the interests, abilities and talents of students, (3) research began to flourish, (4) religious and moral education came to be imparted, (5) importance was given to the three-language formula for solving the language problem, (6) many reforms in the system of examination were carried out. In addition, many steps for student welfare, education of women and related issues were taken.

Jurisdiction. The jurisdiction of the Commission was stated in the following words, "To report on Indian University Education and suggest improvements and extensions that may be desirable to suit present and future requirements of the country. (Report of the U.E.C. Page 1.) This Commission stated the objective of university education in the following terms- it should seek to harmonise life and the various branches of knowledge. Hence it is essential that the subjects taught in the universities should bear a relationship to fife. They should comprehend all elements.

The Education Commission has laid stress upon formation of character. It clarifies that the objective of education is the achievement of justice, liberty, equality and brotherhood upon the foundations of a national discipline. Highlighting the importance of teachers, the Commission has declared that the success of the educational process depends upon the ability and character of the teacher. The most important aspect of any scheme for improvement of university education is the obtaining of able teachers. The Radhakrishnan Commission has reflected upon every possible way for improving the conditions of teachers. It has attached importance to raising the standards of teachers and the expansion of laboratories and libraries, etc.

The Commission has defined three objectives of the curriculum : (1) to provide general education, (2) to provide a liberal education, (3) to provide professional education.

To ensure this, greater importance is given to law and medicine, the commission has made some significant recommendations. It has also stressed the need to develop objective testing techniques. In connection with the we dare of students, the Commission has expressed the view that the prime functions of the university are imparting education to youth and searching for new truths. Students are not created for universities; instead universities are established for formation of the students' character. Hence, it is essential that the university should seek, by every conceivable means and ways, to bring about the integral physical, mental and spiritual development of the student's powers.

Throwing light on the importance of education of women, the Commission opines that without educated women, there can be no educated men or women. General education should not be confined to either men or women. Women, too, should get the opportunity to receive education because, it is only in this condition that knowledge can, with certainty, be transmitted to future generations.

Emphasizing the need for the setting up of rural universities, the Commission has stated that for the general progress of rural

India, it is necessary to bring about a constant extension in skills, limits of training and its quality. In order to provide these, and to satisfy the need for educated citizens, it is necessary to adopt the technique of rural colleges and universities. Hence, work in this direction is very desirable.

Dr. Rajendra Prasad's opinion of this Commission was that the Commission had presented a very valuable document on the achievements of education in our universities, and that it had provided useful suggestions for the attainment of varied specialised skills.

Mudaliar Commission

A Secondary Education Commission was appointed in 1952-53 for the reorganiszation of secondary education. Dr. Lakshmanswami Mudaliar was appointed its chairman. The recommendations of this Commission brought forth the following changes in education—

1. The Higher secondary programme was extended to 11 years.
2. Stress was laid on the establishment of multipurpose schools.
3. The curriculum was made comprehensive and varied.
4. Objective testing was given importance.
5. Schemes for welfare of teachers were proposed.

Jurisdiction. The sphere of operation of this Commission and the issues it was to examine were stated thus- 1. Evaluation of every aspect of secondary education in India and throwing light upon it. 2. Giving suggestions for the improvement and reorganisation of secondary education.

This Commission considered the defects of secondary education and determined its objectives in the light of the following needs-(1) development of qualities of character through education, propagation of nationalism and secularism, (2) increase in productive capacity so as to bring about an increase in national wealth. (3) Improvements in education.

Objectives of Education. (1) Development of democratic citizenship. (2) Training in the art of living. (3) Development of personality. (4) Supply of professional skills. (5) Training for leadership. (6) Propagation of love of country.

The Secondary Education Commission determined the period of education at 7 years, intended for children between 11 and 17 years of age. It was divided into two parts- (1) 3 years for middle education, and (2) 4 years of higher secondary education. Provision was also made for a three-years degree course.

The Commission considered it important that technical schools and other kinds of schools should be developed. It also provided for co-education. Its views on the study of languages were as follows-(1) Hindi has been given the rank of the national language by the Constitution. (2) After some time, Hindi was expected to become the language of exchange between the Centre and the States. (3) Hindi would become the practical language of the majority. (4) As the language of the government, Hindi would bring about a growth of national unity.

Similarly, the Commission put forth the following views on the subject of English—(1) English is popular in the country. (2) English will bring about political unity. (3) English has international importance. (4) English is necessary.

The Commission's views on Sanskrit were - (1) Sanskrit is the mother of Indian languages. (2) It has been responsible for the growth of the cultural and religious attitude. (3) Indian knowledge can be obtained only through knowledge of Sanskrit.

The Commission also gave many valuable suggestions concerning the curriculum. It divided this into two parts-the Core and the optional part. The Commission also advocated the nationalization of the text books. These should be cheap, and of good quality. The Commission has accepted formation of character as the basis of education. It has suggested that schools should have arrangements for consultancy and vocational guidance. It has also recommended physical or health education. In addition to improvements in examinations, it has suggested the proper maintenance of school records. It has also given importance to improving the conditions of teachers. The Commission has also reflected upon the economics of education, and pointed towards many important sources.

Kothari Commission

Under the Chairmanship of Dr. Daulat S. Kothari, a National Education Commission was set up in 1964. It put forward a national education scheme for the next 20 years. This Commission has given Indian education a new direction. The Commission has reflected upon the entire spectrum of education, from its objectives to its economic aspects, and in consequence, it has raised many illuminating questions for the country's educationists to reflect upon.

In the context of the establishment of this Commission, the Central government stated on July 14, 1964, that the Commission had been appointed to reflect upon and advise the government on educational policies, national standards of education, and the potential for development in every sphere of education. The prefatory statement throws light on—(1) Education and national ideals, (2) method of education, its structure and level, (3) the standard of the teacher, (4) teacher training, (5) enrolment and manpower, (6) equality in the opportunities for obtaining education, (7) the parameters of educational problems of schools, (8) method of education, direction or guidance, and evaluation, (9) school education, administration and inspection, (10) environment for higher education and programmes, (11) sovereignty of universities, (12) agricultural education, (13) professional, technical and engineering education, (14) scientific education and research, (15) adult education, (16) educational planning and administration, and (17) the economics of education.

With reference to the prospectus of this Commission, the contemporary minister for education, Sh. Muhammed Karim Chagla, said that the prospectus was a kind of Magna Carta for teachers. In it, thought had been given to national and social service, salaries of teachers, the three language formula, etc. This preface led to many important turning points in the sphere of education. Of these, the three language formula became a subject of considerable discussion.

Goals Achieved

Since independence, there has been a remarkable quantitative increase in the educational sphere. The number of schools has increased, and so have the students, but the objectives of education could not be achieved. Many new professional institutions came into existence, as did many new universities. There were many and varied experiments in education. The scales of pay of teachers underwent numerous revisions. There was progress in the sphere of women's education.

The new achievements in education can be enumerated thus—

1. The Centre has adopted democracy as a form of administration and way of life for the people.
2. It has reduced poverty through the means of education and thus brought about a general improvement in the level of the people.
3. Modernisation has been adopted in industry and agriculture.
4. Obedience to ancient Indian traditions has gone hand in hand with the acceptance of knowledge and science.

5. It has accepted a socialistic pattern of society.
6. Equality has been granted to the opportunities for education.
7. The rate of literacy has increased from 19 to 28 per cent.

In the context of this new age, we must accept that education is the basis of our consciousness, awareness of our society and our nation. According to Acharya Vinobha Bhave, revolution should be introduced into education, so as to bring about a synthesis between knowledge and action. It is the combination. of knowledge and action which can be called education. In view of this, both physical and mental activities are essential for the individual. Every individual should possess the capacity for the complete and balanced development of both aspects. In spite of all these achievements, our educationists continued to feel that our educational structure suffered from some shortcomings.

In fact, the modern system of education was the contribution of British people. Missionaries played a vital role in emerging vast, successful and systematic shape of education. Nurrulah and Nionik say-To the missionaries, belong the honour of being pioneers in modern educational system. of India.

East India Company was employed to perform all the state functions: executive, judicial, legislative and economic. Establishment of schools, Madarasas, Pathshalas, College, a current of education was shown all over the country.

Hunter Commission gave a shape to complete system of education. University Education Commission, Sadler Commission gave a concrete shape to higher education.

We conclude it in the words of Howell- Education in India under the British Government was first ignored, then violently and successfully opposed the conducted on a system now universally admitted to be erroneous and finally, placed on its present tooling.

7

PLANNED DEVELOPMENT

The outcome of the past three decades is before us. We are passing through a period of change in generations. The children of yesterday are the citizens of today, and they wish to bear the burden of the nation on their shoulders, but on observing their attitudes, conduct and bearing, one feels hesitant and suspicious about handing over the reigns of the nation to them, though this will be inevitable. However, some burning questions stare us in the face. If the nation's reigns are given to the present generation, what will become of our nation? Will the values and attitudes of our public men lack our national characteristics? Will the process of national reconstruction continue at its present leisurely pace? All these questions relate to different aspects of life, but there is a common answer to them all-that, we have treated education as a means to selfish attainment. We have not given priority to education. In the absence of desirable plan, the results of education have not produced any long-term results. Because of aimless education, the younger generation has lost sense of direction. The result is that the youth of today is dissatisfied, desparing and doubtful. He wants to do something, but he does not know what he should do. For all this, it is necessary that we initiate plans for improvement of schools.

Fundamental Planning

According to the Kothari Commission, in India the problem of educational planning means simply that we need to evolve a national policy in the educational sphere while, according to our Constitution, education is a state subject, and consequently, educational officials at various levels take decisions on all of its varied aspects. The task before us is not simple, and we also do not have much experience to guide us. Hence, we will have to evolve our own techniques, and change, modify and improve them as we go along'.

The following are the elements of a comprehensive educational plan which have to be improved in order to overcome the problems that arise in the educational sphere-

1. Creation of literature in the modern Indian languages, which is necessary for making these languages the medium of instruction at the university level.
2. Educational Research
3. Preparation of text-books for schools and help-materials for teaching and study.
4. Improvements in the system of examination.
5. Arrangements for the in-service training of teachers and officials of the education department.
6. Improvements in the methods of supervision.
7. Increase in the contact with guardians and the local community.
8. Provision of progressive schemes for brilliant students and programmes of special assistance to backward students.

The Difficulties

The results of education can be good only if educational planning is successful. In our country, educational planning faces the following obstacles—

1. Excessive emphasis upon enrolment and expenditure.
2. Decentralisation of efforts.
3. Indifference towards accepting clearly defined paths of action.
4. Absence of adequate evaluation and research.
5. Failure to initiate programmes of superior quality.
6. Weakness of the educational planning mechanism.

The Planning Commission's Working Group on education has identified the following causes of the failure of planning-

1. Administration of the police kind, obsolete methods, inadequate resources, increased responsibilities of development, and untrained, incapable and inadequate staff.
2. Lack of attraction for trained individuals ; tradition of making appointments from above ; absence of any system of in-service training ; excessive emphasis upon individual and financial administration. There is need for a revolutionary change in the nature and structure of the states department of education. Instead of functioning as groups of individuals concerned with grants, statistics, financial permission, transfers, appointments, study of complaints, etc., these groups have to become organisations of educationists which possess the imagination to visualise the objectives of educational reconstruction, which are sensitive enough to recognise quickly the needs and demands of people immediately, which can prepare satisfactory plans for reconstruction and implement them

successfully, which can fulfil the roles of friends, philosophers and guides for the teachers as well as students and their guardians. However, so far, no effective steps are being taken in this direction.

3. The entire society is responsible for making the educational plan successful. Till the present, there is no effective system for establishing contact between teachers, students, guardians educational administrators and the rest of society, though the existence of such a system is a prime necessity.

4. Co-operation and harmony with other governmental departments and non-governmental agencies is weak and ineffective.

5. Proper utilisation of resources is hindered because of lack of resources, lack of extension schemes, delays in obtaining financial clearance, changes in the proposed amounts or corrupt activities.

6. Political pressures are often seen working powerfully in the appointment and transfer of teachers, setting up of new institutions and location of schools. The same pressures also influence and modify approved schemes.

7. Wherever-suitable leadership has been found lacking, democratic decentralisation has led either to the obstruction of educational schemes or a complete and destructive change in their very nature. Local influences and force often create problems for the teachers.

8. The thought that goes into making a budget or preparing in a plan is the equivalent of a kind of evaluation. Evaluation is made from time to time. The discussion in the organisations of teachers, the press and the legislative assemblies are also forms of evaluation. But, hardly any efforts have been made so far towards introducing a systematic and formal mode of evaluation by individuals directly involved in education.

In view of these factors, the Working Group felt constrained to say that comprehensive educational plans, keeping in view every aspect of education, should be prepared. The existing situation is that the states' departments of education thrust the responsibility for planning on certain officials, who then prepare plans and programmes without getting into touch with anyone. Specialists, teachers, organisations of teachers, or educational officials of the district level make no contribution to such plans. Besides, these plans are full of statistics about goals of appointments and expenses, while other much more important aspects of education are completely neglected. Whatever little is done at the higher levels, without making any effort to find out the views of individuals working in education at the grass-roots.

Detailed schemes and blue-prints are also required for the successful implementation of a plan. No attention is paid to this fact. The Working Group's view is that educational programmes should be treated in the same way in which projects concerning irrigation, industry or power are treated. We should see not merely the clarity of objectives; we must also seek to ensure the achievement of these objectives by considering the time division, need for preparatory work, materials expenditure needed for creating the necessary skills and motivation and administrative requirements, and then try to harmonise them with the time available and conditions existing. At present, there is a complete absence of such projects.

It seems that detailed thinking does not go into the preparing of plans by the education ministry and the Planning Commission, and after plans are once prepared, re-thinking occurs only after a year has passed. Assessments are hardly ever made. Besides, the various agencies looking after education also lack coordination among themselves. At the national level, various ministries, such as food, agriculture, labour, social welfare, home, etc, are also involved in educational planning. Similar agencies exist in the states also, but the co-ordination among them is quite weak.

The Guidelines

It is true that education is the state's responsibility, but it cannot be denied that the nation has an equal responsibility as well as stake in the success of education. Hence, the states and the centre should be regarded as equal partners in education. There are three main agencies of education—(i) the central government, (ii) the state governments, and (iii) local bodies and voluntary organisations. Besides, it is evident that (a) school education involves the partnership of the local government and the state government, and (b) higher education is conducted through the partnership of the state and central governments. A balance can be struck between complete centralisation or decentralisation after these truths are recognised and accepted.

The Working Group has offered the following suggestions for making educational planning successful-

Preparation of Comprehensive Educational Plans. Allocation of resources is all that is actually being done in the name of formulating plans. A comprehensive educational plan is inclusive of the existing situation in education, the objectives, of education, the steps to be taken for achieving these objects, all programmes, those which involve no expenditure or those for which expenditure has to be reduced, etc.

Basis of the Process of Planning. The second necessary reform relates to giving the planning process a wider basis and decentralising it, as well as bringing about co-ordination between the institution, district, state and centre. This will produce a wide range of advantages.

Introduction of Institutional Plans. The basic principle of this new technique will be institutional plans, i.e., plans prepared by the schools themselves. At the school level, plans have to be formulated by considering what can be done within the available resources or by adding a little to them. Good schools in particular should work in this direction.

Work can be started in the states on the basis of the following suggestions:-

1. An essential condition for granting recognition and aid should be that each school should prepare a five-year plan, as well as annual plans, for its own development.
2. These plans should also become the basis of inspection.
3. The department of educational should provide some guidelines in the preparation of the school's plan which should be clearly in consonance with the state's policy on education.
4. The principals of institutions should prepare plans according to the directives of the department.
5. The state educational institution should train principals as well as inspectors.
6. Long-term plans will run concurrently with the state's five-year plans. Schools will re-open at the fixed time, though students will attend school a week latter. During this period, the teachers will consider every aspect of teaching and prepare plans for the forthcoming session.
7. Inspectors should receive detailed information about plans and evaluation well in advance.
8. Inspectors often compel schools to adopt many schemes simultaneously. For this, it is essential that the schemes should be limited in range, and they should be completed before others are taken up.
9. All the related agencies-teachers, students, society, guardians, principal, the management committee, etc., should participate in the preparation of the plan.

We should remember that education is a never ending or inexhaustible source of personal satisfaction. It is related directly to the nation's social and economic development. If education is systematically initiated at every level, and if it is intimately related to national programme, the pace of social and economic development increases.

Official Planning

While reflecting upon institutional planning, we are faced with the following questions- (1) What are your objectives? (2) Is is our purpose to work for the achievement of new objectives? (3) Do we want to bring about a change in individuals? (4) Is it our purpose to replace the old patterns with fresh ones? These questions imply that our thinking on the issue should be clear. The function of institutional planning is to keep an institution occupied in the search for the best possible results in the existing social environment.

In the context of formulating a plan with clear objectives for any institution, it is necessary to reflect upon the existing circumstances. One cannot turn away from the realities of life and society. We must overlook the fact that our universities are tradition bound and that they have to work according to the directives of the department of education. It is the department which formulates the curriculum and also issues orders about its implementation. Thus, if we can still think of an imaginative plan for a particular institution, despite the existence of these circumstances, it must necessarily be appreciated.

The Planks

In order to prepare an educational plan for a single institution, it is necessary to consider the following bases:-

1. Achievement of the best possible results in the given social and physical environment.

2. Reform and progress in technique, materials, resources, etc.

3. Making the best use of the talents of the students and teachers.

4. Generating a suitable atmosphere for the development of creativity.

5. Recognition of innate powers, their use, encouragement of efforts and leadership.

6. Encouraging mutual co-operation without injuring freedom of thought and action.

7. Achieving the maximum utilisation of building, laboratories, libraries and other resources.

8. Practising self-service and self-achievement.

The Working Group of the Planning Commission has suggested the following means of bringing success to the plans of schools:-

1. The states' departments of education will have to begin to think a new in order to recognise or identify good schools and grant them greater aid as well as freedom, to guide the weaker schools towards improvement, and also to encourage competitiveness, creativity and experimentation amongst teachers and students. Instead of uniformity and rigidity, it will be necessary to adopt an approach which is dynamic and flexible.

2. The schools themselves should try to secure the means needed for their development. The best steps in this direction would be (i) the co-operation of local officials, guardians and the local community, (ii) a change in the method of giving grants in order to encourage superiority, and (iii) establishment of experimental schools and autonomous colleges.

3. It is necessary to initiate co-operation and mutual dialogue between schools and colleges, instead of allowing them

to throw allegations at each other. School complexes can be of tremendous advantage in this sphere.

4. Transfers of teachers in government schools should be reduced to a minimum. Organising committees or boards of governors should be created, and in these the teachers should have an important voice, so that their commitment should be to the institution, and not merely to their cadre. Such a situation does not exist in private institutions, and hence they should make efforts to attract the best teachers towards themselves.

5. Teachers have necessarily to shoulder the leadership in the formulation and implementation of institutional plans. Among primary schools, there exists the peculiar problem of single-teacher institutions. For such cases, all institutions within a radius of three to five miles will treat the higher secondary school as the centre, and function as a school complex, and their institutional plan will also be a collective one. From the viewpoint of organisation, each complex should be treated as a unit. At the secondary school level, the form of principals will work to achieve co-operation from the nearest college or university and to ensure mutual co-operation. A complex can also be created by linking a college or even a department of a university with a group of secondary schools.

6. Transfers can help each other in the framing and implementation of plans even through the method of Panel Inspection. The panel can consist of some selected teachers and principals who can give the benefit of their experience and knowledge to other institutions, apart from their own, by giving a little extra time.

7. Colleges will, in general, not have much difficulty in preparing their own plans, but they can seek the guidance of the university. The universities, too, will frame their

own plans. For this purpose, in keeping with the suggestions of the Education Commission, they will create their own 'academic planning boards.'

Various Stages

Institutional planning operates at three levels—(1) District, (2) State and (3) National.

District level Plans. Accepting the district as the fundamental unit of planning, development and administration, work is to be. initiated in some districts in the next year itself. It is to be introduced in every district by the end of the sixth five year plan. Today, the expenditure on education in a single district is more than the total expenditure in India in 1882. The educational plan of a district should comprehend all educational activity below the level of university education-preprimary, primary, secondary and vocational. Towns with a population of a lakh or more can also have their separate plans, in which the municipal boards should also offer co-operation.

State level Plans. Plans at the state level have to become the centre of gravity of the entire planning process, and for this purpose, it is essential that every state department of education must have a powerful and effective planning wing. For the near future, the following programmes have been suggested for immediate implementation: (i) Evaluation of the development from independence till the present, (ii) formulation of a long term plan for fifteen or twenty years, publication of a white paper on the subject, and giving it a final shape in the light of the suggestions received, (iii) framing of an education Act.

National Plans. At the national level, the government of India has suggested the formulation of a national educational policy which should be reviewed every five years. National plans will be based on this national policy. Their main elements will be the following: (i) the synthesizing element of framing a national plan based on all state-plans, (ii) co-ordinated action on the national plan by the centre as well as the states, (iii) central programmes to be implemented either by constitutional directives or the assent of the states. It will be the Centre's responsibility to produce a plan which does away with regional differences, which is balanced, and which is suited for a long term period. For this purpose, special national programmes within the overall national plan will have to be evolved.

The Dual Process of Plan Formulation. Planning has to be done both from above and from below. It is necessary to have two time-tables in the planning process. For example, guidelines and hints about the temporary allocation of resources will flow from the central government to the state government, from the state government to the district level officials and institutions. In the reverse process, the institutions will prepare their own plans in the light of the information given. They will indicate the plans they can implement with the given resources, and what they may be able to do if more resources are made available, etc.

Contribution of Teachers. Teachers are expected to co-operate intimately and effectively in educational plans. Theoretically, this does not appear to be an unusual idea, but in effect, it has been implemented so far because of the following four factors: (i) The government has never shown any interest in this, and in fact the government has never understood either this problem or its importance. (ii) We have, as yet, never seen even a dream of any institutional organisation which makes it possible for teachers to participate in the formulation and implementation of educational plan. (iii) There are so many differences among the various categories of teachers that the whole profession has been weakened, and consequently the teacher's capacity to contribute to educational planning is almost destroyed. (iv) Teachers are also lacking in specialisation and leadership, besides which they have adopted an attitude of indifference towards the problems of education planning. These four difficulties have to be overcome in order to benefit education by raising the status of teachers. which can be done by giving them the leadership in educational planning and development.

For this, the following suggestions have been offered—

(a) School-planning should be introduced in every school.

(b) At the district level, there should be an advisory board council of teachers on which every teacher organisation of the district should have representation. It should be consulted in every matter pertaining to educational planning and development.

(c) Similar advisory boards should also be created at the, state level, and these should be called joint teachers' councils.

(d) The central ministry of education should establish a national committee of teachers on which every teacher organisation of the national level should be represented. In planning and development matters, this committee should be consulted, as is to be done at the district and state levels.

(e) The government should declare, without any reservations and conditions, that it wishes to hand over the leadership in matters of educational planning to the teachers, and, that the responsibility for helping in this work and collecting the necessary resources will fall upon the department of education. Such a declaration will influence the attitudes of departmental officials as well as teachers and lead to the creation of a suitable environment which is essential for the success of this entire programme.

(f) Efforts must be made to win the co-operation of the teachers in administrative activities relating to the school as well as other matters.

(g) The teachers themselves should develop an interest in planning. It is unfortunate that teachers have neglected this important aspect of their vocation. Teachers organisations have shown no interest in the past three five-year plans and three annual plans. They have not indulged in any profound criticism or analysis, though it is expected of them that they would not only subject the government's plans to criticism, but also offer a parallel plan of their own, so that the people may have an opportunity for a comparative study. It is obvious that teachers will have to give up this indifference, and the sooner it is done, the better.

(h) Teachers will also have to develop the necessary skills for planning; both individuals and in groups, through their organisations. Of course, it is true that this will happen only when the plan for decentralisation outlined earlier is implemented and teachers are asked to cooperate.

(i) If teachers of all categories unite and form a single, organised community, their contribution to educational administration can become more effective. For this, the first thing necessary is a change of attitude. At present, the teaching profession is divided into a number of discrete units which, it appears, visit their own classrooms individually without ever entering into a working relationship. It is obvious that there is no place for such an alienated outworn attitude in the new India that we dream of, a country with a social system based on equality, freedom, justice and the dignity of the individual. The community of teachers is one, and all within it are fundamentally equal. Everyone will have to strive to generate the spirit of brotherhood, and create opportunities which may encourage a spirit of unity and foster it.

(j) In order to generate a commitment among the teachers for the institutions in which they teach, it is essential for them to have an effective voice in its administration. Suitable efforts for this will have to be made in private as well as governmental institutions.

Training. It is necessary to train all individuals concerned with the formulation and implementation of plans. Besides, some selected individuals must also be specially trained for formulating and implementing certain specialised projects. A detailed document should be prepared for each scheme, showing the objectives, period of work, finance, individuals involved, description of resources, arrangements for co-ordination, a detailed time division plan, made of evaluation, preparatory work, etc. This task is undoubtedly difficult, and the specialists available will also be few. Hence, the Asian Educational Planning and Administration Institution can be entrusted with providing help in this sphere.

Eradication of the Stress on Money. Every effort should be made to get rid of the stress on money in educational plans. If we imagine that surplus funds will help us to end every conceivable problem in education, the idea only indicates our naivette. After spending substantial amounts of money we have succeeded in expanding the general system of education and in creating new institutions, better scales of pay for teachers, more teaching, putting up more buildings, and expansion of resources. However, those improvements which were not related with finance have met with limited success only. We have almost completely failed in the growth of adult literacy or in preventing wastages and stagnation in primary education. The enrolment at the university and secondary level has not decreased. No noticeable progress in the schemes for qualitative improvement has been noted. For all these activities, what is needed is more and better human resources, not more money. In the sphere of human efforts, our work has been unsatisfactory. In a rich country, the emphasis upon money may not mean a serious loss, but in a poor country like ours, this lavishness is intolerable. We can achieve success in our objectives if we adopt the following major programmes along with our other schemes:-

Cost Consciousness. The money invested should not exceed the profit gained.

Intensive Use of Available Resources. Efforts should be made to derive the maximum profits from the existing investments, instead of seeking avenues for fresh investments.

Research on Inexpensive Techniques. Science should pay attention to this field.

Selective Technique. Instead of taking up numerous schemes simultaneously some selected schemes should be chosen on the basis of priorities.

Human Efforts. The vicious circle lack of education in a poor country itself becoming the cause of further poverty should be broken through enthusiastic and dedicated human effort.

Priorities. It is necessary to determine priorities at the national, state and local levels. Today, there is a tendency to think of everything in terms of the national level. Instead of this attitude, it would be better if, at the national level, priority is given only to some subjects of truly national importance. These can be treated as national schemes. In teaching, production of books and teaching of science can be treated as national schemes for the sixth plan. On these issues, the Centre should finalise decisions after consultation with the states. But once a decision has been taken, the states will compulsorily have to act upon them in the most potent and effective manner possible.

On most of the remaining issues, the states themselves must take their own decisions, and in accordance with local needs, determine the priorities. For instance, at the secondary level, the question of an educational fee can be taken up. There is no need to seek uniformity at the national level in such matters. In many other matters, such as facilities in schools and non-teacher costs, priorities will have to be fixed at the local level, in consonance with local needs and the clearly defined rights and authority of the school or local body, which should also have the necessary freedom to take decisions. There is no need to expect absolute uniformity in all districts. In some matters, freedom must be given even to the schools. Neither is there any need to accept complete uniformity and conformity in all schools of the same category. A system based on co-ordinated and rationally determined priorities separately determined, at the national, state and local levels will be far better than the prevailing system in which, so far, many decisions have been taken, even in matters of regional and national importance, without the least attention to local needs. Such a system has led to the complete obstruction of any tendency to take the initiative and bring improvements. What is needed is relatively better coordination and harmony between all the agencies, departments and ministries concerned with education, rather than any attempt to foist an unnecessary uniformity.

Administrative Reforms

For the proper implementation of educational programmes, it is necessary to bring about improvements in educational administration on the basis of well-defined priorities. At present, the education department focuses its attention only upon maintaining organisational administration, with the result that the duty of developmental administration is not fulfilled at all. For this latter purpose, the departments of education should have full knowledge of educational programmes in all the states of our own country as well as the programmes initiated in foreign countries. Besides they should give suitable importance to all such programmes in their own educational planning, keeping in view the needs, aspirations and ambitions of the people of their region. Such a developmental administration will possess the following characteristics:-

1. Developmental administration accords equal importance to the twin aspects of quantitative and qualitative improvement in education. It makes continuously modifiable and improved schemes for the future, evaluates the experiences of the past and present, and simultaneously provides the administrators with ever increasing opportunities for increasing their professional skills.

2. The existing organisational administration soon becomes involved in its own web of ever-expanding rules and regulations, by laying excessive stress upon control. It is thus unable to spare a thought to progress or development. In contrast, developmental administration gives importance to the independence of teachers and institutions, expansion in extension services and guidance, experimentation, initiative and creativity, and encourages all of them.

3. Organisational administration is suitable for a static or slowly progressing society, because it always sticks to uniformity and insists on obedience to rules. On the other hand, developmental administration concerns itself with the development of the individual in a rapidly changing society, and for this purpose, it does not hesitate to modify its own policy, if this is necessitated by circumstances.

4. Another drawback of organisational administration is that it creates the two classes of teachers and administrators, with greater benefits invariably flowing to the latter. This discrimination invariably has an adverse impact both upon the teacher and the teaching process, as well as development of education. In contrast, developmental administration invariably aims at healthy relations between the two classes so that both of them are able to fulfil their respective duties without coming into conflict with each other.

5. Developmental administration is completely democratic and decentralised. As is the case of organisational administration, it has no place for the centralisation of power or the creation of a bureaucratic approach. Every individual, at every level, has the right to make rules, to work accordingly and to evaluate his activities.

Having been accustomed to organisational administration for almost centuries it now appears difficult to adopt developmental administration. Even today, our administration spends almost the whole of its time in the appointment of workers, their transfers, promotions. and investigation into anonymous complaints and allegations. Whatever time does remain is spent in sorting out financial complications. The consequence of this is that the department soon loses all touch with society, and it turns into an isolated tower standing in a waste land. In order to introduce developmental administration, we will first have to overcome these drawbacks. The suggestions for the improvement of educational administration are based on our assumption that the central and state governments are faced with the major task of making the objectives of education determined by the governments themselves.

Restructuring Process

The outstanding purpose or aim of educational administration is- improvements in educational services. This should be done at the state and central levels. It was with this in view that the suggestion for an Indian Educational Service was mooted, but, for a variety of reasons' it was never implemented. Hence, it has become necessary to think of some other means of achieving the necessary goal. In this connection, the following measures are suggested:-

1. An educational advisory service should be established. A service of this kind, associated with the ministry of education, suffers from many drawbacks, the main one

being that its members are out of touch with existing realities, since they never have an opportunity to work in the practical field. The following programmes can be adopted for overcoming this weakness.

(a) All the posts under the government of India requiring educational expertise as well as such voluntary organisations such as the Central Schools Organisation should be combined under this. If possible, the states desirous of joining the unit may be allowed to do so.

(b) Some posts in the central ministry of education should be reserved for officials nominated by the state governments. In exchange, some officials of the central ministry should be appointed in the states' departments of education. This policy will benefit both the Centre and the states. Officials from the central ministry will get an opportunity to increase their knowledge and experience about the actual conditions existing in the states, and also to make their own attitudes more liberal, while the states will benefit from the diverse and wide experience of the central government's educationists.

(c) The officials of the states' departments of education, principals of schools, vice-chancellors of universities and famous educationists should be appointed to the posts of additional educational advisors. Such appointments should be made only for five years, though they may be extended for another 5 years under exceptional circumstances.

2. For the improvement of the states' departments of education, the following steps can be considered :

(i) The scales of pay of their officials should be improved.

(ii) The number of posts of inspectors should be increased to the extent necessary.

(iii) It is generally seen that the department fills the senior posts in the department by promoting junior officials. Even if direct recruitment is adopted for some posts, priority is still given to promotion of juniors. Consequently, fresh and enthusiastic individuals do not get any opportunity and the qualitative development of education suffers a setback.

(iv) The posts from the level of district education officer to the level of the director of education (where special qualifications and abilities are needed for framing policies and setting down rules) should be filled through offers of five-year contracts to able individuals working in schools, colleges and universities, though few such posts may be reserved for promoted individuals. Those employed on contract may be allowed to extent their contract for another five years, but only if their work in eminently satisfactory in the initial period.

Educational institutions should possess facilities whereby individuals with marked administrative talent may be enables to take up administrative jobs. On the other hand, administrative officials interested in teaching should be allowed opportunities for appointment in schools, colleges and universities.

Education for the Employed

The second very significant programme far important is the provision of in-service education for educational administrators. This is even more important in view of the fact that the condition of the states' departments of education is truly pitiable at present. For this, the following steps have been suggested:-

1. Each administrator or inspector should be required, on being first appointed, to complete a course of training, whose period and subject should be in accord with the posts held by the individual.

2. Education of this kind should have two purposes-one, to acquaint the officials from time to time with the state's educational policies, and two ; to get an opportunity to study improvements in education in India and abroad and to assess them in the light of the conditions in their own state. These officials should participate in conferences or seminars or workshops for at least a week twice a year. Such conferences should be organised, at the district or regional level, by the district officials, for the non-gazetted staff, while for the gazetted staff, they should be organised by the director of education.

3. Each department should regularly publish a newspaper or letter of the highest quality in order to acquaint its officials with the latest government policies as well as the least thinking in the educational sphere by leading educationists.

4. It is essential to have provisions for granting leave to those officials who wish to improve their knowledge or enter specialised studies at regular intervals. Six months leave can be granted after every six years for such purposes. In the past, India did have a system of further studies'. Similar schemes should now be evolved and adopted.

5. Officials of one state should be sent to other states for studying particular problem.

6. The ministry of education, the NCERT, and the Asian Educational Planning and Administration Institute should prepare a programme for in-service training, since such a

programme can bring to the participants the knowledge, experience and guidance of experts and scholars in this field. The states' departments of education should allow their officials to participate in such programmes freely.

7. Both at the national and state levels, there should be arrangements by which officials of other departments concerned with education and its problems can be kept in touch with latest ideas, and also be given training.

The Kothari Education Commission had suggested the establishment of a National College for the training of educational administrators. This is a very valuable suggestion, and it should be accepted and implemented in the present plan-period. Giving opportunities for improving professional qualifications is a good idea, but not all individuals are able to benefit from them. Hence, for encouragement, they should also be given incentives, such as promotions or increase in pay. In view of the existing circumstances, it is essential that, within the next one or two years, massive programmes for the reorientation of our educational administrators should be taken up. In all such programmes organised at the national, regional or local level, the states and the Centre should co-operate with each other.

Constructive Programme

The third programme for the improvement of educational administration concerns the proper organisation of developmental work regarding schools and workers. For the last twenty years, our attention has been focused upon the quantitative expansion of education, but the time is now ripe for concentrating upon its qualitative improvement. Many elements are important for this, for instance—the abilities of teachers, their devotion to duty, the commitment and motivation of students, an atmosphere conducive to truth and hard work, provision of facilities, a developed curriculum, dynamic methods of teaching and evaluation, research, good supervision and guidance work, and a favourable social climate. However, solving the problems of educational administration depends upon two factors- (1) school organisation, and (2) supervision and guidance.

Before 1947, educational authorities were compelled to bear two burdens, those of administration as well as introduction of programmes of qualitative improvement. But after 1950, the work load of administrative activities upon these officers increased to such an extent that they had almost no time to spare for programme of qualitative improvement. Even as early as 15 years ago, it was felt that there was need for establishing special agencies to carry out developmental programmes. It was with this in view that such institutions as the Central Text-book Research Bureau, the Central Educational and Vocational Guidance Bureau, the National Audiovisual Education Institution, the National Basic Education Institute, the National Institute of Primary Education, Directorate for Extension Programmes in Secondary Education, Central English and Hindi Institutes, etc., were established. In a similar fashion, in the states, too, state education institutes audio-visual education institutes, educational and, vocational guidance institutes, evaluation organisations, state science teaching institutes, and the English institute, etc., came to be established.

It is beyond doubt that these agencies have succeeded in those states in which due attention was given to these two conditions, one, the department of education appointed its own highly qualified staff in these institutions, two, these officials were able to win the co-operation of all administrators in education for the fulfilment of their goal and the implementation of their ideas.

On the basis of past experience, the following suggestions can be offered for bringing about qualitative improvement:-

1. In the organisation of the above institutions, those professionally skilled individuals should be appointed who can understand the problems of school education, seek solutions to them and guide the teachers.

2. So far, universities have remained completely cut off from schools. Now, they should offer their co-operation for the improvement of school education through research, improved curricula, search for new and better methods of teaching and evaluation, teacher training, preparation of superior text-books, etc.
3. At the national level, too, there should be an ideal institution capable of working for the improvement of education. At present, the NCERT is performing this function, but it is necessary to make its efforts more fruitful in a shorter time frame.
4. In the states, too, there is the need to establish such institutions as - state secondary education board, teacher training board, text-books improvement centre, curriculum research institute, vocational guidance institute, etc.
5. At the district level, there should be strong organisation under the direction for the district education officer, and the principals of all training colleges in the district should offer him their co-operation.

The following points should be kept in view in order to make the working of institutions more effective ; —

(a) In these institutions, only the most capable and highly qualified officials should be appointed, with suitable attractive scales of pay.

(b) These institutions should co-ordinate and harmonise their activities with each other. For example, the NCERT should associate itself with the state educational institution, departments of universities and district level organisations while district level organisation should devote itself to the assistance and supervision of schools, teachers and school organisations.

(c) The functioning of these institutions should be regarded as an inalienable part of the working of the ministry of education and department of education.

If a system of the kind outlined above is introduced, there is little reason to doubt that classroom teaching and research level activities of the highest order will be linked with each other in a single chain. All the problems of education will be tackled as soon as they arise, and new and superior programmes will be formulated and implemented promptly.

The Vigilance

Although various suggestions have been given for making supervision and guidance of schools more effective and these include formation and implementation of institutional plans, reorganisation of the department of education, adoption of the school complex scheme, introduction of panel inspection, etc., it is equally important to raise the standard of inspection through the proper training of the inspecting staff. For this, the first step is to increase the number of inspectors, because at present, each inspecting officer has the responsibility for inspecting the working of between 22 and 246 institutions, (an average of 51), and between 94 and 1091 teachers (an average of 197). The second step is the appointment of specialist officials, in addition to the general inspection staff, and the former should be capable not only of evaluating the teacher's teaching work but also of guiding him. These specialists should be of two kinds-one, those who pay complete attention to the teaching in specific subjects, such as mathematics, science, English, etc., two, those who possess specific qualifications in such fields as programming, physical education, improvement of examination system, construction of courses, etc. These specialists should be entrusted, not merely with the routine inspection of schools, but with the task of providing in-service training and guidance. Initially, specialist inspectors should be appointed for particular subjects in some selected districts. A panel of between 3 and 5 such inspectors should work at the regional level.

Effective Functioning

The fourth programme for the improvement in administration is the modification and modernisation of the department's method of working, which, at present, is in a deplorable state. For this purpose, the measures outlined below should be adopted:-

1. The National College, whose establishment has been recommended by the Kothari Commission, should provide opportunities for research into educational administration. In addition it should study the following subjects and offer its suggestions-rules pertaining to admission to educational institutions of particular classes, provision of financial grants to institutions, selection of teachers, evaluation of teaching work, determining the internal and external techniques of evaluation, adoption of a convenient method for payment of teachers salaries, preparation of text-books and their acceptance, and analysis of the work of official concerned with inspection and supervision.
2. The department of education in each state should have a wing for the study of organisation and working, and it should offer its suggestions for administrative reforms from time to time.
3. In the annual conferences of educational administrators of various levels, information about departmental policies and programmes should be given, but in addition, they should also be made aware of the changes introduced. Their views on these changes should be invited and discussions initiated.
4. Excessive and unnecessary staff should not be appointed, but at the same time, care should be taken to see that

important officials do not waste their time and energies in routine and minor works.

5. Delays in work and inconveniences are occasioned by an irrational division of authority. Hence, as far as possible, more and more administrative and financial responsibility should be shifted to district level officials. The directorate of education should concern itself mainly with co-ordinating their efforts, formulating policies, and ascertaining whether the authority delegated to them is being properly utilised or not.

In this context, it is to be noted that improvements in departmental working require officials with open minds and hearts. When the organisation suggested above it introduced, it is hoped that these administrators will be able to develop the right attitudes.

Adjustment Factors

The fifth step towards the improvement in administration lies in introducing flexibility and dynamism in administration. The problems of India's education are very complex, and the diversities and variety in the country's economic and social conditions have obviated the possibility of finding a single solution for them all, under all conditions. Even this diversity can be converted into a virtue if the method of working is dynamic and flexible. What will happen in such a situation is that varied experiments will be carried out in different situations and contexts, and with their help, solutions will be found quickly and inexpensively. This important principle can best be illustrated through some examples-

1. Under the present educational system, all the colleges and schools in the state have a common curriculum, and whatever changes are introduced usually produce destructive results in certain plans. The reason for this is that those who formulate the curriculum invariably keep their vision fixed upon the weaker and backward students.

In consequence, the brilliant students and enthusiastic institutions are never benefited. Besides, the rigid curriculum makes it impossible to exploit the institutional advantages that some institutions may have over others. Hence, it is essential that, in a state, more than one, or at least two curricula-one generalist and the other specialised, must be introduced.

2. The second rigid constraint in the existing system is that the child makes his choice of subjects in class 9, at. the age of 14, and then remain tied to this choice for the future. This kind of responsibility, thrust upon the immature child, is as harmful in the long run as the institution of child marriage proved to be. Besides, deciding upon groups of subjects is also counter-productive. In this context, we should be more liberal and the student should be given more freedom in his choice of subjects.

3. Efforts at making secondary education development oriented and reducing the enrolment in research at the university level have both failed. Hence, a plan should be prepared in which the curricula for the first degree synthesizes a number of vocational studies. Later on, specialised education in those vocations should be provided, to the extent of allowing the candidate to obtain his Ph.D. degree in the subject, if he so wishes.

4. No less important is flexibility and variability in the methods of teaching and evaluation. The existing fixed methods, a fixed curriculum and a definite system of education may satisfy the average teacher and the average student. But teachers with creative minds, if prevented from working outside the guidelines fixed by the department, will be completely stultified.

5. There should be flexibility even in the sphere of education. At present, an excessive expansion in secondary and

higher secondary education in certain regions has led to increased unemployment while on the other hand in some regions, these levels of education have been introduced quite recently. In the future, expansion of education should be limited only to the underdeveloped regions only. Besides, those subjects should be encouraged for study which have remained neglected so far.

6. There should be a practical and flexible approach towards the medium of education. So long as regional languages remain incapable of shouldering the burden English should be retained as the medium of education, in order to maintain standards.
7. The current fashion is to give financial grants upon certain fixed principles to all educational institutions, with the result that the superior as well as the inferior institution obtain under the same rules and conditions. This policy of uniformity should be modified so as to make provisions for additional grants to the better and more progressive institutions.

It is of course true that it is as difficult and problematic to implement a flexible and dynamic method of education as it is easy and convenient to implement a rigid and uniform system of education. But, in modern society, we just cannot make progress without a flexible and dynamic system. In fact, we must now grant freedom to every student, every teacher and every institution. This is a difficult task, but it is not impossible. In order to make it possible two aspects must be strengthened the teacher, and the administrator.

The Assessment

The need for a continuous evaluation of programmes is self-evident. In fact, planning, implementation and evaluation are mutually correlated functions. They help in overcoming the obstacles that arise during implementation. Besides, they also help in finding solutions to the problems that remain. Unfortunately, we have not laid sufficient stress upon evaluation and research, as yet. We suggest that in the next few years, special emphasis should be laid upon evaluation and educational research.

There are three modes of evaluation, which will have to be adopted simultaneously and continuously:-

1. One simple form of evaluation is that, in which each teacher, administrative official of the department and educational institution will have to become involved. In the context of school planning and implementation, the institution should itself periodically evaluate its own progress. Similarly, teachers and administrators should also evaluate their own work. The state as well as the central governments should also evaluate their programmes from time to time to discover whether their policies are being promptly, effective and economically implemented or not.

2. There is need for the evaluation of the programmes and schemes adopted by district level organisations, central government and the state governments. Realistically, periodical evaluation should be necessarily provided for in every important programme. This provision should provide a clear statement of the aims of evaluation, its process, agency and period. Briefly stated, just as teaching and evaluation are inseparably related, in the same way policy formulation and evaluation should also be regarded as inseparable.

3. There are certain aspects of planning which must be evaluated at the highest level. For instance, there is the very important question how does education contribute to national development, or what contribution can it make?

Equally important are the questions of the use of manpower, the need for it, and the opportunities for planning its utilisation. In addition, there is the problem of standards in education. In connection with brilliant students at the various levels of education as well as in different kinds of institutions, it is necessary to discover the extent to which they achieve the desired standard. It should be the duty of the Ministry of Education and the Planning Commission to encourage research into this aspect. Famous departments of universities can be beneficially associated with these programmes of evaluation.

Universities at Work

The administrative problem of universities are no less complex neither are they in any less need of attention. In this connection, the recommendations and suggestions of the Education Commission should be implemented. We suggest that the Indian branch of the Asian Institute of Educational Planning and Administration, with the cooperation of the University Grants Commission, should take into its hands the work of research into this aspect, and also prepare programmes for the proper, training at the university level. It is also our suggestion that the Planning Commission should establish a working group, under the guidance of the Asian Institute, for a detailed study of these problems, and on the basis of its findings, it should also promptly take definite and concrete steps for the improvement of university administration.

It is desirable that specific programmes concerning educational planning, administration and evaluation should be evolved on the basis of priority in the present plan period. In the last 20 years, the states' departments of education have not expanded at the same rate as that at which facilities have expanded. For instance, in 1946-47, only 3.2% of the total expenditure on education was expanded upon supervision and inspection, although at least 5% should have been spent. In 1965-66, this expenditure increased by 6 times, but during this period, the expenditure on education had risen from Rs. 50 crores to Rs. 600 crores, with the result that the percentage spent upon inspection and supervision fell to only 1.9.

This tendency of spending less and less on educational administration has continued over the years, and in the last three, plan periods, it has become even more marked. In the states' plans, no money is at all allocated for administration and inspection in the first place, and even when some provisions are made, deductions are made in it, whenever there is any need to reduce expenditure. The outcome of this short-sighted policy is that although a small amount of administrative expenditure is saved, a much larger sum is wasted on education because of the lack of proper administration, and inspection.

It is most sadding to note that there is very little awareness of the great ,harm that has been caused to educational administration. In many matters, the quality of administration has deteriorated sharply, while in many others, administration has completely vanished. For instance -

1. The director of education is usually so completely occupied by his work in the office that he is unable to undertake regular tours of schools, as he did in the past. He is also unable to establish close relationships with district officials, and thus, he is unable to stimulate or direct them fruitfully. Regional officials also suffer from similar handicaps.

2. The result is that even district officials are often unable to inspect schools for long stretches of time.

3. Many very important responsibilities have been thrust upon the departments of education, but they have failed to evolve an efficient machinery for implementing their schemes. For instance, text-books have been nationalised, but there is no efficient machinery to over-see the

production of text-books of the desired quality or standard. Consequently, in some places, the district inspector has been converted into a mere bookseller, while at other places, he wastes two-thirds of his time in paying the salaries of teachers.

Not only is it necessary to reverse this flow, it is essential to achieve this promptly. Hence, it is suggested that, for the purpose of improving and strengthening educational administration, 5 per cent of the educational budget should be earmarked, on a priority basis, for educational planning, administration and evaluation, and this should also include research and the training of educational administrators, principals, as well as the in-service training of teachers.

Recommendations

1. Instead of allocating funds for a few selected schemes, complete educational plans should be formulated.
2. Well co-ordinated and harmonised plans should be framed at the district, state and national levels in order to meet the need for a decentralised approach to educational planning.
3. Institutional plans will provide the basis for this novel process of educational planning.
4. The district should be regarded as the basic unit of educational planning, administration and development. From the very next year, district plans should be initiated for purposes of guidance, and these should be adopted within a five-year period.
5. State plans must be made the basis of the entire process of educational planning.
6. It is the responsibility of the Central Government to adopt and maintain a balanced viewpoint and foresight regarding

education development as well as the eradication of regional imbalances among states in the matter of education. From this viewpoint, specific programmes should be included in the national plan. Planning should have a dual aspect-planning from above, and planning from below.

7. It is necessary to involve teachers, intimately and effectively in the formulation and implementation of educational planning.
8. All individuals concerned with educational planning and implementation should be given suitable training.
9. In preparing plans for educational development, the technique of preparing projects should be adopted.
10. The tendency towards heavy investments and negligence of costs in educational development programmes should be curbed; instead, programmes more in keeping with the conditions of a developing country should be prepared.
11. Priorities at the district, state and national level should be clearly defined for effective educational planning.
12. There is an acute need to establish co-ordination and harmony between the various agencies concerned with educational planning. The states and the centre, too, should co-ordinate and harmonise their activities in plan formulation and implementation.
13. For improvement in the implementation of educational plans, it is essential that the existing organisational administration should be immediately replaced by developmental administration.
14. Under the new concept of developmental administration, there will be great need for re-organisation in the state and central educational services.

15. Programmes for the in-service training of educational administrators should be given a high priority.

16. Giving the highest priority to the Education Commission's suggestion for the establishment of a national college for training such administrators, we recommend that this should be established immediately and developed fully within the five-year plan period.

17. There is need to encourage departmental officials to increase their professional competence.

18. In addition to developing programmes for in-service training, it is also necessary to adopt a programme to complement such training. In this the administrative officials at every level should be acquainted with the complex problems of educational reorganisation.

19. If educational administration is to be improved, proper provisions of institutions and able individuals for the supervision of programmes for qualitative improvement must be made. These should include the NCERT at the national level, state educational institutes at the state level, and other institutions and school complexes at the district level.

20. Effort must be made for providing better supervision and guidance to schools.; For this, wherever necessary, the staff for inspection must be increased and subject-inspectors appointed.

21. Departmental working, which is unsuitable for developmental administration must be improved quickly.

22. The mode of working of departments of education should be dynamic and flexible.

23. In the forthcoming years, due emphasis should be placed upon evaluation and educational research. In these fields, some determined progress must be made.

24. The Indian branch of the Asian Institute for Educational Planning and Administration, with the co-operation of the University Grants Commission, should conduct research into the problems of university administration, and also introduce programmes for the suitable training of university teachers.
25. Priority must be given in the present plan to schemes for reforms in educational planning, administration and evaluation. For this, 5 per cent of the expenditure on education should be set apart for this purpose.
26. It is our suggestion that a sum of Rs. 26 crores should be provided for developmental schemes relating to educational planning, administration and evaluation.

8

FIVE YEAR PLANS

The development of a nation depends upon its mode of education. Even the development of a young nation like India depends upon its educational approach. The leaders of our nation put forward a blue-print for India's development through the medium of Five Year Plans. It was felt that society would have to resort to modernisation to educate itself. It would have to endeavour to create, in order to raise the educational level of the common citizen, a class of educated persons containing individuals from every section of society, whose beliefs and aspirations bore the deepest imprint of Indianness. In a democracy, the end is the individual himself. Hence, the main function of education is to grant him the greatest possible opportunities for the growth of all his powers.

At present, India's future is being formed and shaped in its class rooms. In the world of today, a world which is founded upon science and technology, it is education alone which determines the level of prosperity, well-being and security of every individual. The success of our endeavours at national reconstruction depends upon the qualities of our students emerging from our schools and universities. Evolution of a national consciousness should be an important objective of school education. We should seek to fulfil this goal by bringing about a growth in the knowledge of our cultural heritage, by encouraging constant revaluation and re-examination of it, and by generating firm faith in its future. Attempts to achieve this objective have been made through the Five Year Plans. The following paragraphs outline the form and nature of education in our country under the successive five year plans.

In the First Five Year Plan, it was perceived that the first problem before the country was that of eradicating the economic imbalances created by war and the partition of the country. The aim of the plan was to utilise fully the basic sources for rapid economic development in the future. The problem of rehabilitating the refugees was intimately connected with both these aspects. It was decided that the fundamentals laid down in the Constitution for the achievement of social justice had to be kept in view.

The First Five Year Plan had its beginning in 1951. In the sphere of education, its various objectives were the following:—

1. Reorganisation of the educational system into various branches and stages.
2. Expansion in the various spheres of education, particularly basic and social education; modification of the form of professional and technical education.
3. Organising the existing secondary and university education so as to make it adaptable to and useful for the rural sector.
4. Expansion of women's education.
5. Making provisions for the training of teachers in basic schools.
6. Providing aid through grants to backward states and areas.

The priorities in the programme of the First Five Year Plan were as follows:—

1. Expansion of basic or primary education.
2. Consolidation of secondary and university education.
3. Consolidation and development of the teacher's facilities.
4. Teacher training.
5. Experiment and Research.
6. Creation of literature for children.
7. Providing the necessary facilities for social education.
8. Providing the necessary facilities for professional and technical education.

At the initiation of the Plan, the level of literacy was respectively 40,10 and 1 per cent in the age groups 6-11. years, 11-19 years, and 19-23 years, while the average literacy was 16.6 per cent. Because of this, great attention was paid to achieving significant progress in the educational sphere during the plan period. At that time, the expenditure on higher education was more than that on primary education. There was vast difference between education in rural areas and that available in urban areas. There was considerable wastage of funds, and also a number of obstacles.

The achievements of the First Five Year Plan can be stated thus—

Pre-school Education. In the First Year Plan period, responsibility was tulfilled, to a limited extent, in the following spheres of pre-school education- (1) training of teachers, (2) giving aid to private institutions, (3) introduction of creches in every state, (4) giving grants to local bodies for establishing creches and pre-school institutions, (5) providing aid for the construction of buildings.

Primary and Basic Education. In the First Five Year Plan, primary and basic education were understood to mean the national scheme for education. Efforts were made for the expansion of primary and basic education, for training teachers and providing aid.

Secondary Education. A Secondary Education Commission was appointed for the reorganisation of secondary education, and on the basis of its report, text-books were produced and organisations established for the guidance of education.

Social Education. In the sphere of social education, Janta Colleges (public colleges) were established and training given to social educators and workers. New literature was produced, social education centres were established, libraries were created, youth camps were organised, inter-university youth festivals were organised, and provisions made for setting up students' hostels.

Others. Among the other activities were the establishment of training centres for the blind, provision of higher education in rural areas, creation of social and child welfare centres, and the establishment of national society of drama, and a fundamental education institution.

It is apparent from the foregoing table that the figures for the beginning and the end of the plan period clearly show progress, and also that the achievements of the plan had an impact upon public life.

The history of planning in India is rapidly becoming the history of our social, cultural and economic progress. The second link in this chain was the second Five Year Plan, which began in 1956 and continued till 1961. It was stated in the Plan document that the educational system had a definite impact upon economic achievements, and many advantages could be derived from it. Economic development naturally demands human resources. In a democratic system, education is an essential element in the generation of values and attitudes.

In this plan period, notable work was done in the spheres of basic education, expansion of primary education, diversification of secondary education, expansion of technical and professional education, and programmes for social education and cultural progress. The allocation for education in the first Plan was Rs.169 crores, while Rs. 307 crores (Centres-95 crores; States 212 crores) were allocated in the second plan. The notable characteristics of the plan was as follows—

1. Stress on basic education.
2. Definition of Initial education.
3. Diversification of the curriculum at the secondary level.
4. Improvement of the standard of education at the college and university level.
5. Development of professional and technical education.
6. Development of social education and cultural programmes.

In our Constitution, we have visualised a socialistic and democratic pattern of society, and for the achievement of this objective, specific objectives were defined in the second plan. Referring to this, it is stated in the Plan document that the concept of a socialistic pattern of society means that at various levels, there should be public participation and constructive leadership in every activity. In the second plan, Rs. 307 crores were provided for education, out of which Rs. 95 crores were to be spent by the Centre and Rs. 212 crores by the States. The allotment of these resources in the first and second plans are shown in Table 1.

Allotment of Funds (1, II, Plan) in Crores.

Educational Items	*Ist Plan*	*IInd Plan*
Elementary	93	89
Secondary	22	51
University	15	57
Technical and Industrial	23	48
Social	5	5
Administration & Others	11	57
Total	**169**	**307**

Story of Achievements

Initial or Primary Education. In this plan, primary education underwent adequate growth, which was the result of the proper use of the Double Shift system by local bodies and voluntary institutions. The percentage increase in education is reflected in Table 2.

Sl. No.	*Age Group*	*1st Plan %*	*IInd Plan %*
1.	6-11	51	63
2.	11-14	19	23
3.	6-14	40	49
4.	6-14 Girls	23	28

Basic Education. Many efforts were made for the growth of basic education. These took the form of training of employed teachers, refresher courses, research and training establishment for basic teachers. A Basic Education Council was also formed.

Secondary Education. A sum of Rs. 50 crores was spent upon the development of secondary education, and a large number of secondary schools were converted into higher secondary institutions. By the end of the plan, 60% of the teachers in secondary schools had received training. The number of girls receiving education went up. from 4 per cent to 11.5 per cent.

University Education. The University Grants Commission took numerous important steps for the improvement and development of university education. Emphasis was given to professional and technical education.

Social Education. The level of literacy, which was 16.6% at the end of 1951, rose to 24%.

Teachers. The number of institution for training teachers rose from 730 to 1307.

Other Achievements. The other achievements of the second plan were as follows: (1) Provisions were made for granting scholarships to brilliant students, and those belonging to the backward and scheduled tribes. (1) Hindi and regional languages were developed. (3) Sanskrit universities were established at Banaras and Kurukshetra. (4) Music, dance, drama and art underwent development. (5) A National Child Museum, a modern art Gallery, a child centre. and central library were established.

A glance at the entire plan brings to light the following important facts- (1) An educational programme is inevitable for the future of the nation. (2) Mutual co-operation and confidence between the government and the people is essential for the achievement of these objectives. (3) For the success of programmes for economic development, it is essential to formulate, implement and control education programmes.

For the fulfillment of all these goals, the Planning Commission pointed out that the problem of reorganisation of education has numerous practical aspects, e.g., increase in the number of those for whom educational facilities are available; creation of more opportunities for girls and women; variety in education at the secondary level; implementation of the method of basic education in place of the traditional primary education; growth of social education; proper organisation of technical and professional education, and an improvement in university education. There are many fundamental objectives implicit in these activities. In order to get rid of backwardness and to move forward at a rapid pace, the nation needs unity, co-operation in every sphere and the maximum possible efforts. For modern economic development, it is desirable that the attitude of the people should be more scientific, there should be a feeling of respect for labour, there should be a sense of discipline in the services, and new techniques and new knowledge should be easily accepted by the public. On the whole, this second step towards progress was indicative of success, since there was progress in every sphere. The main reason for this was that an image of public consciousness was reflected in the educational plan.

The third stage of national development begins with the introduction of the Third Five Year Plan. In this Plan document, it was said, in the context of education, that the major objective of the third five year plan should be expansion of education and an increase in its intensity so that education may become the focal point in the economic growth in every sphere of national life.

The achievements of the third five year plan are as follows—

Primary Education. In this plan, arrangements were made for efforts to extend these arrangements to children in the 6-14 years age group. Housing facilities for lady teachers and other allowances were given in rural areas. Provisions were also made for a condensed curriculum. Sixty thousand primary schools were converted into basic schools.

Secondary Education. The number of school-going children of the 14-17 years age group increased. Many high schools were converted into higher secondary schools. Various curricula came into force. There was growth in vocational education for women.

University Education. During this plan period, almost a dozen universities and 400 colleges were established. Vocational, technical, and scientific curricula were initiated, along with correspondence courses. Rural Institutes were established.

Women's Education. Rs. 175 crores were allocated for the education of women. The number of girls and women receiving education increased considerably.

Social Education. During this period, literacy rose from 17% to 24%. Arrangements were made for social education in Panchayats, many social education officers, social education organisers and workers for voluntary institutions were appointed. Aid in various forms was extended to them.

Technical and Professional Education. In this period, the Institute of Manpower and Planning was set up. Engineers, technicians, veterinary graduates, administrative officers and forestry workers were trained.

Other Achievements. Other educational programmes during the third plan period were- (1) scholarships were provided, (2) Sanskrit and Hindi were developed, (3) Cultural programmes were organised through the Sahitya Academy, Lalit Kala Academy, the National Museum and the National Art Gallery.

Allotment of Funds (Three Plans) in crores

Sl. No.	***Distribution***	***I***	***II***	***III***
1.	Elementary Edn.	85	87	209
2.	Secondary Edn.	20	48	88
3.	Higher Edn.	14	45	82
4.	Cultural	—	4	10
5.	Other items	14	24	29
	Total	**133**	**208**	**418**

The Table shows the expenditure upon education during these three plan periods.

The notable features of the Third Five Year Plan can be stated briefly as follows:- (1) In this plan, an effort was made to provide educational facilities for all children in the 6-11 years age group. (2) Education in science was expanded and developed. (3) Facilities for training of teachers were expanded. (4) Technical education underwent notable development. (5) For the growth of basic education, the ordinary primary schools were converted into basic schools. (6) Ideal basic schools were set up in urban areas. (7) At the secondary level, there were improvements in education in science, increase in the number of multipurpose schools, conversion of secondary schools into higher secondary schools, introduction of practical curricula in handicrafts secondary schools, improvements in examinations, etc. (8) Provisions were made, at the university level, for three-year degree courses, improvements in laboratories and libraries, research, post-graduate research, hostels, scholarships for research and other scholarships, improvements in the scales of pay of teachers, student welfare, establishment of evening colleges, and correspondence courses. (9) in the field of technical education, technical curricula for mechanical, chemical, electrical, minerals, metals, engineering and other disciplines were evolved and facilities for training provided.

Smooth Progress

In this plan, technical education and training, medical care, public health, housing facilities and a public supply system were given attention with a view to increasing public welfare. Investments in human resources for national economic development produce political democracy and social justice. Provisions were made for crores of rupees for the implementation of the following programmes in the public sector.

1. Provision of universal primary education for eradicating wastages and stagnation through proper work orientation.

2. Expansion of the education of women, provision of various curricula, such as scientific, vocational, etc., at the secondary level.

3. At the university level, improvement in standard and quality, by greater precautions at the time of admission.

4. Provisions for the training of teachers through correspondence courses on the basis of full-time work, and the development of training establishments.

5. Expansion of professional education on the basis of the demand for engineers and technicians. Expansion of research and post-graduate level academic activity and establishment of specialised technological institutions.

6. Creation of text-books, reorganisation of school curricula, development of research in teaching.

7. Organisation of social education, adult literacy, creation of literature and reading matter, and establishment of libraries.

In this plan, education was defined in economic terms. Education came to mean investment in those public resources which occupy an important place among the factors contributing to economic development. During the period of the three preceding plans, there was a remarkable increase in registration at every level of education, but the standard of education declined with the increase in population. It was determined that the prevailing defects in the educational structure, lack of coordination between education and economic development, lack of satisfactory progress in women's education, wastages and stagnation, lack of harmony between curriculum, manpower resources and planning, etc., would be eradicated during the fourth plan. In this plan, arrangements were made for providing lunch to 190 lakh children. The following table shows the expenditure of the State and the Union government on education.

Allotment of Funds in Fourth Plan, in crores

Sl. No.	Particulars	Amount
1.	Elementary Education	322
2.	Secondary Education	243
3.	Higher Education	175
4.	Teacher Education	92
5.	Social Education	64
6.	Technical Education	253
7.	Cultural	15
8.	Others	46
	Total	**1210**

J.P Naik's views on the fourth five year plan are- "A major weakness in our educational planning has been to adopt the comprehensive approach, the trend to do something in every sector, however small. This is really an attitude of escapism from the difficult problem of deciding priorities. It also finds considerable support in the democratic context."

Great emphasis was laid upon eradicating the existing weaknesses in education and making it more effective, putting an end to internal pressures and moulding education in accord with society. The achievements of the first four plans are outlined in tables.

It is because of this that J.P Naik points out that "The educational problems of a developing country can be solved only if there is a large band of idealistic workers who are willing to devote themselves to the tasks of moulding the rising generation. It may not be easy to plan for the creation of such a band of missionaries, but it is doubtful if anything worthwhile can ever be achieved by a nation which cannot create it."

In 1972, the Ministry of Education and Social Welfare, for the first time announced an official Blue Print for education in the Fifth Five Year Plan. In this document, thought was given to education from the primary to the university level, in the context of modernization of Indian society, and in the light of the process of national development. Every possibility of progress has been considered. Provisions were made towards an expenditure of Rs. 3200 crores on education. This sum was divided into various heads, which included numerous schemes, including the establishment of model schools. The document also threw light on the professionalization of education at the secondary level. The following points have been considered in detail in this plan.

Improvements in the Curriculum. Great importance was attached to the reorganisation and improvement of curricula at every level of education, in the context of national development., Emphasis was laid upon cultural instruments in education. Arrangements were made for imparting knowledge about the national movement for independence, the achievements of the country after independence, developmental programmes, exchange of views on national problems, etc., with a view to achieving education for citizenship.

1. At the primary level, the school curricula is intimately related to the environment, which is important for children. In addition to the teaching of the Three R's, children should obtain experience of local developmental activities and programmes. Students of classes 9 and 10 were to be given compulsory education in Crafts, so that students become engaged in socially useful activities.

2. Two main directions were delineated in the reconstruction of the curriculum at the higher secondary level. (1) For those students who wish to study various subjects so as to prepare themselves for university education, provisions were made for such subjects as mathematics, natural sciences, humanities, social sciences, etc. (2) For other

students who wish to prepare themselves for service or self-employment, provisions were made for education in agriculture, industry, etc., so as to,enable them to seek employment therein.

3. In the restructuring of the curriculum at the university level, attention was paid to (1) Relevance (2) Flexibility (3) Diversification, and (4) Modernization. Even today, many universities have curricula which are between 30 and 50 years old, and they do not fulfil the needs of the present times. Hence, there is great need for modernizing the curricula. In higher education, at the postgraduate level, the emphasis was upon training and research. This educational programme paid attention to teaching methods, improvements in examination techniques, improvements in the standards of text-books, and the generation of vocational or professional skills.

Changes in Education. In the Fifth plan, a need was felt for changes in the methods of education in the light of existing facts. It was because of this that importance was given to Informal and Liberal education. So far, there was only one recognised path-starting from the primary level. However, the second path, for those who did not get any educational opportunity- consists of opportunities of informal and liberal education: An important reform intimately linked with this method would be the linking of education with the Informal Agency. This would lead to the growth of mass education and improved potential for games and sports, arts and the development of culture. This would make the curriculum more effective.

Model Schools. The establishment of ideal schools by the universities, on the basis of the Seed-Farm Technology, is an important step in this direction. Initially, these schools will be of an experimental nature. Later on, with an increase in the number of teachers and greater possibilities of their availability, such schools will increase. The second step will be initiated after the successful completion of the first stage, i.e., after passing through the primary and secondary stages, the student will enter the third stage and get an opportunity for progressing towards professional and enlightened education. These model schools will perform the function of Pace Setting. Hence, it will be best to establish comprehensive secondary schools. In such schools, 25 per cent of the seats will be reserved for children from poor families. They will be given scholarships. Because of this, opportunities will become available for the unprivileged, apart from the privileged, and thus an important step towards socialism will have been taken. Under this programme, 10 per cent schools will be allowed to develop to the level of model schools. These schools will also function as Demonstration Centres while neighbouring schools will function as Extension Centres. Another programme aims at the development and improvement of other schools also. For this purpose, local co-operation will be sought.

University Level. In order to encourage programmes of the kind and nature of contact programmes at the university level also, it will be best that Pace Setting Institutions should be run by the universities themselves. Another programme under this scheme envisages the setting up of Autonomous Colleges, which perform the function of Contact Institutions. Such Institutions will be given adequate aid to raise their standards.

Compulsory Education. It has been made clear in this plan that the objective of compulsory education which, according to the Constitution, should have been achieved by 1960, has now been extended to 1980-81. For achieving this objective, the following changes will have to be made in the system of primary education-(1) Multiple Channels will have to be accepted for admission to education at the 6 + 11 + and 14 + age levels. (2) Many full-time as well as part time programme will have to be adopted for those children who could not receive formal education for some reason. (3) For this purpose, the services of retired teachers, able individuals from society and voluntary workers of the national service will have to be utilized.

Development Programmes. A sum of Rs. 1,190 crores was spent upon this programme. More money was spent upon qualitative improvement in education at the primary and secondary level. Experienced teachers, teachers of science and additional teachers were appointed for this purpose. Rs. 558 crores were spent on this alone. Provisions were made for Rs. 990 crores and Rs. 585 crores, i.e. Rs.1575 crores, which were to be spent on Qualitative and Quantitative programmes respectively. Rs. 400 crores were earmarked for secondary education. For the expansion of higher education 15 universities and 50 university-centres were set up during this plan period, and provisions was made for an expenditure of Rs. 100 crores. Advanced Centres of Studies were also developed. 100 such centres were established at a cost of Rs. 20 crores.

Total Expenditure. In the fifth plan, Rs. 3200 crores were provided for education. In this, Rs. 1250 crores (3.2% of the national income) will increase every year, and by the end of the plan period, this increase will amount to Rs. 2250 crores (4.5% of the national income). If the education programmes of other ministries are also included in this head, this increase will amount to 4.7% of the national income.

The Evaluation

In India, our five year plans are the medium of national development. The objective is to take the nation to the desired level through these plans. So far, in each one of these plans, there has been expansion and development in the educational sphere, at every level. However, at times, these plans have been subjected to criticism also.

The following view was expressed in the *Hindustan (Dainik)* on this subject. It was said that the education ministry had prepared a plan for the expenditure of Rs. 3200 crores on education from the primary to the university level. How much of this would be spent was a secondary question. The central question was whether any fundamental change would occur in the structure of education. The system of education introduced by the British into this country aimed at the creation of workers who could help the British rulers in their work. It is a matter of the greatest shame and sorrow that, even 32 years after independence, the same old structure of education continued to function, an education which had no national basis, and which could not help the student to become an ideal citizen. The education imparted through English, a foreign language, was completely removed from everything Indian. It did not include even those means which could help the student become a lover of industrious effort and independence, which are necessary for success in the struggle for existence.

In India, only that mode or system of education can be successful as well as purposeful which has deep roots in Indian culture. India's youth can be put on the path towards Indian national unity, unlimited faith in its destiny and self-reliance, only when they are given knowledge of Indian literature, art and culture. Towards these, they must have deepest feeling of attachment. What right have they to call themselves Indians if they study Shakespeare, but are completely ignorant of Kalidas, if they are learned in the political philosophies of ancient Greece and modern Europe but do not have even a nodding acquaintance with the names or ideas of Kautilya, Shukracharya, Vidhur, Brahaspati and other Indian philosophers? It is a strange anomaly that in India today we can find many Indian students spouting the revolutionary theories of Karl Marx, but we cannot discover even a few who have any knowledge of the revolutionary changes that Rama and Krishana brought about by their ideals, courage and revolutionary activities, and the light that they thus shed upon human ignorance. Our schools tell our students of the adventurous journeys of Columbus and Vasco-de-Gama, but they are not informed of the prestigeous ships and travellers enjoyed in the ancient world, and the fact that our travellers went to the countries of South East Asia, China and other countries, both for trade and for propagation of their religion.

Undoubtedly, there is need for revolutionary changes in the education of women in India. From the very beginning, it is essential to impart that education which introduces our students to our glorious Indian culture, so that our students may glory in its grand achievements, may develop attachment for it and thus may develop well-rounded personalities and character. Besides, the student should be put into possession not only of theoretical knowledge, but should also be given practical knowledge of various trades and industries so that, in his future life, he may be self-reliant. The Basic education of Gandhiji's concept aimed at nothing more than this.

In 1977, the Opposition parties formed the governments at the Centre and in many of the States for the first time since independence. These new governments put an end to many of the programmes and ideas of their predecessors. They put forth their programmes for the first time in the form of the Sixth Five Year Plan (1978-83), which possessed the following characteristics:—

(i) Eradication of illiteracy, universal primary education, introduction of job-oriented education, were the prime objectives of this plan. In order to introduce the programme for adult education at the national level (for the 15-35 age group), the co-operation of universities, other institutions, trade unions, voluntary and governmental institutions, etc., was expected.

(ii) In the sphere of primary education, provisions were made for the admission of 320 lakh children, since in the 6-14 age group, 90% of the above number is made up of this figure. At present, this percentage is 69. In this sphere efforts were made to minimise wastages and stagnation. Arrangements were made for the provision of informal education. In the same way, the plan envisages, at the higher secondary and university levels, the diversification and enlargement of the curricula, progress towards vocationalization, and encouragement of a scientific attitude in the rural popoulation, etc.

By the end of the fifth plan, the number of schools and colleges increased from 2.31 lakhs to 5.72 lakhs, while the number of students rose from 273 lakhs to 876 lakhs. In 1973-74, a sum of Rs. 1311 crores was spent on education, a sum which was 18 times the sum spent in 1950-51.

Structure of the Educational Policy. In the educational policy for the sixth plan, there are six important points—

(i) Introduction of adult education at the national level for which 10 per cent of the education budget was set apart. This education is intended for the 15 to 35 age group.

(ii) 50 per cent of the education budget was allocated for providing free and compulsory education at the primary level for the 6-14 age group. Many important improvements in this sphere were suggested.

(iii) At the higher secondary and university level, attention was paid to the quantitative expansion of education. In this sphere, importance was given to making admissions systematic, and to turning the students towards vocationalization.

(iv) The education falling outside the sphere of the government's programme registered a rise of 12 per cent, and hence suggestions were made for taking effective steps to make this education more beneficial.

(v) It was suggested that the state governments would have to make special efforts for the extension of universal and compulsory education.

(vi) It was planned that educational programmes must comprehend rural bases also, by virtue of which scientific education and the scientific tendency could be fostered through the medium of informal education.

Elementary Education. In the four years of the fifth five year plan, 106 lakh children were granted admission at the elementary stage. In the 6-11 age group, admissions have risen to 85%, and in the 11-14 age group, to 69%. Keeping these facts in mind, and also Article 45 of the Constitution, much thought was given to this matter in the sixth plan.

(i) So far, the emphasis has been upon granting admissions to classes 1-5 and 6-8, a process in which there is a wastage of 65% at the elementary level and of 75% in the classes 1 to 8. Because of this, the figures should consider not only admissions but also average attendance. And students should be allowed to move forward on the latter basis. Special programmes should be framed and adopted for putting an end to the wastage.

(ii) There are arrangements for elementary education in urban areas, but in rural areas, on an average, primary schools are available at only distance of 1.5 kilometres and secondary schools at 3 kilometres, though population is higher in rural areas. Hence, during this plan period, priority was to be given to the proper choice of the location, in the opening of new schools.

(iii) In order to fulfil the aim of universal education, every school was required to make an assessment of all children of the 6-7 age group in its region and to encourage greater admissions.

(iv) The present system, which is based on single-point entry and completely full-time education, suffers from the following drawbacks:- (1) Older children do not get admission again in schools, (2) Those children who perform the function of an economic unit in the family are compelled to leave their education incomplete. Hence, two improvements were suggested.

(a) Part-time, informal education for the 9-14 age group should be initiated for those children who either fail or leave school. Children in the 11-14 age group can be admitted directly to class V after being given education for 12 or 24 months.

(b) A multi-dimensional admission policy should be adopted. In this, informal and part-time education should be encouraged.

(v) With the adoption of this programme, there is now hope that 220 lakh children will get admission to classes 1 to 5, and 100 lakh children will secure admission to classes 6 to 8. This would lead to an increase of 110 per cent in educational opportunities for the 6-11 age group, 57% for the 11-14 age group, and 97% for the 6-14 age group. This situation is expected to come into existence by 1982-83.

(vi) Special arrangements should be made for the girls who do not go to school, and for the children belonging to scheduled tribes, landless farmers and other weaker sections of society. These arrangements include appointment of new teachers, distribution of free text-books, lunch uniforms, etc.

(vii) Efforts are to be made for eliminating regional imbalances.

(viii) Educational research in certain selected spheres would be conducted.

(ix) Impetus will be given to the adult literacy movement. The role of teachers will be made more important. The number of inspectors will be increased.

Qualitative programmes will be implemented for improving the standard of primary education. Education will be linked to life through useful productive activities and changes in the curriculum. The latest techniques and ideas in education will be implemented for this purpose. Importance has been attached to low cost, greater benefit and the best use of local resources. A sum of Rs. 900 crores has been provided for this purpose.

Adult Education. It has been pointed out in the sixth plan policy on adult education that such a programme, along with a scheme for the eradication of illiteracy, has remained neglected since independence. Not even one percent of the total educational budget was invested on this. Considering the importance of this programme, it has now been given a high priority. In the second plan, there was a provision of Rs. 200 crores for the extension of adult education. In the fifth plan, only Rs.18 crores were spent on adult education. In the sixth plan, the following schemes were give great importance—

1. Schemes of functional literacy for farmers in rural areas.
2. Polyvalent adult education centres and labourer's schools in urban areas.
3. Adult education departments in universities.
4. Nehru Youth Centres.
5. National Service Scheme
6. Financial aid to voluntary institutions providing adult education.

The adult education programme in the sixth plan aims at the mobilisation of intense efforts for the education of the 15-35 age group, at the national level. In the past, 5 lakh people were made literate every year, but the aim of this plan is to secure literacy for 11 lakh in the first year, 45 lakh in the second, 90 lakh in the third, 180 lakh in the fourth and 320 lakh in the fifth year.

In this scheme, special attention has been given to the fact that the benefit of adult education should flow to the scattered and far-flung people of all castes and classes in rural and urban areas. The programme also aims at eradicating the illiteracy ingrained in women, landless workers, agricultural labourers, and the backward and Scheduled Castes and Tribes. The purpose of the plan is to generate, in the illiterate, the capacity to solve problems of daily life, and a consciousness of reality, as well as consciousness of self. For this reason, provisions have been made for adopting a mixed programme of general education. This programme includes literacy, education for citizenship, health education, family welfare, development of occupational skills, awareness of general science and technology, physical education and cultural activities. Its success depends upon the motivation imparted to adults, the selection of workers, suitable educational material, learning through doing and living, public participation, proper guidance and superintendence. The programme can be given a suitable momentum through voluntary organisations, educational organisations, youth organisations and other such institutions. For this reason, it is planned to involve retired teachers and regular teachers as well as students in this programme.

The emphasis is upon organising the entire programme on a decentralised basis. A council for National Adult Education has been constituted to implement the programme systematically all over the country. It is proposed to appoint identical councils at the state, district, block and city level.

The first year is primarily reserved for making preparations for the programme. These preparations include holding consultations for this programme from the block to the national level, motivating youthful workers, retired individuals and regional instruments, mobilizing all such tools, studying the pre-conditions pertaining to adults, training teachers for adult education, and preparing teaching materials, etc.

Secondary Education. The main objective of the sixth plan is the expansion of secondary education. so far this expansion has been haphazard and ill-planned, because of which some places have numerous educational institutions while a few have none at all. The new programme includes the qualitative development of secondary education, and its vocationalization and expansion. Provisions have been made for establishing secondary schools in backward areas, and it is hoped that during this plan, 30 lakh children will get admission to the secondary stage. In seeking qualitative improvement, the aim is to adopt schemes and plans which do not involve excessive expenditure. It is hoped that, by this programme, socially useful productive work, the teaching of language as a means of communication, teaching of mathematics and sciences in expensive laboratories, social service, literary work, adult education, teacher training, duty to one's work, etc., will find a place in the educational structure.

The education ministry has made provisions for the preparation of and implementation of new curricula at the secondary stage so as to make education job-oriented. Arrangements for training of teachers have been made at various levels. In this context, the possibilities and potential for self-employment have also been given much thought. In addition, it is proposed in this plan to keep control over those institutions which charge high fees, because many brilliant students fail to get admission to such institutions for lack of financial support.

A sum of Rs. 300 crores has been provided for the development of secondary education. In addition, other resources will also be tapped. There are arrangements for development fees, work experience, teaching of science, construction of school buildings, etc. Every class of society is expected to make its contributions in terms of money and resources. Scholarships will be liberally provided to students.

Higher Education. During the first four plans, general higher education has progressed and spread, but unsystematically and without planning. It was only in the fifth plan that some obstacles were placed in admissions. The new plan does not envisage the establishment of any new university between 1978 and 1983. It is pointed out that when setting up a college, attention must also be paid to its means and resources. An increase in the fees in higher education is also held to be justified, since this will put a stop to the race for higher education. Two factors should be kept in mind, in this context—(1) It should be noted that the dominance of the weaker sections in higher education, which is the medium of horizontal mobility, has increased instead of decreasing, (2) There should be growth in the informal means of higher education so that every one should get an opportunity for higher education and for this every university should have provisions for private students.

The plan pays full attention to qualitative improvement, and to the fact that individuals coming for higher education should be possessed of the requisite abilities and be prepared to stay in the institution for their entire time. It is proposed that the degree and post-graduate curricula should be restructured. In this, there should also be diversification. Indian languages should be made the medium of education through inter-disciplinary movement and other facilities. Thus U.G.C. will aid the colleges in raising their standards. Extension education is regarded as an inevitable part of higher education. It is held that there should be arrangements for research and post-graduate education in universities, in order to encourage research in every discipline, Rs. 265 crores have been provided for the development of higher education.

Technical Education. In India, the development of technical education depends upon the supply and demand for manpower in the modern industrial sphere. Because of stagnation in this sphere, it was not possible to find employment in industries for 25000 technical degree holders and 50,000 diploma holders. Since the existing facilities for technical education are sufficient for the next years, there is no need to establish new colleges or expand existing ones. What is needed is that the situation at every level should be surveyed carefully. Attention has been paid in the plan to unification and qualitative improvement. There are provisions for setting up specialised research institutions for the study of energy, materials, oceanology and resource surveys. Special financial provisions have been made for the development of science and technology.

Major Heads of Education (7th Plan Outlay in Crores)

Sl.	Heads	Centre	States	U T.	Total
1.	General Education (of which MNP Component)	1518.64	2863.18	393.48	4775.30
	(a) Elementary Education	100 00	154905	181-40	183045
	(b) Adult Education	130 00	227.66	2.34	36000
	Total outlay on MNP Component	(230.00)	(1776.71)	(183.74)	(2190.45)
2.	Technical Education	220.00	388.12	73.67	681.79
3.	Art & Culture	350.00	114.86	17.26	482.12
4.	Sports & Youth Services	300.00	122.55	20.88	443.43
	Grand Total	**2388.64**	**3488.71**	**505.30**	**6382.65**

Other Programmes, Art and Culture. Such aspects as physical education, games of sports, development of languages, art and culture etc., have been maintained at their existing levels. Special attention has been given to the preservation of our culture, preservation of archeological material, protection of ancient manuscripts and cultural activities.

In the sixth plan, there is greater emphasis upon the expansion of primary and secondary education, and adult education while higher education has been discouraged in a period of democratic awareness and self-development. Considering technical education to be adequate, the provision is for avoiding excessive expenditure upon it. As far as the subject of adult education is concerned, incurring expenditure does not automatically bring about an expansion of education, since what is needed is devoted workers and suitable instructions, an aspect on which the plan is silent.

The sapling of the plan is foreign, whereas the soil is Indian, and in it, this sapling cannot take root. What is needed is that the sapling should also be completely Indian.

9

STRESS ON ELEMENTARY EDUCATION

Seventh Five Year Plan (1985-90) gave much emphasis on the following aspects of education.

1. Eradication of illiteracy among the age group of 15-35 years upto 1990.
2. To achieve the objective of universal primary education.
3. To provide facilities in each district to develop qualitative improvement of education.
4. To make upto date the system of education to meet the challenges of science and technology education and to make it modernise.
5. To make wider arrangements for vocational education.
6. To reconstruct the system of education for the development of human resources.
7. To provide new shape to education to meet the challenges in 21st country.

During the plan period Rs. 6,382.65 crores were allotted, out of which centre had to share, 2, 388.64 and state was to share 3, 488.71 crores of rupees.

The Prologue. The large amount of social consciousness and political awakening which are seen in India, is due to the changing factors. These factors responsible for the socio-political and economic change are the outcome of industrial and technological progress and expansion of education. Social consciousness and awakening for rights created the conditions by which India made her place among the powerful nations of the world.

National Planning Commission was appointed for the planned change in the country through Five Year Plans. Now. In the Seventh Plan the concept of education has been changed. Man is considered as resource for the development of the country. Therefore, a separate ministry of Human Resources was established and education put under it as a part of it.

Objectives of seventh plan were (i) production programme (ii) rural development (iii) increase in employment (iv) industrial employment (v) high rate of growth of industrial development (vi) development of transport, power etc (vii) Technological development (viii) environment (ix) control over inflation (x) mass consciousness (xi) administrative reform (xii) basic priorities, i.e., food, work and productivity.

The Background. Human resources development has necessarily to be assigned a key role in any development strategy, particularly in a country with a large population. Trained and educated on sound lines, a large population can itself become an asset in accelerating economic growth and in ensuring social change in desired directions. Education develops basic skills and abilities and fosters a value system conducive to, and in support of, national development goals, both longterm and immediate. In a world where knowledge is increasing at an exponential rate, the task of education in the diffusion of new knowledge and, at the same time, in the preservation and promotion of what is basic to India's culture and ethos, is both complex and challenging. It is, therefore, appropriate that the commencement of the Seventh Plan coincides with a comprehensive review of the education policy.

The resolution on the National Policy on Education adopted in 1968 pointed out that the great leaders of the Indian freedom movement realised the fundamental role of education and, throughout the nation's struggle for independence, stressed the unique significance of education for national development. The Resolution further declared that the radical reconstruction of education as envisaged involved (i) a transformation of the system to relate it more closely to the life of the people; (ii) a continuous effort to expand educational opportunity; (iii) a sustained and intensive effort to raise the quality of education at all stages; (iv) an emphasis on the development of science and technology; and (v) the cultivation of moral and social values. According to the Resolution, the educational system must produce young men and women of character and ability, committed to national service and development.

There has been a great deal of accomplishment in the field of education since 1947. Any number which may be picked up as a parameter to define growth in education will show the magnitude of the massive quantitative expansion that has taken place (Annexure 1). The number of recognised institutions has increased from 2,31,000 in 1951 to an estimated 7,55,000 in 1984-85. The total enrolment over the same period in these institutions increased from 24 million to nearly 132 million. The national stock of educated manpower is estimated to have increased from less than 4 million to about 48 million at present, the annual increment to the stock now being of the order of 3.5 million. It is significant to note that facilities have not only increased but also diversified at all levels and in different subjects. The enrolment for postgraduate studies, for instance has grown from a mere 20,000 in 1951 to over 300,000 by 1984-85 while that in science subjects is estimated to have increased from 4,400 to about 73,000. Extensive facilities are available for education in a variety of branches of engineering and technology. The output of this system has contributed significantly to our achievements in areas like atomic energy and satellite communication and provides the trained manpower for our economic development.

The expansion of educational facilities has also helped to some extent in the correction of regional and other imbalances and in achieving progress towards equality of educational opportunity and social justice. The annual non-plan expenditure on education from the Central and State budgets has increased more than fifty times over the last 35 years, from Rs. 114 crores in 1950-51 to more than Rs. 6,000 crores in 1984-85.

Although the Indian education scene since independence has been characterised by massive quantitative expansion at all levels, it is still to undergo the kind of transformation envisaged in the National Policy. It is faced with a staggering backlog; the level of illiteracy is as high as 63 per cent to achieve universal elementary education, as enjoined by the Constitution. There will be need to enroll fifty million more children; vocationalisation of secondary education has yet to make headway there is very significant pressure on the higher educational system and a decline in the standards of quality. There is an urgent need for a new design for education. The Approach to the Seventh Plan has emphasised that one of the primary task is the harnessing of the country's abundant human resources and improving their capability for development with equity. It is recognised that programme for alleviation of poverty, reduction of social and economic inequalities and improving productivity can and should be integrated with educational development. further, the strategies for educational programmes and training and their organisational designs should particularly focus on women, youth and economically weaker groups so that they can make increasing contribution to the socioeconomic development of the country.

Sixth Plan Review. The Sixth Plan provided, inter alia, for mass education through programmes of elementary education (formal and non-formal streams) and adult education. The Plan also envisaged increased bias towards practicals in secondary education, vocationalisation of higher secondary education and restructuring undergraduate courses with a vocational bias. Forging beneficial linkages between education, employment and development was another objective in the field of higher education.

An enrolment target of 18 million additional children was set for the Sixth Plan period under the formal system of elementary education. According to the available reports, the additional enrolment is likely to be nearly 22 million. Although the target has been exceeded on an all-India basis, there have been shortfalls in a few States, especially in regard to the enrolment of girls. Also, the enrolment ratio in 1984-85 was 92 per cent for primary and 53% for middle stages of education. For girls it was only 69 per cent and 38 per cent respectively. Some of the notable measures taken for the promotion of elementary education were : 'earn while you learn' scheme, mid-day meals for children, innovative curriculum renewal schemes, and special emphasis on appointment of women teachers. Funds available under National Rural Employment Programme (NREP) and Rural Landless Employment Guarantee Programme (RLEGP) were also utilised for construction of school buildings.

Under the programme of non-formal education although no specific targets were laid down, 8 million children were expected to be enrolled during Sixth Plan. This was an experimental programme under which diverse models were to be worked out to suit the area-specific or beneficiary-group specific requirement. It is estimated that over 3 million children would have been enrolled under this programme. Beside the non-formal education centres organised by State Governments, innovative and experimental projects were taken up by a number of voluntary and academic institutions. Syllabus and instructional material for use of learners enrolled in non-formal centres were. developed following the integrated approach covering areas of health, hygiene, home science, agriculture, physics, chemistry, biology, history, geography and civics.

The position at the end of the Sixth Plan is that 80 per cent of the out-of-school children are in the nine States of Assam, Andhra Pradesh, Bihar, Jammu and Kashmir, Madhya Pradesh, Orissa, Rajasthan, Uttar Pradesh and West Bengal, but there is need in all States and Union Territories to improve the quality, relevance and effectiveness of the elementary education system, to improve enrolment and retention rates and to promote girls' education.

The Sixth Plan indicated the goal of reaching 100 per cent literacy in the age-group 15-35 years by 1990. While no definite physical target was laid down for the sixth plan, the adult education programme was to be developed on a large scale for the age-group 15-35 years to combat the problem of illiteracy among the productive segment of the population in general and, in particular, among the rural poor. The Central Government funded 386 rural functional literacy projects in the States besides giving assistance to 380 voluntary agencies and 49 universities for adult education programmes. In additional there were programmes of the State Governments. It is estimated that 20 million adult illiterates would have been covered by these programmes during the Sixth Plan. Fifteen States Resource Centres provided the resource support to adult education centres in terms of curriculum formulation, preparation of teaching and learning material, development of methods and media, training of functionaries, monitoring and evaluation, and research and innovation. Development of learning materials for women and weaker sections was given special attention.

Enrolment in secondary and higher secondary levels has increased from about 10 million in 1979-80 to about 17 million in 1984-85. The 10 + 2 pattern of education has been adopted by 20 States and 9 Union Territories although it is yet to be fully implemented in some of these States. The National Council of Educational Research and Training, the State Councils of Educational Research and Training and the State Institutes of Education continued their efforts towards improvement in science and environmental education, value-orientation including national integration and curriculum reforms. Propagation of community singing in schools was launched as a national movement.

In the context of INSAT utilisation, State Institutes of Educational Technology (SIET) were set up in six States, namely, Andhra Pradesh, Bihar, Orissa, Gujarat, Maharashtra and Uttar Pradesh to produce educational television programmes. A Central Institute of Educational Technology (CIET) was set up for the production of programmes, training of personnel from the States as well as for providing guidance in the development of the programmes.

Vocationalisation of education at the higher secondary stage was one of the important reforms included in the Sixth Plan. This programme has made limited progress with an enrolment of about 55,000 students in vocational education, confined to nine States and three Union Territories where it has been introduced. Measures have been initiated to establish the necessary links combining vocationalisation, skill training, in-plant apprenticeship and placement in gainful employment as composite parts of an integrated effort to raise the level of utility of the programme, and its wider acceptance and success. The organisational requirements for the planning, implementation, supervision and evaluation of the integrated programme, along with the mechanism for effective coordination among the concerned agencies, are being assessed and defined.

Enrolment in higher education is estimated to have increased from 2.5 million in 1979-80 to 3.5 million in 1984-85. Efforts were made for the consolidation of existing institutions and to equip universities and colleges with essential facilities within the limited resources available. Other important programmes taken up during the Sixth Plan included restructuring of under-graduate courses, improvement in standards of teaching of sciences and the humanities, strengthening of postgraduate education and promotion of research within the university system. A one hour daily telecast on higher education was also initiated for the benefit of colleges. On the recommendation of. the Science Advisory Committee to the Cabinet, a new scheme was introduced in 1983-84 for strengthening the infrastructure facilities for research and post-graduate education in science and technology within the university system.

During the Sixth Plan period, the major emphasis in technical education was on diversification and optimum utilisation of existing courses and institutional resources. Efforts were made to provide facilities in areas such as computer sciences, instrumentation, product development, maintenance engineering, bio-sciences, and material sciences. Forty-six selected polytechnics were assisted and supported to develop them into a network of "community polytechnics" which would help transfer and apply available technology with the object of modernising rural structures. New manpower training programmes were undertaken for emerging areas in technology such as micro-processor application, remote sensing, laser technology, atmospheric sciences, and energy sciences. Programmes of management, education, particularly in the Institutes of Management were reviewed by an Expert Committee and on its recommendation, the establishment of a new Institute at Lucknow was taken in hand.

The Resolution on National Sports Policy was laid before Parliament in 1984 to serve as a policy frame for the Central and State Governments and all organisations connected with sports. The policy gives a new thrust to sports activities towards achieving excellence in as many areas of sports and games as possible and at the same time making "sports for all" a reality. The Eastern Regional Centre, Calcutta, of Netaji National Institute of Sports, Patiala (NIS) started functioning from 1983 providing additional training courses for coaches. The national coaching scheme now has an authorised cadre strength of 800 coaches. 25 Regional sports coaching centres have been developed in State capitals and district headquarters. Besides its regular training programme, NIS implemented on behalf of the Central Government programmes of National Sports Festivals for women, All India Rural Sports Tournament and Sports Talents Search Scholarship.

The Sports Authority of India was established in 1984 and undertook several sports activities in addition to maintaining and managing infra structure and other facilities created for ASIAD 1982. Sports Councils with the assistance of Central and State Governments have jointly undertaken programmes for improving and developing facilities for the promotion of sports and games. Specifically, assistance was given for development of playfields, construction of Stadia and swimming pools, construction of sports complexes, establishment and maintenance of rural sports centres, running annual coaching scheme and for purchase of sports equipment. The ceilings of financial assistance for these purposes were also enhanced. National Sports Federations were also told for organising coaching camps for preparing the Indian teams and competitors to participate in appropriate international competitions. Under the scheme of National Sports Organisation, financial assistance was provided for developing physical facilities for sports and games in colleges and universities, especially for developing playfields, and construction or gymnasia.

Youth programmes for student and non student youth were continued and expanded during the Sixth Plan. A National Service Scheme originally launched in 1969-70 was a pilot scheme with 40,000 students, covered over six lakh students in the year 1984-85. The scheme enabled students to participate during their first degree studies in various programmes of social service and national development and provided them an opportunity to understand the conditions and problems of social environment. The activities undertaken by the students included environmental conservation, plantation of trees, cleaning of village ponds, construction of wells, health and family welfare programmes, family welfare education of rural women and sanitation drives in urban slums. They also undertook some production-oriented programmes. Nehru Yuvak Kendras set up to cater primarily to the needs of rural student and non student youth, organised several social service camps, slums clearance schemes and environmental awareness schemes as well as programmes for training of youth leadership. In the year 1984-85,120 youth leadership camps and 180 work camps were organised, involving 65,000 participants.

Programmes for preservation of monuments and sites of national importance were taken up on a priority basis. An expert group on archaeology carried out a professional study to prepare an overall plan of action. The number of archaeological circles which look after the preservation of monuments and sites of national importance was raised from 12 to 16. The number of excavation branches was also raised from three to five; Assistance was also provided to Indian National Trust for Art and Cultural Heritage (INTACH) for promoting the conservation and propagation of works of Indian art and culture. A large number of conservation programmes were taken up for repair and preservation of monuments and sites of national importance. The facilities at the National Museum, New Delhi, were further improved through taking up the first phase of its construction programmes. The National Museum organised several aided tour and short-term in-service course. The Indian Museum, Calcutta, the Salar Jang Museum, Hyderabad, the National Gallery of Modern Art, New Delhi, the Nehru Memorial Museum and Library, the National Museum of Man and the National Archives were the other institutions whose programmes received support during the Sixth Plan. The National Council of Science Museums was also supported to undertake the task of popularising science and technology, among students in particular, through a wide range of programmes. The National Research Laboratory for Conservation of Cultural Property in Lucknow undertook a number of research programmes for technical studies with a view to improving conservation methods.

The Anthropological Survey of India was supported through funding of its several research projects on physical and cultural anthropology and allied disciplines. The Survey also undertook exploratory studies in the Himalayas, Narmada Valley and Coastal Andhra Pradesh.

Library programmes were another area of importance during the Sixth Plan. The construction programme at National Library, Calcutta, was taken up. The Raja Rammohun Roy Library Foundation which renders assistance to States and Union Territories for development of public libraries was further strengthened. Promotion and dissemination of culture was another major programme of the Department of Culture. The Sangeet Natak Akademi, the Sahitya Akademi and the Lalit Kala Akademi, besides the National School of Drama, undertook several programmes in this area. The Center for Cultural Resources and Training, New Delhi, organised a number of in-service training programmes for the benefit of teachers drawn from primary and high or higher secondary schools in different parts of the country. Financial assistance was also provided to dance, drama and theatre ensembles and to selected cultural organisations.

Strategy and Thrust Areas in the Seventh Plan. The Seventh Plan provides for reorientation of the education system so as to prepare the country to meet the challenges of the next century. The main thrust areas in the Seventh. Plan would be: (i) achievement of universal elementary education; (ii) eradication of illiteracy in the age-group 15-35 years; (iii) vocationalisation and skill-training programmes at different levels of education;

(iv) upgradation of standards and modernisation at all stages of education with effective links with the world of work and with special emphasis on science and environment and on value orientation; (v) provision of facilities for education of high quality and excellence in every district of the country and (vi) removal of obsolescence and modernisation of technical education.

The major strategies for achieving these objectives would include effective decentralised planning and organisational reforms, promotion of non-formal and open learning systems, adoption of low cost alternatives and optimum use of resources, forging of beneficial linkages with industry and development agencies, and mobilisation of community resources and societal involvement.

Basic Education

Overriding priority will be given to realising universalisation of elementary education for children in the age-group 6-14 years by 1990; this will continue to be part of the Minimum Needs Programme. The emphasis will shift from mere enrolment to retention of pupils in schools and to the attainment by them of basic elements of learning. The objective is sought to be achieved through a combination of formal and non-formal methods, focussing sharply on the needs of girls and of children belonging to the economically and socially weaker sections.

The enrolment at the elementary stage was estimated to have reached nearly 112 million by the end of the Sixth Plan period. For achieving the goal of universalisation by the end of the Seventh Plan, over 50 million children will have to be additionally enrolled. A projection of enrolment in full-time elementary schools is given in Table. Increasing enrolment in full-time schools beyond this level of 137 in classes I to VIII might not be feasible due to socio-economic reasons and other factors. Even to achieve this level effectively, sustained efforts will have to be made to reduce the number of dropouts.

Expansion of Elementary Stage Education

(Enrolment figures in million)

Sl. No.	*Classes/ Age Group*	*Likely enrolment (1984-85)*	*Projected enrolment (1989-90)*	*Additional enrolment (1985-90)*
1	2	3	4	5
I.	I-V (6-11)			
	Boys	51.20 (11748)	55 00 (110 00)	3.80
	Girls	34.17 (6920)	40 - 96 (8815)	6.79
	Total	85.37 (91.84)	95 - 96 (99 89)	10.59
II.	VI-VII (11-14)			
	Boys	17.46 (66.90)	25-12 (92.56)	7.66
	Girls	9.27 (38.19)	16. 55 (65.44)	7.28
	Totai	6.73 (53 07)	41.67 (79 46)	14.94
III.	I-VIII (6-14)			
	Boys	68-66 (90 96)	80 12 (104 24)	11.46
	Girls	43.44 (64.02)	57.51 (80.28)	14 07
	Grand Total	112.10 (78 21)	137.63 (92.60)	25.53

Note : Figures in parentheses indicate enrolment ratio relative to population in the corresponding age-group.

Non-formal education would be the other important programme for the achievement of universalisation of elementary education as this can be useful to those who are not able or willing to attend full-time schools. The number of children to be covered by the non-formal programme is reckoned to be of the order of 25 million. Non-formal education in the Seventh Plan will, therefore, have to be expanded at a fast pace and made acceptable with a variety of forms to suit the varying needs of the target groups. Non-formal system should be made flexible and appropriately linked to the formal system. Adequate textual material with area-specific background and supplementary reading material would be developed and made available to students. Adequate teacher-training arrangements will be made for teachers participating in the non-formal system. For optimum use of resources, the schools, non-formal education. centres and adult education centres should develop linkages and be educationally integrated with development programmes.

The enrolment projections in are indicative figures, worked out. at the macro-level and disaggregated to the State level. Specific operational targets will require to be worked out by the State Governments concerned block-wise and village-wise through decentralised planning. Once such target was worked out for the catchment area of each school or a cluster of schools, it would be expected that the authorities responsible for the achievement of the target would adopt the most appropriate strategies of implementation and monitoring of progress.

The role of the teacher is most crucial in achieving universal elementary education, especially in the motivation of children as well as their parents. 'they can play a leading role in improving the quality of primary education, bringing in environmental and health education and value orientation. In-service training of teachers thus becomes a programme of high priority. The training of teachers will include, apart from pedagogy, the use of mass media, science and technology, planning and curriculum design for local environment-based courses, mobilisation and use of community resources and other relevant subjects. There will also be special emphasis on teaching methods and other measures particularly required for first generation learners and for reducing the number of drop-outs. Teacher training institutions will be developed and strengthened accordingly.

Facilities will have to be created for the training of additional teachers required during the Seventh Plan period. There is as yet no infrastructure in the country for training of teachers in non-formal and early childhood education. Training of such teachers would have to be organised by suitably strengthening the existing teacher training centres.

Considering the numbers involved (over 2.5 million teachers), institutionalised in-service education of teachers will be difficult to organise not only due to the huge costs involved but also due to lack of facilities for training. It is, therefore, necessary to think of a variety of training arrangements. Among others, these would include

(a) In-service education by utilising the mass media, as was done during SITE;

(b) adoption of schools of lower levels of education by institutions of higher levels for upgrading of teacher competencies;

(c) despatch of teacher guidance notes by training schools;

(d) publication of bulletins informing teachers of new developments; and

(e) use correspondence course materials supported by occasional contact.

Drop-outs and non-attendance of children at the primary stage of education are due to poor school facilities, unrelated curriculum, poor methods of teaching and poverty. The reorientation of teacher training referred to above will help to a large extent in tackling these factors. In addition, suitable supportive programmes for the provision of incentives, the improvement of facilities, increasing community awareness, curricular reforms, adjusting of school timings, utilisation of local community resources and earn-while-you-learn scheme, etc., will be introduced or expanded selectively according to local requirements.

Enrolment of girls has been lagging behind despite special measures taken in the past. towards' the end of the Sixth Plan some steps were taken to promote enrolment of girls and for providing non-formal education to them wherever necessary. In the Seventh Plan, the focus of effort will be on promotion of girls' education through appointment of women teachers, attachment of pre-school centres, provision of free uniforms and other incentives.

Special emphasis will be given to the enhancement of quality and efficiency of elementary education. The Seventh Plan will seek to provide specific funds for those programmes which will enhance the efficiency of the system. There is need to have a fresh look at the design and construction of school buildings as well as the text-books in use. Various projects like population education, environment and wild life education and curriculum renewal have helped in the preparation of suitable teaching-learning material and this material will be utilised.

Due to the difficult resource position and the magnitude of the task involved in the implementation of the programme of universalisation of the elementary education, optimal use should be made of the available infrastructure and funds. The Plan and non-Plan budget provision for elementary education and the existing teacher resources should be reviewed and redeployed on the basis of actual requirements and attendance in classes. Part-time teachers or helper-teachers on fixed salary, selected from among locally available educated men and women will be utilised to augment teaching resources and also improve relevance and cost-effectiveness of elementary education. Community support and financial contributions will be mobilised especially for clearing the backlog of physical facilities and school buildings. The construction of school buildings will be taken up also under the National Rural Employment Programme (NREP) and similar programmes.

Early childhood education is important both from the point of view of the personality development of the child and for inculcating in the children a healthy attitude to school-going to help increase their retention rate in schools. This programme will be dovetailed with nutrition, health care and social welfare as a package within the broad frame work of the programme of Integrated Child Development Service (ICDS). Voluntary efforts to undertake innovative experiments in respect of early childhood education will be supported.

The National Policy Resolution on Education recommends the placement of disabled children in regular schools. The scheme of integrated education of disabled children was started by the Ministry of Social Welfare as a Centrally-sponsored scheme where handicapped children were sought to be integrated in the normal school system with a view to promoting their psychological acceptance. The scheme is now being implemented by the Ministry of Education. One of the difficulties facing this scheme is the lack of trained teachers in special education. As such, during the Seventh Plan, greater emphasis will be laid on teacher training.

Education for Adults

Eradication of adult illiteracy and the development of a programme of continuing adult education is a major thrust area in the Seventh Plan. The task of covering all the illiterates in the age-group 15-35 years by 1990 is a formidable one. As motivation of the learner is crucial for success and as the number to be covered is about 90 million, the strategy to achieve the goal can only be through a mass movement involving social institutions, voluntary organisations, students, teachers, employers and the community. This programme will also have to be linked effectively with various development programmes especially the Integrated Rural Development Programme (IRDP). Active participation of village panchayats, mahila mandals, community centres, etc., is essential. Employers will be required to impart necessary functional education to all their illiterate employees. The programmes of Nehru Yuvak Kendras (NYK) and the national Service Scheme (NSS) will also focus on eradication of illiteracy. Programmes for motivating the learners by holding community meetings and through publicity, through posters, films, broadcasting, etc., will be implemented on an adequate scale and with sufficient intensity to create a conducive climate. A network of libraries and the development of literature for neo-literates will also be initiated as a follow-up programme to avoid lapse into illiteracy. Community participation in all literacy programmes will be an essential feature from village level upwards to give proper direction and orientation and lend effective support to this national programme.

Another aspect of education of adults relates to training in functional skills relevant to their respective economic activities. Programmes for this purpose will be strengthened and adequate resource support provided for organising technical and vocational skill-based courses for the benefit of adult learners through Shramik Vidyapeeths and other similar institutions. As a part of the post-literacy and follow-up services, short-duration condensed training courses will be organised for upgrading the skills of the neo-literates and for increasing their awareness of various social events. The existing programmes on rural functional literacy and State adult education programmes and various training programmes for adult learners will be consolidated and dovetailed in the new mass movement programmes of adult education. Citizenship education including adult education, will be a necessary part of the entire education system, and will be specially promoted.

Secondary Level

The demand for secondary education has been growing. The expansion and effectiveness of elementary education will provide a further impetus to this growth. The projected demand for additional facilities will, to some extent, be met by better utilisation of resources in the existing schools. Provision has been made for this purpose and for promoting distance learning techniques and open school system. Unplanned growth of high/higher secondary school will be checked. Norms for the establishment of secondary school will be evolved and strictly observed in order to avoid proliferation of economically non viable and educationally inefficient institutions. In expanding the facilities, special attention will be given to the needs of backward areas, of under-privileged sections of the population and of girls. Girls education will be free upto the higher secondary stage.

The teaching of science and mathematics at high/higher secondary stage of education will be strengthened and made universal. Efforts will be made to update and modernise science curricula, improve laboratories and libraries in schools and ensure the quality of science teachers through large-scale in service training programmes. Environment education will form an important aspect of science education.

The socially useful productive work (work experience) programme component seeks to highlight the link between work and education and to develop positive work ethics and work habits. The programme would allow for better utilisation and integration of community expertise in the teaching-learning process and the use of facilities available with local industry and development institutions. Besides, the support system for development, training, management and supervision available for vocationalisation programme will also be utilised for the programme of social useful productive work at the secondary stage. Semi courses/activities of pre-vocational character will also be introduced for more effective implementation of the programme.

In view of the importance of linking education with productivity, a major impetus was given in the Seventh Plan to vocationalisation of the higher secondary stage. Facilities for vocational education were suitably diversified to cover a large number of fields in agriculture, industry, trade and commerce and services. It was ensured that there was no duplication of courses between technical and vocational institutions and the schools. The skills imparted, were to be of adequate standard for securing gainful employment or self-employment. At the same time opportunities for pursuing higher general and professional education would be provided.

Vocational career courses in education institutions will be introduced in a flexible manner linked to emerging work opportunities. The current intake will be considerably increased by introducing vocational courses in many more institutions.

Based on the evaluation of the on giving scheme of vocationalisation, States are taking steps to re-organise and improve the programme. An Expert Committee has been set up to suggest ways and means of implementing an expanded programme of vocationalisation fully coordinated with the educational system and manpower needs of economic development. The report of this Committee will provide guidelines for further development.

The present wide reach of the media will be used for improving education, especially at the secondary stage. Facilities for production of the requisite audio-visual material including educational software for broadcasting and telecasting will be augmented substantially in the Seventh Plan. During the Sixth Plan, a small beginning was made in providing computer literacy to students in selected secondary schools, based on this experience, steps will be taken to extend the programme to cover different aspects of computer appreciation and application.

One of the essential conditions for continuous improvement in the quality of secondary education is an effective system of in-service training of teachers. The existing facilities were to be assessed, additional requirements identified and steps taken to meet them. The opportunity provided by the new communication technology will be explored for this purpose. Here again, special attention was to be paid to the development of requisite software. Training of personnel required for effective use of modern communication technology and computers in education was to be given very high priority. The NCERT which has already initiated programmes in this regard , would help the State build a network for this purpose.

Education has a crucial contribution to make towards promoting national integration, understanding and a sense of togetherness and harmony. There is, therefore, great need for an integrated and value oriented education with a national perspective. This programme should be so designed that its various threads can be woven into the curricular and co-curricular activities. Suitable revision of text books, strengthening of school libraries and training of teachers would be important from this point of view.

Higher Level

The main emphasis in higher education will be on consolidation, improvement in standards and reforms in the system to make higher education more relevant to national needs and to forge forward and backward linkages of higher education with employment and economic development. Expansion of general higher education facilities will be carefully planned so as to take care of the need to provide larger access of weaker sections and first generation learners from backward areas. In doing so, emphasis will be laid on providing access to existing institutions through appropriate reservation, scholarships, provision of hostel facilities, etc. A network of facilities will be provided through open universities, correspondence courses and part-time education to meet social demand and the needs of continuing education.

The need and urgency for restructuring of undergraduate courses so as to bring in the necessary concern for relevance and use, application, orientation, flexibility and diversification is well recognised. The guidelines for restructuring of courses of study indicated by the University Grants Commission (UGC) provide for addition of groups of courses that may be relevant and useful according to local or regional needs. Extension activities will be developed as components within each subject/discipline. Beneficial linkages will be developed between colleges and development institutions and programmes. Application oriented courses will be given due emphasis.

The Indira Gandhi National Open University, which has been established as a pace setting institution, will besides offering' courses in higher education based on the principles of the open learning system, be also responsible for training of personnel, production of programmes and development of material for utilisation through the electronic media. The National Open University will function as a nodal resource centre for coordination of programmes and development of models for distance education, documentation and dissemination of information and organisation of appropriate support programmes. Besides this, six centres of educational technology being developed by UGC would serve as regional centres for the production of software for educational technology and training of personnel engaged in the programme of distance education and correspondence courses for higher education.

In the area of post-graduate education and research, emphasis will be placed on promoting quality programmes, inter-disciplinary studies and on new emerging frontiers. Research within the university system will get due emphasis and be coordinated with national research efforts under the Science and Technology programme. The programme of strengthening infrastructure facilities for research in science and technology and of postgraduate education within the university system which has started on the recommendation of the Science Advisory Committee to the Cabinet, will be further developed.

Training of teachers in higher education is another area which needs special attention in the Seventh Plan. The faculty improvement programmes will be designed to impart knowledge of new methods and techniques of teaching, learning and evaluation, to develop a national value system, and to prepare the teachers for the task of restructuring undergraduate courses.

Many of the reforms initiated earlier, such as autonomous colleges and examination reform, seem to have faced obstacles and delays in the process of implementation. The Seventh Plan will give high priority to the speedy implementation of various reforms already initiated and to the modernisation of university administration.

Besides concerted efforts to increase the enrolment of Scheduled Castes/Scheduled Tribes students, the most significant programmes for these students will consist of remedial teaching, preparatory training and special coaching. These programmes will be implemented on a large scale by institutions with sizeable student population drawn from the Scheduled Castes and Scheduled Tribes and other weaker sections. These institutions will be strengthened to impart a better quality of education. The scope of these programmes will also be enlarged to include training for employment, coaching for competitive examinations for recruitment to various services and adult and continuing education programmes.

Vocational Education

In the context of the rapid modernisation of the economy envisaged in the near future and given the Seventh Plan objective of improvement in productivity, technical education has to play a leading role. The main emphasis in the field of technical education during the Seventh Plan period was on the following—

(i) Consolidation of infrastructure and facilities already created;

(ii) Optimum utilisation of the existing facilities with attention to cost effectiveness;

(iii) Identification of critical areas with a view to strengthening the facilities in the fields where weaknesses exist in the system at present;

(iv) Creation of infrastructure in new areas of emerging technology vital for the development of the country and provision of necessary facilities for education, training and research in those fields;

(v) Improvement of quality and standards of technical education;

(vi) Removal of obsolescence;

(vii) Modernisation of engineering laboratories and workshops in the technical education institutions;

(viii) Effective management of the overall system of technical education for an optimum return on investments made;

(ix) Innovative measures to improve existing facilities to provide low-cost alternatives to achieve various goals and objectives laid down in the Plan; and

(x) Institutional linkages between technical education on the one hand and rural development and other development sectors, on the other.

To achieve these objectives there would be a balanced development of institutions of technical education at all levels. The Indian Institutes of Technology which have been set up as pace setting institutions, would be further developed as advance centres of excellence. The Institutes have already initiated research work in a number of new areas. An expert committee has been set up to look into the requirements of these Institutes in the context of the challenges ahead. The regional and other engineering colleges would also be developed further particularly with a view to their modernization and to making their courses relevant to the emerging requirements. The upgradation of standards and modernisation of polytechnics will also be accorded a high priority. A major task in the Seventh Plan will be the removal of obsolescence in equipment and revision of courses in all technical education institutions, many of which were drawn up more than two decades ago. The All India Council for Technical Education has recommended that it is necessary also to restructure polytechnic education with a view to—

(a) improving the standard and contents of technical courses;

(b) providing a lateral entry to the vocational stream from 10 + 2 stage;

(c) restoring the balance in the employment pattern of engineering graduates and diploma holders; and

(d) providing multi-point entry to the various courses.

Besides the improvement on these lines, polytechnic education for women was to be given greater attention to meet their special requirements. Further as a result of reorganisation of school education in the 10 + 2 system and with vocationalisation becoming the major thrust in it, the polytechnics will play a significant role in the promotion and development of vocational education, particularly in engineering and allied trades. Besides modernising polytechnics and removing obsolescence in courses and equipment, special attention will be paid to emerging technologies and computerisation. Development of interaction between the technical institutions and industry will be taken up. Removal of regional imbalances would be another major objective in the development of technical education at all levels. The faculty in the technical institutions have to keep themselves abreast of the latest knowledge and advances taking place elsewhere in the world and also have to be in constant touch with industry. A number of schemes have already been instituted under the quality improvement programme including M. Tech. and Ph.D. courses, short-term and mid-term courses and industrial training for engineering college and polytechnic teachers. However, these arrangements need considerable strengthening. Special attention will be paid to the problems of staff training and retraining and to continuing education for staff, including those of the polytechnics, to facilitate academic and professional advancement.

A reliable manpower information system is a pre-requisite to planning in the field of technical education. A national manpower information system is being developed for storage, updating, retrieval and analysis of manpower information to assist in technical education planning. It has at present 17 nodal centres and is coordinated by the Technical Education Division of the Department of Education with the assistance of the lead centre located at the Institute of Applied Manpower Research. The manpower information system will be considerably strengthened and integrated with the planning of technical education.

Besides general improvements, polytechnics will be assisted to undertake extension services for the benefit of the community. The programme of community polytechnics, already initiated in the earlier Plans, will be expanded in the Seventh Plan to cover as many polytechnics as possible.

Curriculum changes need to be introduced periodically in the light of emerging trends in technology. This will require more effective collaborative linkages with industry and research and development establishments and agencies. The allocations provided from budgetary funds for technical education have to be supplemented by contributions from user industries and organisations, which will be facilitated when closer collaborative arrangements are established.

Technology and Science

Considerable emphasis will be laid on the improvement of the quality of teaching science and technology at all levels of education. At school level NCERT at the centre and SCERTs/SIEs in States will provide training to teachers on all aspects of science and technology including design, development and production of science kits and strengthen science laboratories of secondary schools. A National Science Centre will be established for displaying experimental models and projects.

The quality of higher science and technology education has to match the best in the world. In this connection, university departments and colleges will be selected for providing special assistance to bring about improvements in science education.

Modernisation of laboratories in Indian Institutes of Technology, Regional Engineering Colleges and other institutions of technical education will be accorded priority for providing research in' technology. An International Centre for Science and Technology Education will be established. This will operate through a network of existing institutions and serve as a resource centre for cooperative research, and will also disseminate ideas, methods and materials to bring about basic improvement and modernisation in Science and Technology education. The total estimated outlay for S & T component in the education sector will be of the order of Rs.180 crores, including Rs. 35 crores for the programmes recommended by the Science Advisory Committee to the Cabinet.

The Assessment

The present examination-oriented system has distorted the very character of education and has converted it into a mere system of certification to regulate the flow of manpower to the labour market. The dominance of the examination system over the educational processes has led not only to the wrong type of learning, but has also led to many attendant malpractices. Examination reforms to remedy the present malaise would be given the utmost priority. At the same time, the employing sector should be helped to devise its own selection procedures, lay down academic qualifications, prepare assessment tests and evaluation systems in keeping with job content and the ability and skill for performance of the tasks attached to a job.

New Schemes

The Seventh Plan provides for the continuation and limited expansion of on-going programmes relating to scholarships, development of languages, book promotion, educational planning and administration as well as to effective monitoring, particularly of elementary (including non-formal)and adult education.

The existing schemes of scholarships will be reviewed and, if necessary, re-oriented to help talented students to develop their full potential. The Central Government schemes of national scholarships including that for talented children from rural areas will continue in the Seventh Plan. Financial assistance by itself is not adequate for the development of talented children, especially from the poorer sections of society and from backward areas. Their access to, and placement in, good academic institutions is equally necessary. Placements in residential schools will be particularly helpful and a scheme for this purpose is already in operation.

To provide good quality modern education with Indian values to talented children, particularly from the rural areas, it is proposed to set up 432 model secondary schools, one in each district, during the Seventh Five Year Plan. These schools will offer a common core curriculum, ensuring comparability in standards and promoting National Integration and National Values. They will bring together students from different parts of the country, providing opportunities to talented children to fully develop their potential. Admission to these schools will be through a test conducted at tehsil/block level, in which the best performers from every primary school in the district will be eligible to appear. The test would be designed by the NCERT, and it will be associated in conducting and evaluating the test. Residential facilities will be provided in these schools. An autonomous organisation, registered under the Registration of Societies Act, will be set up for establishing and running these schools.

Problem of Language

The development of languages is of basic importance for all educational development programmes. The activities and programmes undertaken in the field of languages comprise: (i) promotion of Hindi (as envisaged under Article 351 of the Constitution); (ii) promotion of modern Indian Languages (as provided in National Policy of Education); (iii) promotion of English and other foreign languages; and (iv) promotion of Sanskrit and other classical languages such as Arabic and Persian. Other languages for which the Centre has special responsibility, like Urdu and Sindhi, have also received attention. These activities will be further developed in the Seventh Plan, with special attention being paid for raising the standards of language competency, spoken as well as written.

The capabilities of existing institutions will be strengthened, particularly, with a view to enabling them to undertake a much larger programme of in-service training, publication of textual and other materials, production of software for transmission through radio and television and to work at the grass-roots level. A selective approach will be adopted in respect of publications, so as to ensure that materials of good quality become available and are widely disseminated. Instead of entrusting publication of dictionaries, terminologies, text-books, etc., exclusively to governmental agencies, it is proposed to involve creative scholars, university departments and literary organisation with publication activities. Voluntary organisations working for the development and promotion of various languages will be supported, particularly, for undertaking innovative and experimental projects the experience from which will assist in more effective teaching and learning of languages, whether by formal or informal methods.

In Sanskrit, emphasis will be given to activities which will ensure preservation of Shastric and Vedic traditions in oral and written forms, preservation, editing and cataloguing of rare manuscripts, publication of rare and out-of-print books, and training of teachers. It is proposed to assist selected institutions for audio and video taping of recitations of various sakhas which for want of continuing training of scholars in the oral tradition, are becoming extinct. Support will be provided for interdisciplinary research, particularly with a view to identifying the scientific and technical advancement that had taken place in the past and has been recorded in various Sanskrit texts.

The programmes being undertaken for the development of modern Indian languages, including Urdu and Sindhi and also classical languages, in Arabic and Persian will be continued and additional support provided to increase their coverage.

Art and Culture

In Art & Culture the main thrust in the Seventh Five Year Plan would be on the development of culture in all aspects, with emphasis on dissemination, and on the promotion and development of regional cultures and building up of a sense of oneness and underlying unity and cohesiveness of Indians. This would require the involvement of the masses in cultural activities. In order to achieve these objectives, the programmes of the Seventh Plan would include:

(i) Zonal Cultural Centres being set up at different regions of the country. The essential thrust of the creative development efforts of these zonal centres would be to bring about awareness and participation at the grass root level, cutting across-territorial/linguistic boundaries.

(ii) The existing activities of various cultural organisations for dissemination of culture would be stepped up on a wide scale with adequate financial inputs.

(iii) Introduction of a cultural component into the educational system at different levels. The Departments of Education and Cultural Affairs would work together in close coordination for inter-linking education and culture through appropriate programmes.

(iv) Cultural inputs would be integrated in youth activities, rural development activities, domestic tourism, etc.

(v) For the dissemination of culture to the masses, the mass media would be utilised.

(vi) Besides the national cultural organisations, the State agencies would also strengthen their programmes. The Central and State agencies would work with greater coordination towards this objective.

It is proposed to set up seven zonal cultural centres which while developing the unique cultural identities of various areas in the states would also stress and explore their cultural kinship in relation to the totality of India's composite culture, highlighting the essential unity in diversity of the Indian cultural heritage. The Centres would provide facilities for creative development of arts; with special emphasis on folk arts as also the revival of vanishing arts.

The traditional fairs and festivals which provide the continuing link with the rich traditions of the past would be supported through the State agencies and Zonal Cultural Centres. Appropriate programmes would be taken up to provide exposure to youth to the cultural diversity of the country to raise their awareness of the rich heritage that exists in the country.

Preservation, documentation and conservation of our rich and varied cultural heritage would continue to receive priority in the Seventh Plan. This would mean greater attention to the development of archaeology, museums, archives, manuscript libraries, Buddhist/Tibetan studies, and to folk-lore and oral traditions. It is recognised that strands of cultural heritage run through a wide range of development sectors and programmes. These need to be identified and demonstrated as diverse aspects of our rich traditions. Art forms and cultural institutions provide a powerful medium to foster national integration as well as national development. Necessary co-ordination links will be established and cooperative programmes will be undertaken for this purpose.

Greater emphasis will be laid on strengthening of arts through institutions, such as the Academies. Assistance would continue to be provided to voluntary organisations engaged in the promotion of art and culture. Library systems would be strengthened throughout the country with special attention to improving the facilities in the National level institutions.

Some of the rich art forms existing are in the realm of tribal and folk art. The development of folk and tribal arts, especially those which are facing extinction such as the folk art of the Himalayan regions, threatened ecologically as also culturally, would be supported through assistance to voluntary organisations engaged in these fields and areas.

In the field of anthropology, new projects have been identified to study the people of India and promote dissemination of culture. The Rashtriya Manav Sangrahalaya which is expected to be completed in the Seventh Plan, would recreate the history of human evolution, the evolution of culture and the range of living cultures in India.

The Indira Gandhi National Centre for Art will be set up at New Delhi as a resource centre and data base for the arts. It will also develop a major informatics library of cultural materials. The National Theatre will also be established on the same premises to support and project activities particularly in the field of visual arts, including folk and tribal arts.

Youth and Sports

According to the 1981 census, 220 million or about 30 per cent of our population is in the age-group of 15-34 years, with 73 per cent living in the rural areas. The majority of them do not have the benefit of formal education. the problems of youth, therefore have to be identified, with existing programmes being strengthened and new programmes devised to involve their participation and development. The two existing programmes of National Service Scheme (NSS) and Nehru Yuvak Kendras (NYKs) have proved useful in promoting the involvement of youth, both student and non-student, and urban and rural, and in creating awareness among them of nationally accepted objectives and motivating them to work towards their fulfilment. Both these programmes will be further developed and expanded in the Seventh Plan. The strength of the NSS will be raised from six hundred and ten thousand at the end of the Sixth Plan to one million at the end of the Seventh Plan. Activities of Nehru Yuvak Kendras will be expanded to cover all the districts in the country and will also be diversified. The organisational structure of the Yuvak Kendras will also be revamped to impart greater flexibility in the development of programmes for youth, their speedier execution and closer monitoring. The aim will be to make the Kendras effective by ensuring coordinating links between youth and the various agencies of Government and public sector in the national development effort. Programmes of scouting and guiding, mountaineering and adventure, Common-wealth youth programmes and International Youth Exchange Delegations, and National Service Volunteer Schemes will be continued.

A major step will be taken during the Seventh Plan to translate into action the newly adopted Resolution on National Sports Policy, by giving high priority to the development of infra structure and facilities for sports and games at grass-root levels and developing the potential of our human resources both in the rural and urban areas. Efforts will be made to raise national standards in games and sports. Programmes for spotting and nurturing potential sports talent through coaching, training and nutrition required for helping the talented to realise their highest level would be continued. Present schemes like Rural Sports Tournaments, Women's Sports Festivals, National Talent Search Scholarships, grants to National Federations and State Sports Councils, etc., will be expanded. The activities of the Netaji Subhash National Institute of Sports, Patiala will be intensified and its coverage enlarged. The Sports Authority of India will be assisted to pursue its main objective of promotion and broad-basing of sports in the country and creation of health consciousness among citizens through appropriate and meaningful schemes.

Fiscal Provisions

The Seventh Plan outlay for education is of the order of Rs. 6383 crores of which the States sector outlay is Rs. 3994 crores.

The provision for education is mainly in the States' sector. The Centre will play a coordinating role and provide leadership and guidance for new and innovative programmes. Out of the total non-plan budget estimates of education in 1983-84, amounting to Rs. 5229 crores, nearly 91 per cent was in the States Sector. Nearly 87 per cent of the total national expenditure on education is incurred on non-Plan side. In view of the constraints on resources for education, the structure and pattern of utilisation of Plan and non-Plan funds needs to be reviewed, to ensure the optimal use of funds in relation to the goals of the Seventh Plan. It is proposed to adopt low cost designs and devices for effecting economy and for reducing unit costs. Besides, non-budgetary resources have to be tapped and substantial resources mobilised from the community especially for replenishing and augmenting physical facilities in educational institutions.

It is also necessary to emphasise the non-monetary inputs in educational development, i.e., better planning, advanced technologies and practices, careful block level and institutional planning, and school mapping; better systems of supervision and administration; monitoring and evaluation a good information system; dedicated efforts by teachers, students and educational administrators; intensive utilisation of existing resources and facilities; and above all, commitment and active involvement of the local community. Educational research and training and planning and administration of education needs to be streamlined. The State level capabilities particularly require to be built up under the leadership of the National Council of Educational Research and Training and National Institute of Educational Planning and Administration.

ANNEXURE 1

Educational Development From 1950-51 to 1984-85

S. No.	Item	Year 1950-51 (Actual)	1960-61 (Actual)	1970-71 (Actual)	1980-81 (Actual)	1984-85 (Actual)
1	2	3	4	5	6	7
1.	Institutions (Number)					
(i)	Primary	2,09,611	3.30,399	4,08,378	4,85,538	5,50,000*
(ii)	Middle	13,596	49,663	90,621	1,16,447	1,40,000*
(iii)	High/Higher Secondary	7,288	17,257	36,738	51,594	60,000*
(iv)	College					
	(a) Art, Science & Commerce	548	1,161	2,587	3,393	3,500*
	(b) Professional	147	381	1,017	1,382	1,500*
	(c) Universities and Deemed Universities	28	44	93	123	135
2.	Enrolment by Stages (in '000)					
(i)	Primary (I-V Classes)	19,155 (42-6)	34,994 (62-4)	57,045 (76-4)	72,688 (83- 1)	85,377 (9184)
(ii)	Middle (VI-VII Classes)	3,120 (12-7)	6,705 (22-5)	13,315 (34-2)	19,846 (40'0)	26,729 (5307)
(iii)	High/Higher Sec./ Intermediate	1,481	3,483	7,167	11,281	16,800*
(iv)	University-end Above (Ist Degree)	174	557	1,956	2,752	3,442*
3.	Expenditure (Rs. in scores)					
	Total	114	344	1,118	3,746	6,000
	Plan	20	90	115	520	800
	Non-Plan Estimates	94	254	1,003	3,226	5,200

Source: (i) For School Education sir Expenditure—Ministry of Education & Planning commission.

(ii) For Higher Education IOC Reports.

Notes: Figures in parentheses indicate Gross Enrolment Ratio, as percentage of the total population in each category.

ANNEXURE 2

Major Heads of Education (7th Plan Outlay in Crores)

Sl.	Heads	Centre	States	U.T.	Total
1.	General Education (of which MNP Component)	1518.64	2863.18	393.48	4775.30
	(a) Elementary Education	100 00	154905	181-40	183045
	(b) Adult Education	130 00	227.66	2.34	36000
	Total outlay on MNP Component	(230.00)	(1776.71)	(183.74)	(2190.45)
2.	Technical Education	220.00	388.12	73.67	681.79
3.	Art & Culture	350.00	114.86	17.26	482.12
4.	Sports & Youth Services	300.00	122.55	20.88	443.43
	Grand Total	**2388.64**	**3488.71**	**505.30**	**6382.65**

10

STRESS ON SECONDARY EDUCATION

Education for All

It is now universally acknowledged that the goal of Plan efforts is human development, of which human resource development is a necessary prerequisite. Education is the catalytic factor, which leads to human resource development comprising better health and nutrition, improved socio-economic opportunities and more congenial and beneficial natural environment for all. There is already enough evidence in India to show that high literacy rates, especially high female literacy rates, are associated with low rates of population growth, infant mortality and maternal mortality besides a higher rate of life expectancy. Although the country has not so far achieved the goals of universalisation of elementary education (UEE) and eradication of adult illiteracy. (EAI), the 1991 census results reveal a literacy rate of over 52 per cent, with a higher rate of growth for female literacy. This is highly encouraging and the country. can hope to achieve the broader goal of 'Education for All' (EFA) which has incidentally received international recognition at the world conference on EFA held at Jomtien in March, 1990. The commitment of the Government to the National Policy on Education (NPE), implemented from 1986-

87 onwards and reviewed in 1990, has been reaffirmed with revised formulation in respect of a few paras, placed before the Parliament on 7.5. 1992. On the eve of Eighth Plan, therefore, the country is poised to make a real breakthrough in achieving its long-cherished educational goals as well as in supporting the drive for higher rate of economic growth.

Story of Success

The development of education in terms of institutions and enrolment from 1984-85 onwards is indicated in the Table.

Elementary Education

The Seventh Plan gave overriding priority for the realisation of the objective of UEE by 1990. It was estimated that for achieving the goal, over 5 crore additional children would have to be enrolled. By 1991-92, however, about 2.53 crores were actually enrolled in the formal system and even after taking account of 0.72 crores in the non-formal system, the target could not be achieved. At the end of 1991-92, the gross enrolment at the primary and upper-primary stages is likely to have reached 10.09 crores and 3.44 crores respectively. The details of enrolment at the elementary stage are given in the following table.

Enrolment in Elementary Education: Additional and Cumulative Achievement During 1985-92

(Figures in Crores)

Sl. No.	System/Stage	7th Plan (1985-90) Addnl. Achivmt.	Annual Plans (1990-91 & 1991-92 Addnl. Achivmt.	Cumulative Enrolment at the end of 1991-92
1.	Formal:	1.95	0.58	13.53
	(a) Primary	1.34	0.36	10.09
	(b) Upper Primary	0.61	0.22	3.44
2.	Non-formal:	0.61	0.08	0.72

The latest data show that in 1990-91, the gross enrolment ratio (GER) had reached 101.03 per cent at the primary stage and 60.4 per cent at the upper primary stage. Considering that the number of overage and underage children in the GER data was in the range of 16-23 per cent and the dropout rate for primary stage in 1987-88 was 46.97 per cent and for elementary stage as a whole 62.29 per cent, we are clearly far away from the goal of universal enrolment and retention, much less achievement.

The strategies of the Seventh Plan underwent a change in the middle of the Plan period with the adoption of the NPE in 1986. The new thrust in elementary education emphasized the aspects of (i) universal enrolment and universal retention, and (ii) substantial improvement in the quality of education. As part of implementation of NPE, the new scheme of Operation Blackboard (OB) was launched. Besides, the scheme of Non-Formal Education (NFE) was revised and a number of schemes for teacher education were also taken up. By March, 1992, the scheme of OB covered about 80 per cent of the blocks and 49 experimental, innovative NFE projects were sanctioned. There were 27.342 NFE centres run by 419 voluntary agencies and there were 2.72 lakh State run NFE centres.

Teacher Training

In 1987-88, a Centrally-Sponsored Scheme (CSS) for restructuring arid reorganisation of teacher education was started, which included Mass Orientation of School Teachers (MOST), strengthening of Secondary Teacher Education Institutions (STEIs), State Councils of Educational Research and Training (SCERT), setting up of District Institutes of Education and Training (DIETs) and establishment and strengthening of Institutes of Advanced Studies in Education (LASE) in Universities. Between 1987-88 and 1991-92,12.96 lakh teachers were covered under the scheme of MOST and Central assistance was extended to set up 287 DIETs, 25 STEIs and 12 IASEs. The scheme of strengthening SCERTs did not, however, make headway.

Education for Adults

The NPE and the Programme Of Action (POA) envisaged that the Adult Education Programme (AEP) would cover 4 crore illiterates by 1990 and another 6 crores by 1995. With the launching of the National Literacy Mission (NLM) in 1988, the targets were reformulated and strategies recast. Accordingly, 3 crore illiterates were expected to be covered by 1990 and 5 crores by 1995. While Rural Functional Literacy Programme (RFLP), the post-literacy the teaching-learning process were modified, new strategies like area-specific and time-bound approach to achieve 100 per cent total literacy (TL), massive participation of non-governmental organisations (NGOs) and students and effective utilisation of traditional and folk theatre forms in literacy work were evolved. By 1991-92, the post-literacy programme was institutionalised in the form of 32,000 Jan Shikshan Nilayams (JSN). Apart from the introduction of Improved Pace and Content of Learning (IPCL) method, which reduced the duration of learning from 500 to 200 hours, technology demonstration programmes were initiated in 42 selected districts. The scheme of Shramik Vidyapeeths (SVs) was reviewed, suggesting a need for expansion. The number of State Resources Centres (SRCs) increased from 19 to 20. A National Institute of Adult Education (NIAE) was set up in January 1991 to augment the technical and academic resources support to adult education and to undertake quality research and evaluation studies.

Area-specific and time-bound mass campaigns for TL first launched in Kottayam town and Ernakulam district in Kerala in 1989 with the active participation of students and voluntary agencies have been extended to other districts. By March 1992, twenty-five districts had achieved total literacy (in the sense of 85 per cent literacy) and TL campaigns were at different -stages of progress in 80 districts in Andhra Pradesh, Bihar, Gujarat, Haryana, Himachal Pradesh, Karnataka, Madhya Pradesh, Maharashtra, Orissa, Punjab, Rajasthan, Uttar Pradesh and West Bengal covering over 3 crore illiterates with the help of about 30 lakh volunteers.

Secondary Level Education

As part of NPE, new CSS for vocationalisation of higher secondary stage, improvement of science education and environment orientation to school education were started. The new Central schemes of Navodaya Vidyalayas (NVs) and National Open School (NOS) were also initiated. The existing schemes of Integrated Education, Educational Technology and Computer Literacy Studies (CLASS) Project were strengthened.

By the end of 1991-92, about 8.7 per cent of the higher secondary students (5.85 lakhs) would have been diverted to vocational stream. The Open School affiliated to Central Board of Secondary Education (CBSE) was converted into an autonomous NOS in 1989 and by 1991-92, the total enrolment was in the neighbourhood of 1.50 lakhs. Under the Class Project, 2598 schools were equipped with computers, with 60 institutes providing resource support to these schools. As many as 275 NVs designed to provide good quality school education to talented rural children have been established in 29 States/Union Territories. As on March 31,1991, there were 64 ,517 students in the NVs and the pass percentage of the first batch, which took Class X examination was 95.77. The National Council of Educational Research and Training (NCERT) brought out the National Curriculum Framework for all stages of education and undertook a massive revision of text books for classes I-XII on the basis of the revised syllabi designed as per the framework.

New Schemes

The Central language institutions relating to Hindi, Indian Languages, English, Urdu, Sanskrit and Foreign Languages implemented a variety of schemes relating to training of language teachers, publication of language teaching materials, assistance to voluntary organisations, support for Urdu Calligraphy Centres etc. The National Book Trust (NBT) was involved in the work relating to preparation of literature for neo-literates under the NLM and preparation of a Central list of books for the libraries of 5.5 lakhs primary schools under the OB Scheme. The NBT's Nehru Bal Pustakalya and Adan-Pradan Schemes have also made a mark. Besides continuing the schemes relating to national scholarships and scholarships for the talented children from the rural areas, in 1988-89 a new scheme for upgradation of merit of SC/ST students through remedial and special coaching was started as part of NPE.

Universalisation of elementary education, eradication of illiteracy in the age group of 15 to 35 and strengthening of vocational education (VE) so as to relate it to the emerging needs in the urban and rural settings are the major thrust areas of the Eighth Plan in the Education Sector. Utilisation of formal, non-formal and open channels of learning would be the strategy for this purpose. The changed approach, improved methodology of teaching, increased participation of NGOs and student volunteers have infused a new vitality into the literacy programme and have given it a fresh momentum. The aim would be to impart a similar vitality and momentum to the universal primary education programme with a definite edge in its favour. The programmes of AE and UEE are complementary and there are situations where the Elementary Education (EE) programmes may benefit from the spin-off effect of the AE programmes. The improvement in the literacy percentage in the decade 1981-91, after allowing for statistical adjustment due to the exclusion of age group 0 to 6 is as much due to the higher literacy rate of school age cohorts and attrition of old-age cohorts with low level of literacy as to the special efforts on the AE front. The need for according the highest priority to UEE is, therefore, well-established. Within the overall school-age population, the focus would be on girls, who account for two-thirds of target, and among adults the focus would be on women's literacy which has a beneficial impact on children's literacy as well as other national objectives like population control and family welfare.

So far as UEE is concerned, the NPE stress on retention, participation and achievement, rather than mere enrolment, would be reinforced. Enrolment data are easily available and enrolment is a pre-condition for any further action. However, special attention would be paid to increase retention, improvement of quality, specification of minimum levels of learning (MLL) and their attainment by the learners.

Elementary Education: Projected Enrolment for Eighth Plan (1992-97)

(Figures in Crores)

Sl. No.	*State*	*Population by 1997*		*Population with average/ underage children*		*Enrolment achieved upto 1991-92*		*Addnl. Population to be enrolled by 1997*	
		Total	*Female*	*Total*	*Female*	*Total*	*Female*	*Total*	*Female*
1	2	3	4	5	6	7	8	9	10
1.	Elem. Edn	16.64	8.09	19.14	9.30	13.53	5.54	5.61 (67%)	3.76
	(a) Primary (I-V)	10.53	5.12	12.11	5.89	10.09	4.24	2.02 (82%)	1.65
	(b) Upper Primary (VI-VIII)	6.11	2.97	7.03	3.41	3.44	1.30	3.59 (59%)	2.11

In regard to literacy, the emphasis would be on sustainability of literacy skills gained and on the achievement of goals of remediation, continuation and application of skills to actual living and working conditions.

In view of the employment orientation of the Plan and the need to establish meaningful linkages between the world of work and the world of learning, VE would be another priority area. This would not be confined to higher secondary stage but permeate the whole arena of secondary education and non-formal education/training. A combination of vocational and academic courses would be offered at secondary stage with open education (OE) as an important channel, preparing the students for wage employment and self-employment. In the service sector, expansion of health-related courses having a rural orientation would be emphasised. In the rural areas, agro-based and technology-based vocational courses would be developed by combining the strengths of existing institutional structures with OE institutions.

Goals and Actions

It is estimated that additional enrolment to be achieved during the Eighth Plan to reach universalisation is approximately 5.61 crores children. These data are based on the assumption of 15 per cent incidence of overage/underage phenomenon both at the primary and the upper primary stages. Enrolment of about 4.38 crores would be achieved through formal schools, about 1 crore through non-formal centres and the rest through the open learning channel of upper-primary stage. These targets are much higher than the Seventh Plan achievement. They are, however, within the realm of possibility, if the requisite will and mobilisation of organisational and financial resources are brought to bear on the task and innovative schemes like voluntary primary schools and OE at the upper primary stage are introduced. The NDC Committee on Literacy recently appointed is expected to give a lead in this regard. Working targets in relation to retention and achievement based on institutional capabilities and consultations with State Governments need to be laid down. The details of enrolment targets are given in Table.

According to the 1991 Census, the number of illiterates in all age-groups is 33.6 crores. It is estimated that there will be 11.2 crore illiterates in the 15-35 age group of whom 70 lakhs would have become literate by the end of March 1992. Thus, the target to be covered during the Eighth Plan will be about 10.5 crores, compared to the achievement of 2.65 crores during the Seventh

Plan. In the context of the emphasis on sustainability of literacy and on continuing education, suitable targets in this regard need to be laid down after consulting State Governments.

In the VE, the target is to cover 15-20 per cent of students of higher secondary stage by the end of Eighth Plan.

The main strategy for achieving the targets would be : (a) adoption of the decentralised approach to educational planning and management at all levels through Panchayat Raj (PR) institutions; (b) combining this approach with a convergence model of rural development involving integrated utilisation of all possible resources available at Panchayat, Block and District level for activities relating to elementary education/literacy, child care/ development, women's socio-economic empowerment and rural health programmes; (c) large scale participation of voluntary agencies and (d) development of innovative and cost-effective complementary programmes including open learning system (OLS) supported by distance education techniques.

In specific terms, the following measures will be adopted :

1. The formal school system will be expanded and improved.
2. The non-formal system mainly catering to the needs of children working for wages, children working whole-time in domestic or household duties and children in schoolless habitations will be expanded, improved and strengthened in the matter of supply of teaching-learning materials, instructional delivery and achievements.
3. A voluntary school scheme will be introduced. At present, elementary education is considered a responsibility of State and local bodies. However, there is scope for providing part-time non-formalised education to a large number of learners who are not able to avail of the facility of formal full-time school or non-formal education centres. Voluntary agencies would be encouraged in a big way to

start non-formal part-time schools, thus catering to the learning needs of urban working children and children in the tribal, hilly and inaccessible areas.

4. A well-defined open learning system will be developed with a network of educational opportunities relevant to the needs and circumstances of learners, especially girls, women, SCs/STs, and the poor, the unemployed and the untrained. The major thrust of OLS would be on the acquisition of life-skills, vocational skills, directly contributing to productivity and inculcation of habits of self-learning.

5. The MLL with reference to class III, V and VIII will be laid down for improving learning achievement. The educational system will be required to ensure that every child who completes any of these stages of learning reaches the minimum level of achievement. Measures for improving classroom teaching like introduction of a comprehensive evaluation system and a continuous in-service training of teachers will be taken up simultaneously. The MLL approach will be decentralised, each planning unit being able to determine its present levels of achievement, adopt appropriate MLLs and define a realistic timeframe within which to achieve the mastery level, through additional efforts and inputs where necessary.

6. District Boards of Education (DBEs) would be set up. They are conceived as the nodal agency for planning and management of education at the district level comprising formal education, AE, NFE and teacher training, vertically linked to Block/or Mandal Education communities and Village Education Committees (VECs) in a decentralised framework.

7. The school complexes would be developed as the basic unit for educational planning, mobilisation and super-

vision, building organic linkages between educational institutions, DBEs and the Panchayati Raj Institutions.

8. The involvement of the people in school management would be operationalised by giving VECs a more prominent role in planning and management of educational programmes at local level so that VECs, which know the micro-level problems, needs and expectations of the local community, will be accountable for the enrolment, retention and achievement of children and teachers.

9. The methodology of Mahila Samakhya (MS) project of mobilising women's groups to voice their needs would be extended in conjunction. with the involvement of local community to create a favourable environment to serve as a monitoring mechanism for promoting UEE and adult literacy.

10. The district will be treated as a unit of educational planning in the Eighth Plan. For grant of central assistance under CSSs during Sixth and Seventh Plans, a number of States were characterised as educationally backward. The Gross Enrolment Ratio was considered as a benchmark for the identification of backwardness. It was considered that there is a need for special assistance to the educationally backward States to overcome the historically obtaining disadvantages and also for reduction of regional disparities in educational development. The district-wise data of various indicators of educational development, however, show that the inter-District variations are more significant then the inter-State variations. Moreover, the State is too large and variegated an area to serve as a homogeneous unit for educational planning. Therefore, educationally backward districts would be identified and special inputs would be provided in proportion to the degree of backwardness. The Working Group on early childhood and elementary education had ranked the districts in

terms of a composite indicator giving equal weight to four parameters of general/female literacy and general/female GER - primary. Although, almost all districts in the top 200 backward districts were from backward States, there is no guarantee that assistance to backward States will necessarily flow to backward districts within them. During the Eighth Plan; accordingly, the backward districts irrespective of the State where they are located, will be targetted. A more systematic study to identify the criteria for educational backwardness of districts and the ranking of the districts in terms of the selected indices on the basis of latest Census data, as a basic tool for investment decision would also be initiated.

11. Special efforts will be made to bring down construction cost of school buildings and other educational structures using available materials and adopting locally relevant architectural styles. Attention will be given as much to full utilisation of resources as to larger allocation, e.g., more intensive use of buildings by operation of double shifts in schools and of equipment by inter-institutional sharing.

12. In the case of teacher education, the stress will be on improving the standard of pre-service teacher education institutions and the quality of its programmes, providing continuing education of a suitable kind to every teacher educator and to a substantial number of teachers and on creation of a system to discourage setting up of substandard institutions and phasing out of existing substandard ones.

13. Time-bound, area-specific and cost-effective TL campaigns by involving all sections of society, specially students and non-governmental organisations would be expanded. While the whole adult education programme will be debureaucratised, the strategies of ensuring continued political commitment, strong administrative support, use

of traditional and non-traditional media and cultural and art forms will be adopted. Students and teachers of universities, colleges and schools would be involved in a big way not only by awarding marks to students for their literacy work but also by making literacy work as a part of curriculum.

14. Apart from consolidation, and expansion of secondary education increasingly through the open channel, the stress during the Eighth Plan will be on qualitative upgradation of secondary education through reorientation of its content and process, examination reform, diversification by way of vocationalisation and modernisation by way of technological inputs.

N.B: The revised policy formulation relating to the NPE, 1986 which was placed before parliament on 7th May., 1992 should be kept in view while working out details of programmes under General Education, University and Higher Education and Technical Education.

The Eighth Plan is being launched in the backdrop of acceptance by the NDC of the recommendations of the Report of the Narasimha Rao Committee which has removed the uncertainties regarding the continuance of CSSs in Education Sector. All the existing CSSs will be continued. Introduction of new CSSs would require approval of full Planning Commission but they may be taken up in the priority areas when justified.

Primary Education

Early Childhood Education (ECE). It would be expanded by attaching pre-primary classes to selected primary schools. Voluntary agencies and other NGOs would be encouraged and provided financial assistance by reorganising the scheme of ECE. Integrated Child Development Scheme (ICDS) model would be supplemented by Balwadis, Creches and Vikas Wadis.

Non-formal Centres. Primary schools or alternatives to primary schools like non-formal centres etc. would be provided to every child within a walking distance of one kilometer, with suitable adjustment for special cases. Voluntary agencies, factories, cooperatives etc. would be encouraged to set up part-time primary schools to serve several groups of children belonging to hilly, desert, marshy, forest areas and nomadic tribes, seasonal migrants, urban poor etc with freedom -to adjust the number of school days, instructional hours and appoint teachers on contract basis.

Shikshakarmi. Innovative programmes like Shikshakarmi which have given good results in an experimental project in Rajasthan would be expanded. Besides, a range of activities that suit the requirements of specific groups of learners, who are usually left out of the ambit of large scale projects, would be taken up. Opening of night schools in urban areas, pre-primary and lower primary centres for children of 3-9 years of age, 'half-time' instructors and special projects to tackle educational problems of areas with concentration of child labour would be tried out.

Open Schools. Open schools would involve themselves in the post-primary stage education on an experimental basis to provide wider access to children who are working or not in a position to attend regular schools due to socio-economic or any other reasons.

Increase Enrolment. Special efforts will be made to increase enrolment rates and improve participation rates at the upper-primary stage especially in respect of girls. Hence, while ensuring effective universal access to all children at the primary stage, the infrastructure at the upper-primary stage will have to be considerably expanded.

Quality of Education. Besides expansion of school facilities, there will be need to improve the quality of education by providing existing schools with sufficient facilities. Therefore, the "Operation Blackboard" scheme will not only be continued and completed during the Eighth Plan in relation to primary schools but also extended to upper primary schools. The eventual aim would be to move towards a situation where every class has a classroom and a teacher.

Universalisation of Education. In order to expedite universalisation of middle stage education and increase the enrolment of girls, the ratio between primary and upper primary schools would be brought down from the existing 1: 4 to at least 1: 3 with the ultimate aim of 1: 2.

Tribal Sub-plan. Apart from expanding Tribal Sub-Plan (TSP) and Special Component Plan (SCP), special measure are required for promotion of education of SCs/STs Certain sub-castes, tribes and communities need particular attention because literacy rates among them are extremely low. The existing scheme of residential ashram schools will be expanded to cover classes from I to X and scholarship schemes for talented children at the secondary level would be expanded. This will be supplemented by the scheme of voluntary schools wherever possible. Suitable incentives will be provided to all educationally backward sections of society, particularly in rural areas. Hill and desert districts, remote and inacccessible areas and islands will be provided adequate institutional infrastructure. Greater attention will be paid to the educationally backward minorities keeping in view the recommendations of the·Empowered Committee on Minority Education (1991).

Infrastructure

A system of incentives to overcome social, economic and educational handicaps, which lead to high incidence of dropout has been an integral part of educational planning for universalisation since long. A recent evaluation of these schemes has made a positive assessment but has also emphasised the need for paying adequate attention to management aspects of the system so that they yield the desired results. A comprehensive package of incentives and support services for girls, SCs, STs and children of the economically weaker sections of society will be provided. The emphasis will be on provision of facilities that have special relevance for retention of girls, such as establishment of Day Care Centres for pre-school children and infants, provision of free uniforms, textbooks and stationery, attendance allowance and coordination of support services such as drinking water, fodder and fuel to release children, especially girls as well as women from related domestic chores.

The Assessment

A National Evaluation Organisation (NEO) will be set up to undertake assessment of student learning on national scale on a sample basis to implement the strategy of MLL.

The Vigilance

Annual sample studies to estimate the completion rates as envisaged in NPE, vis., "number of children of about 11 years of age completing five years of schooling or its equivalent through the formal/non-formal stream" will be undertaken. The data of completion rates and MLL will be used to set targets for the States under the 20-Point Programme also:

A comprehensive computerised institutional and related data base at the district level will be developed so that information, relevant not only to monitor the internal efficiency of the educational system, both formal and non-formal, but also to improve the planning and management at the district level, is available in time. Computerisation would be extended to all districts of the country in phases.

Training Facilities

Statutory status will be accorded to the National Council for Teacher Education (NCTE) to lay down and maintain standards in institutions and courses. The schemes of DIETS, STEIs and

IASEs would be continued and their coverage expanded with a view to strengthening the institutional infrastructure and programmes of teacher education. The scheme of strengthening of SCERTs would be sanctioned and implemented and suitable measures for selection and professional development of staff in SCERTs, DIETs and IASEs will be undertaken. A large number of teachers will be covered through in-service programmes, both institutional and distance education, and reputed professional organisations will be encouraged to conduct inservice and refresher courses for teachers.' Open universities at the national and State level will be encouraged to introduce induction teacher training courses to supplement the efforts of the existing training institutions. The bulk of seats in teachers' training colleges would be reserved for rural women.

Literacy programmes will be launched in districts/regions which are educationally backward or have high concentration of SC/ST population or have low female literacy. By the close of the Eighth Plan, 345 districts including about two-thirds of all districts in the educationally backward States would be covered by the TL campaigns, while the centre-based approach would be gradually phased out and confined to hilly, tribal and sparsely populated regions. The strategy for backward districts would be two-fold. First, a few blocks would be selected where the literacy campaign can achieve success within a reasonable period. The demonstration effect of the blocks would influence the backward blocks which, in course of time, could develop appropriate literacy programmes. Secondly, the voluntary base in educationally backward districts being somewhat weak, ways and means of identification, strengthening and expansion of the same would be evolved in consultation with the respective State Governments. It is also necessary to develop technical competence among voluntary agencies so that the partnership between the Government and the operating agencies becomes meaningful.

The possibility of further enhancing contributions from the community especially in urban areas and industrial towns would be explored so that apart from voluntary service, at least 20 per cent of the total expenditure on the campaign may be met.

In States, where library movement is strong, rural libraries should be integrated with the JSNs which are envisaged as innovative post-literacy and continuing education centres. Reputed NGOs, educational institutions, distinguished individuals, ex-servicemen, war widows, award winning teachers, etc., will be encouraged to set up and run JSNs. Particular attention would be paid to the availability of a variety of quality materials in adequate quantity to the neo-literates. Reputed printing presses and publishers would be motivated to print gratis literacy materials, posters and charts.

The academic and technical support to Adult Education programmes would be provided by the newly set up NIAE, which would be involved to a greater extent in various aspects of training, action research and monitoring, so that the Directorate of Adult Education can be phased out by the end of the Eighth Plan. At the State level, the State Resource Centres will be strengthened.

The scheme of SVs, which provide a variety of training programme to the industrial workers and their families would be extended to cover workers in unorganised sector and would also experiment with a variety of training models including distance education.

The contents of adult education would also include inculcation of values like secularism, national integration, scientific temperament, small family norm, concern for environmental conservation, cultural appreciation, and so on.

The expansion of secondary schools would be regulated and new schools opened on selective many avenues for continuing education in the context of the march towards a learning society, in which open schools and open universities would play an important role.

Basis, particularly to cater to the needs of deprived sections like girls and SCs/STs and in rural areas generally. Quality improvement and the raising of the internal efficiency of the existing (10 + 2) system would be emphasised. While an increasing number of students may like to discontinue their formal studies either temporarily or permanently after 10 + 2, there would be provision for there re-entry into the education system at a later stage. For this purpose, education would be linked to the world of work by expanding the facilities and improving the quality of vocational education as also provision of subjectwise examination credits.

For widening the reach, an open channel of education would be provided to those who do not have access to regular institutions because of socio-economic and locational constraints and those who have already entered the world of work but are keen to improve their skills and income generating capacity. Open education programmes will be imparted with the help of multi-media packages and contact centres.

Open Education

The NOS will continue its existing programmes and revise the syllabi and textbooks for the secondary/senior secondary courses and bring out a fresh set of instructional materials for the bridge course. It will develop and introduce vocational courses, especially in the areas of health, agriculture and rural development in collaboration with the concerned departments. The coverage is expected to increase progressively with registration of more and more accredited institutions, which now number 191. It should also coordinate and standardise the work of similar State-level mechanisms. The idea of starting state level open schools in all the States as recommended by the Conference of Boards of Secondary Education should be pursued. The NOS is expected to provide programme and resource support to State-level Open Schools. The setting up of a national Consortium on Open Education to facilitate accreditation of courses and of maintenance of quality through a process of networking and evaluation should be pursued by NOS in cooperation with the Indira Gandhi National Open University (IGNOU).

Professional Education

The courses which have already been started would be consolidated. Special attention will be given to paramedical vocational courses to meet the needs of health manpower in the Eighth Plan. In addition to vocational courses. In addition to vocational courses forming part of the higher secondary courses, efforts would be made to offer varied courses of suitable duration to women, rural and tribal students and deprived sections of society. These courses may be coordinated with the working of Krishi Vigyan Kendras/organisations which offer training for self-employment. Non-formal, flexible and need-based vocational programmes would be made available to neo-literate youth who have completed primary education, to the school dropouts, to persons engaged in work and to the unemployed or partially employed persons. Institutions of Open Education will be actively involved in this area. Suitable programmes would also be started for the handicapped.

Candidates who have completed vocational courses should have ample opportunities for career improvement and professional growth. For this purpose, bridge courses which would give them an opportunity to take up higher technical and professional courses should be a necessary component.

It is essential that experimental projects with other vocational education models are also tried out, e.g., pre-vocational education at the lower secondary level, exposure to various occupations right from the primary level for attitudinal change, etc. It is also proposed to involve major industrial houses and all large projects and to prevail on them to include human resource development as part of project cost. The services of commercial agencies and NGOs will also be utilised.

The target for the Eighth Plan would be to cover about 200 blocks by following the composite area approach to the planning and implementation of the integrated education for the disabled. Crucial areas like health, physical and art education should be made an integral part of school curriculum and accorded parity with other subjects. It is necessary that the work of NCERT in the area of Value Education is supplemented by work at the State level by SCERTs and measures to enrich teacher education. The CSS for introduction of Yoga in schools should be implemented more effectively and comprehensively. The activities of the national Population Education Project would be directed, in addition to the formal schools, towards the non-formal sector for which the curriculum, material development and facilitator orientation would have to be specially developed. It is proposed to continue assistance to State Institutes of Educational Technology (SIET) and to extend in a phased manner facilities for Educational TV programme production. The government is committed to the establishment of Navodaya Vidyalayas in each of the districts of the country. The construction work for the existing 275 Vidyalayas would be completed. The possibilities of reducing the cost of construction and expenditure towards infrastructure will be explored. The-setting up of new NVs in all the remaining districts will be appropriately programmed keeping in view the stipulated target date. In view of the key role of computers in modernisation of Secondary Education, the CLASS Project will be. continued in a modified form and would cover 15,000 higher secondary schools by 1997. The project will be implemented with the collaboration of private agencies, with the elements of accountability and monitoring built in. The physical facilities and characteristics of the selected schools will be ascertained prior to the launching of the project. Full-time teachers will be provided for computer literacy by the private organisation and this subject will be taught during the normal school hours unlike the earlier practice of teaching it beyond school hours. The existing schemes of improvement of science education and environmental orientation to school education would be strengthened by improving teacher training inputs. A new scheme for improvement ox teaching of Mathematics at school level is being started. The NCERT would undertake Sixth Education Survey and a scheme for examination reforms apart from watching implementation of National Curricular Framework and MLL.

Promotion of Languages

For the implementation of the Three Language Formula in a uniform manner, 100 per cent financial assistance for appointment and training of modern Indian language teachers in Hindi-speaking States is envisaged. The Bureau for Promotion of Urdu would be accorded an autonomous status as per the recommendations of Jafri Committee. The long pending Sindhi Vikas Board would be established. The Education Department would collaborate with the Department of Electronics (DoE) in the project 'Technological Development in Indian Languages'. For promotion of classical languages, a national level body is proposed to be set up for maintaining, coordinating and improving teaching of Sanskrit and classical languages as also Arabic and Persian.

Sanskrit organisations for promoting Sanskrit learning would be fully utilised by reorganising and developing the existing ones. Vedic learning and its linkage with modern scientific development under the Rashtriya Veda Vidya Prathisthan (Vedic Endowment) will be strengthened. The scheme of scholarships to upgrade the merit of SC/ST students would be revised with respect to number of awards and amount in consultation with State Governments.

The number of awards under other schemes would be suitably enhanced so as to increase coverage and make them attractive. To foster book mindedness in the country, a Readers' Club Movement would be introduced. The National Book Trust intends to set up a National Centre for Children's Literature with the aim of producing 3000 titles every year. Under its Adan Pradan Scheme, translations of a large number of significant books from various Indian languages would be brought out. Besides developing manuscripts for neoliterates and school dropouts by organising workshops in various States, the NBT would provide assistance to publishers and voluntary agencies for production of books. The school Library Programme under OB would continue. A National Society of Authors is envisaged to oversee the interests and needs of authors.

Educational Administration

The Eighth Plan would focus on decentralisation of planning and management activities; providing autonomy to educational institutions; building capabilities for the involvement and participation of the stake-holders in the educational process and building up of capabilities and professional competence among the administrators and voluntary associations and NGOs. The State Advisory Board of Education (SABE) would provide strong advisory support for training, research and dissemination of information on methodologies of planning and management strategies appropriate to the State level and to the district-level bodies, namely the. DBEs referred to earlier. The existing bodies like Central Advisory Board of Education (CABE), UGC, NCERT and NIEPA would be strengthened. The CABE needs to be reorganised and should have a number of sub-committees to continuously review and monitor the progress in specific areas of education. A standing committee of CABE on Open Education is proposed to be set up. For streamlining the flow of information and developing the planning capacity at the district level, an Educational Management Information System (EMIS) covering all the districts in the country needs to be operationalised by the end of the Eighth Plan. The National Informatic Centre (NIC) has already developed a comprehensive computer network linking all the districts with computers. There is need to coordinate the working of educational management information system with NIC network. Following steps are also necessary to improve the system of educational statistics:

(1) Compulsory registration of non-reognised educational institutions; (2) More extensive use of sample surveys to monitor. the progress in respect of some critical indicators of educational development; (3) Continuation of educational surveys conducted by NCERT by clearly defining their frequency and objectives vis-a-vis other sources of data; (4) Construction of composite indicators of educational development of various States/districts and periodical monitoring of their behaviour; (5) Coordination between various sub-sectoral agencies for sharing of information; (6) Development of a comprehensive methodology and a sound data base on private costs of education to rationalise and to improve the efficiency in the use of financial resources.

Fiscal Provisions

The NPE statement that from the Eighth Plan onwards, the outlay on Education would uniformly exceed 6 per cent of the national income would be treated as a guideline for allocation of resources during the Eighth Plan. The present public sector allocation is much lower and requires to be appropriately stepped up. a conscious effort to tap various avenues for raising resources for education needs to be made. In view of the paucity of domestic resources, vigorous efforts to attract external assistance for financing educational programmes, especially priority programmes without compromising country's basic educational policies is necessary. While the external funding would be an additionality to the resources for education, the externally-aided projects would be in total conformity with the national policies, strategies and programmes and drawn up on innovative lines emphasising people's participation, improvement of quality, equality of education and substantial upgradation of facilities. The project formulation would be the responsibility of implementation agencies. At present, India is availing of bilateral assistance for Shiksha Karmi Project in Rajasthan and Mahila Samakhya Project in Uttar Pradesh, Gujarat and Karnataka. Within the broad objectives of the Eighth Plan, it is proposed to take up externally-aided projects, both bilateral and multi-lateral in various educationally backward States for promotion of basic education which includes : primary schooling, non-formal education, adult literacy, women's education and development and post-literacy and continuing education. Such projects are at various stages of development in respect of Bihar, Rajasthan, U.E and South Orissa.

The actual expenditure on general education sector in the Seventh Plan was Rs. 6549.57 crores, of which Rs. 2294.57 crores were in the Central Plan and Rs. 4255.00 crores in the State Plan.

Higher Education

Improvement of quality and consolidation continued to be the main concerns in the field of higher education during the Seventh Plan. The enrolment of students in 1991-92 was 44.25 lakhs — 36.93 lakhs in affiliated colleges and 7.32 lakhs in university departments. Women students totaled 14.37 lakh (34.2 per cent) and the enrolment, of SCs/STs was about 10 per cent. The growth of student enrolment which was 5 per cent per annum upto 1985-86, declined from 1986-87 onwards to around 4.1 per cent. The enrolment in the Correspondence Courses and Open Universities at the end of the Seventh Plan was approximately 5 lakh students, out of which the Indira Gandhi National Open University (IGNOU) alone accounted for more than one lakh students. The number of universities rose to 177, including 29 "deemed" universities.

The NPE had suggested: (1) creation of autonomous university departments and colleges; (2) State Councils of Higher Education (SCHE); (3) enhanced support to research; (4) strengthening of Open Universities (OUs) and Distance Education (DE); (5) consolidation of existing institutions and improvement of quality of teachers and teaching; (6) mechanism for delinking degrees from jobs; (7) establishment of a new pattern of Rural Universities; and (8) establishment of an apex body covering higher education in all areas.

Eleven more colleges were granted autonomous status, thus bringing the total number of such colleges to 106 till December 1991. Under the Academic Staff College Scheme for orientation of newly recruited and in-service college/university teachers, 48 academic staff colleges have been established, which organised 464 Orientation and Refresher Courses covering 12,970 teachers upto December 1991. An SCHE, may be elaborated, was established in Andhra Pradesh. The University Grants Commission (UGC) provided developmental grants to Central universities and 95 State universities, besides assisting more than 3000 colleges for general development programmes and for implementation of special programmes. About 295 departments received special assistance under different programmes such as Centres of Advanced Study (CAS), Departments of Special Assistance (DSAs) and Departmental Research Support. Under the Programme of Coordinated Strengthening of Infrastructure in Science & Technology (COSIST), 112 departments were assisted. To support educational broadcasts, the UGC has set up 7 audio-visual research centres and 7 education media research centres for production of softwares. As many as 2332 programmes, popularly known as Country-wide Classroom Programmes, have already been produced. A new organisation called Inter-University Consortium of Educational Communication (IUCEC) is being set up. Programmes like Teacher Fellowships and Research Fellowships for SC/ST candidates and remedial teaching for weaker sections including minorities were continued. The UGC provided assistance for installation of mini/macro-Computer Systems to 110 universities and 1216 colleges. In collaboration with the Department of Electronics (DoE), several courses in Computer Science were run. An information and library network called "INFLIBNET" has also been proposed. With a view to providing common research facilities and services of the highest quality, inter-university centres in Nuclear Science, Astronomy & Astrophysics and Atomic Energy were established. The IGNOU widened the access to higher education by providing opportunities to learners from disadvantaged groups like women, people living in backward regions and hilly areas with an enrolment of 1.64 lakhs by March, 1992. The Research Councils — Indian Council of Social Science Research (ICSSR), Indian Council of Historical Research (ICHR) and Indian Council of Philosophical Research (ICPR) continued their activities relating to support of research in respective areas.

The Priorities

The higher education system at present suffers from several weaknesses, such as proliferation of substandard institutions, failure to maintain academic calendar, outdated curriculum, disparities in the quality of education and lack of adequate support for research. Recent consultations including the "Brain-Storming" session organised by the Planning Commission to consider future directions have underlined the following thrust areas :

(1) Integrated approach to higher education; (2) Excellence in higher education; (3) Expansion of education in an equitable and cost-effective manner, in the process making the higher education system financially self-supporting; (4) Making higher education relevant in the context of changing socio-economic scenario; (5) Promotion of value education; and (6) Strengthening of management system in the universities.

The strategy for achieving the goals in these thrust areas would be as follows :

1. At present, the higher education, system comprising of general, technical, medical and agricultural streams, is fragmented in terms of structures and policies. Greater cooperation among the streams should be encouraged by promoting networking, sharing of facilities and

development of manpower including teachers' training/orientation facilities. There should be greater coherence in policy and planning. To adequately meet these requirements, the NPE had envisaged the establishment of a National Council of Higher Education (NCHE). This has, however, not made progress so far and a coordination mechanism should be constituted during the Plan period.

2. Several measures will be taken to promote excellence. The, NPE\POA proposal for establishment of a National Accreditation Council (NAC) would be followed up. Apart from continuing the existing programmes of CAS/DAS, COSIST and the inter-university centres, IUCEC and the proposed INFLIBNET, new inter-university centres would be established to provide facilities in the emerging areas like Biotechnology, Atmospheric Science, Oceanography, Electronics and Computer Sciences. Facilities for computer education would be further strengthened in collaboration with the Department. of Electronics. Model curricula for all disciplines have already been prepared but their implementation needs to be monitored. The suggestions of the working Group constituted by the Planning Commission to improve undergraduate courses in science and the teaching of mathematics at Indian universities/colleges would be implemented in a phased manner.

3. The additional enrolment in higher education during the Eighth Plan is estimated to be around 10 lakhs of which 9 lakhs will be at the undergraduate level. This expansion in higher education, keeping in view the present resource crunch has to be accommodated in an equitable and cost-effective manner mainly by large-scale expansion of Distance Education system and providing opportunities to larger segments of population, particularly the disadvantaged groups like women and people living in backward and hilly areas and by measures for resource generation.

The programmes of Distance Education should absorb at least 50 per cent of the additional enrolment during the Eighth Plan and their cumulative enrolment should reach 15 lakhs, including 5 lakhs adult learners beyond the normal age-group 17-23 who have left school long back. Open universities should also start innovative programmes of a vocational nature for meeting the learning needs of rural areas. Opening of new conventional universities and colleges should not be encouraged. Simultaneously, involvement of voluntary agencies and private sector participation in the opening and conduct of higher education institutions would be encouraged with proper checks to ensure maintenance of standards and facilities to make higher education as far as possible self-financing. However, the quality of education is not to be compromised at any cost. Upward revision of fee structure has to be considered but at the same time, the fees charged should not be exhorbitant and should be supplemented by the provision of scholarships and other financial assistance to SCs\STs and students below the poverty line and loans to other students.

4. The tremendous potential of 44.25 lakhs students enrolled in higher education has to be utilised by actively involving them in the programmes of adult literacy, continuing education, population education and other constructive activities. Such extension activities of the universities and colleges would be expanded to cover 95 universities and 2,500 colleges during the Eighth Plan.

5. The significance of Value Education has been highlighted by several committees and commissions on education. The Planning Commission has recently constituted a Core Group on value orientation in education. The recommendations of the Group will be considered for implementation in consultation with the Ministry of Human Resource

Development, UGC, Association of Indian Universities (AIU) and NCERT

6. Stress would also be laid on modernisation and restructuring of the management of university system which entails vigorous pursuit of the programmes of autonomous colleges and autonomous university departments. Facilities in universities and colleges, including research facilities, would be consolidated and strengthened. The schemes of redesigning and restructuring of courses to meet the developmental needs of the country, examination reforms and teachers' training would be expanded.

The research activities of ICSSR, ICHR, ICPR and Indian Institute of Advanced Study (IIAS), Shimla will receive specific attention for promotion of inter-disciplinary research. Action to support research in humanities which at present is neglected, would be taken up.

With a view to delinking degrees as a requirement for recruitment to services, the NPE visualised establishing a National Testing Service (NTS) to conduct tests on a voluntary basis and evolving norms of comparable competence across the nation to determine the suitability of candidates for specified jobs. Towards this end, the idea of setting up of an appropriate national organisation will be pursued.

A strong need has also been felt for providing training to personnel dealing with university administration, for which the existing infrastructure will be further strengthened rather than creating a separate organisation.

Controlling Finances

The Seventh Plan's actual expenditure on higher education was Rs.1201.13 crores, of which Rs. 659.96 crores was in Central Sector and Rs. 541.17 crores in State Sector.

Strategies, thrust areas and programmes as highlighted above, represent the priorities for implementation during the Eighth Plan. They are by no means exhaustive. Higher education is a vast sector and its significance as a source of new knowledge, research and manpower for preceding stages of education namely, elementary and secondary, should not be minimised. Adequate resources should be mobilised and provided to support the higher education sector so that the nation is fully equipped to face the challenges of the future, which is increasingly becoming information and knowledge-intensive.

Technical Streams

Technical education including Management education is one of the most potent means for creating skilled manpower required for developmental tasks of various sectors of the economy. Technical education incorporates the technological dimension which is a vehicle for development. While this implies high costs of construction, laboratory equipment, library books and journals and high rate of obsolescence, such high cost, being directly related to development, should be viewed as an essential productive investment, yielding valuable returns to the society and contributing to socio-economic development.

The Seventh Plan emphasised consolidation and optimum utilisation of existing infrastructural facilities, their upgradation and modernisation, identification of critical areas and creation of infrastructure in new areas of emerging technology, effective management of the overall system and institutional linkages between technical education and other development sectors.

Under the thrust areas programme of technical education 510 projects with a grant of Rs. 53.43 crore were supported for strengthening of facilities in the crucial areas of technology where weaknesses exist, 685 projects involving a grant of Rs. 76.84 crore were supported for creation of infrastructure in areas of emerging technologies and 202 projects involving of Rs. 27.1

crores were supported for programme of new technologies. A comprehensive report of requirement of instrumentation engineers at national level for the period 1990-2000 has been prepared by the National Technical Manpower Information System (NTMIS). The number of Community Polytechnics (CPs) increased to 159 with an annual training coverage of 20,000 rural youth and women.

The following new schemes were started as part of the implementation of NPE :

Continuing Education : The scheme envisaged preparation and dissemination of course material packages suited to the needs of. industry. Under the scheme implemented by 5 Indian Institutes of Technology (IITs) 4 Technical Training Teachers' Institutes (TTTIs), 1 Indian Society of Technical Education (ISTE), 4 engineering colleges/university departments and 4 polytechnics, more than 30,000 working professionals have undergone training.

Institution-Industry Interaction : Under the scheme, Proposals of 21 engineering colleges and 11 polytechnics have been approved for interaction with the industry.

Research & Development in Technical Education : 126 R & D Projects were supported.

New Perspective

The perspective of development of technical education for the Eighth Plan would have to take into account the following imbalances and distortions :

(i) During the past four decades, there has been a phenomenal expansion of technical education in the country. Today, we have over 200 recognised technical education institutions (TEIs) at the first degree level and more than 560 polytechnics at the diploma level with annual admission capacities of 40,000 and 80,000 students, respectively. About 140 institutions offer facilities for postgraduate studies and research in several specialised areas with an annual capacity of 9400 students. (ii) The quantitative expansion has resulted in the lowering of the standards and there exists a structural imbalance of skill requirement of the business sector and the traditional curriculum followed by the educational institutes. These factors give rise to problems of unemployment and under-employment. The wastage in the system is enormous, being 30 per cent at degree level, 35 per cent at diploma level and 45 per cent at post-graduate level. The situation in unrecognised institutions is still worse. A related phenomenon is that of brain-drain involving migration abroad of those trained in emerging areas in excellent institutes. (iii) The infrastructural facilities available in the vast majority of TEIs are extremely inadequate. There is an acute shortage of faculty with about 25 to 40 per cent of faculty positions remaining unfilled. In most of the institutions, there is hardly any R & D activity. (iv) The TEIs are functioning in isolation. Linkage and interaction between TEIs and user-agencies, such as industries, R & D and design organisations and development sectors are not sufficiently strong. Neither is there a strong interaction among institutions by way of sharing of facilities like equipments, libraries, teaching faculty and other resources. (v) There has been an enormous increase in public expenditure on education but little attention has been paid to the strategies for raising non-budgetary resources and maximising people's participation.

Fixed Goals

The thrust areas for the Eighth Plan have, therefore, been identified as follows :

(1) Modernisation and upgradation of infrastructural facilities. (2) Quality improvement in technical and management education. (3) Responding to new industrial policy and industry-institution R & D labs interaction, (4) Resource mobilisation (5) Institutional thrusts.

The strategy to be adopted to achieve these objectives would be on the following lines:

New Avtar

Modernisation relates both to technical equipments and teaching methods. Technology development is a capital-intensive process. The country cannot afford to go on changing the technology every year. It is, therefore, imperative to adopt futuristic approaches for achieving modernisation and self-reliance in a sustained manner. coordinated and concerted efforts would have to be made to upgrade and consolidate the infrastructural facilities in the existing institutions. The process of removal of obsolescence would include enhancement of computer facilities and establishment and interlinking of large computer systems with educational and research institutions through appropriate telecommunication facilities. Steps would be taken to strengthen and create the facilities in crucial areas of technology where weaknesses exist, in areas of emerging technologies and in new specialised fields. Upgradation of infrastructure would also include a crash programme for recruitment of about 10,000 teachers in polytechnics and colleges and strengthening of arrangements for teacher training.

Better Polytechnics

Central Government has launched a massive project with the assistance of the World Bank to enable the State Governments upgrade their polytechnics in capacity, quality and efficiency for the period 1990 to 1999. The project is being taken up in two phases with a total outlay of Rs. 1,892 crores. The first phase would cover 296 polytechnics recognised by the AICTE in eight States- Bihar, Gujarat, Karnataka, Kerala, M.P, Orissa, Rajasthan and Uttar Pradesh. The second phase would cover 262 polytechnics in Andhra Pradesh, Assam, Haryana, Himachal Pradesh, Maharashtra, Punjab, Tamil Nadu, West Bengal and

Delhi. The project has also a Central Sector Component for establishment of a national project implementation unit.

Improvement in Quality

A holistic and need-based approach would be adopted to reorient the technical and management education (TME). A more, broad-based flexible system with provision for multi-point entry is required to enable a better response to the unspecified demands of the future. At the micro-level, the curriculum would be developed to encourage creativity and innovation in experimental work by introducing problem/process oriented laboratory exercises. New technology-oriented entrepreneurship and management courses would be introduced in selected institutions having adequate infrastructural facilities. There would be greater emphasis on production engineering towards design and product development.

Technology on Path of Progress

The Government has recently established a Technology Information Forecasting and Assessment Council (TIFAC). Its objectives include : evaluation of existing technologies, preparation of technology forecast reports and estimation of the nature and quantum of likely demands for goods and services in future. It would be desirable to couple the technology forecasting system with the system of manpower forecasting and planning. Universities and IITs are familiar with the frontiers of knowledge and hence should play an important role in technical forecast and technological assessment with the fruitful involvement of TIFAC, Institute of Applied Manpower Research (IAMR) and the Indian trade and industries associations. It should be possible to develop the right type of indigenous technologies to assess the related manpower requirements and to produce such trained manpower.

The existing facilities for continuing education and retraining are inadequate. There is a need to formalise the retraining programme for engineering and technology personnel engaged in all sectors and to make them mandatory. Increasing use of modern communication devices should be made. Programme-learning packages need to be created and distance learning methodologies employed to enable self-development and training of all scientific and technical personnel.

Policy on Industries

There is a need to establish linkage between industry, national laboratories, developmental sectors, professional bodies, technical education, vocational education and craftsmen training and to bring about networking among institutions. In the context of the new industrial policy, the priority may be assigned to interaction with industry as it holds the key to industrial competitiveness in a global market. A strategy may be evolved for effective interaction between industry and institutions and for promotion of interaction through apprenticeship opportunities, consultancy and sponsored research, continuing education programmes for industry personnel, adjunct professorships in institutions for willing and capable personnel from industry, seconding of institutional faculty to industry, involvement of industry in the development of curricula and courses etc. for this purpose, organisational mechanisms such as Industrial Liaison Board, Industry-Institution Cells, Industrial Foundation etc., will have to be set up. The R & D activities may be taken up through the support of industry.

In this context, a reference may be made to a model for university-industry symbiosis conceived and implemented at Jawaharlal Nehru Technological University, Hyderabad for bringing about a greater and more effective interaction between technological university and industry. The model envisaged the setting up of a Bureau for Industrial Consultancy and Research and Development (BICARD) in universities/technical institutes of higher education, preparation of a comprehensive directory of technology experts to operationalise various aspects of interaction like orientation of university curriculum, exchange of experts between teaching institutions and industries, involvement of teaching staff in industry, technological database and self-reliance of institutions, etc. A national cell to promote and coordinate the linkages between the promotional agencies university, industry and R & D organisations has also been suggested. The revised model could be adopted/adapted with benefit by other TEIs.

Search for Resources

Since technical education is inherently expensive, concrete steps to ensure cost-effectiveness as an aspect of resource mobilisation are of vital importance. These include :

1. Avoidance of duplication of investment in TEIs located close to each other and proper maintenance of available facilities and instruments;
2. Developing institution-wise specialisation in respect of courses and technical manpower so that the institutions can have the most sophisticated and modern library and laboratory facilities in their chosen fields;
3. Weeding out of outdated and stereotyped courses and introduction of relevant courses in emerging areas;
4. Multiple use of infrastructural facilities through part-time courses, continuing education programmes and consultancy and testing services;
5. Marginal increase in intake capacities in areas of scarce manpower and decrease in intake of low demand areas. In this connection, an increase in the intake in better institutions by 10 per cent should receive urgent attention;
6. Introduction of multiple or at least double shifts in TEIs;
7. Maximum use of non-monetary inputs, like better planning, advanced technologies and practices, better system of supervision and administration, monitoring and review etc; and
8. Commercialisation of research work of the institutions.

The Task Force appointed by AICTE to go into the question of laying down tuition and other fees and to suggest other sources of mobilisation of resources for technical education has suggested raising of fees in relation to Government, Government-aided and unaided institutions on a graduated scale. A beginning has been made by raising fees in the IIMs. The IITs and other TEIs are also required to raise the fees. The measure of raising fees, however, should be coupled with scholarships for SCs/STs and for students below poverty line and a loan scheme for other students.

Creation of a corpus fund can be another way of mobilising resources for an institution, especially in the case of IITs. Contributions to the corpus fund will have to come from various sources viz. industry, alumni, charitable trusts, etc., as well as Government.

Another way of enhancing investment is to implement NPE/POA idea of requiring development departments to allocate a fixed percent of their annual budgets for development of TEIs. The question of collection of education cess from industry, which can thus share the cost of educating technical manpower and of giving tax exemption to industry for contributions made by it to development of technical education should also receive serious consideration.

Thrust of Organisations

The AICTE was given statutory status in 1988 in view of the need for maintaining and developing standards. It would be further strengthened to ensure coordinated development with its four regional committees located at Kanpur, Madras, Bombay and Calcutta. A Board of Accreditation is expected to be set up shortly and most of the schemes implemented by the Technical Education Bureau of the Department of Education are expected to be taken over by AICTE.

Technical Institutions

The UGC provides financial assistance to 32 institutions in engineering and technology for their overall development.

Although some of the institutions in this sector like Indian Institute of Science, Bangalore, are centres of excellence and this sector as a whole accounts for 1,600 M.E/M. Tech students, the financial allocations tend to be limited, as they are part of the overall UGC allocations. A separate mechanism may be set up which would advise UGC regarding the financial needs and priorities of these institutions and the Planning Commission should allocate appropriate earmarked outlays for this sector covering not only post-graduate education as in the past but also undergraduate education on a selective basis.

Institutes for Higher Studies

Sixteen State Governments and 24 non-Government post-graduate institutions are being assisted by the Central Government with a view to developing specialised fields of engineering/ technology having national relevance. The intake for post-graduate courses per year in engineering and technology is proposed to be increased from 10,000 to 11,000 by the end of Eighth Plan.

The new Industrial Policy has created an environment which requires IITs to adopt a new role as leaders in current and futuristic technology development. The following four areas for further action have been identified in the light of consultations held by Planning Commission :

(1) Thrust areas of technology development, (2) International consultancy, (3) Resource mobilisation and setting up of Corpus Fund and (4) Industrial Foundation.

The IITs

The technology development through innovation and its subsequent transfer to industry by five IITs would be the first step towards the identification of project mission and creation of appropriate environment. These project missions are conceived in three groups :

1. Areas where gains are likely to be visible in the long-term such as biotechnology, fuel-efficient engines, micro-electronics, photonics.
2. Areas where short-term gains can be planned, such as communication and software technology, food processing, instrumentation and central integrated production engineering and design, non-conventional energy, remote sensing and transportation.
3. Areas where results in the intermediate term are possible like coal, computer, integrated manufacturing, natural hazard mitigation and new materials technology. It is expected that each of the IITs would select a few areas from among those to work on during the Eighth Plan.

Global Consultancy

The IITs have a potential to offer educational and industrial consultancy services at international level. The consultancy would cover: institution building, establishment of specialised laboratory facilities, development of curricula, organising continuing education/joint research projects and faculty development etc. There is good scope for international consultancy assignments for IITs in South-East Asian and other countries. This can be a source of additional resource mobilisation.

Corporate Finances

Resource mobilisation measures would be taken up on the lines mentioned earlier, including corpus fund to which Government could contribute a block grant annually over a period of years subject to contributions from other sources. Ideas specific to IITs are: permitting them to charge from foreign students a full cost tuition fee in foreign exchange and obtaining an endowment grant from countries with an explicit commitment to training specified manpower for that country.

Industrial Basis

In order to facilitate interaction and collaboration with industry and other user-organisations in programmes of mutual interest, an industrial foundation needs to be set up in each IIT. The foundation would function as a registered society/corporate body linked to the parent-IIT, with financial and administrative autonomy and adopt industrial culture and methods. Resource generation of these foundations would be through Government grant/ corporate membership fees/overheads on projects and service/ donation and gifts etc. These foundations would render technical support to small scale industry and engineering entrepreneurs and develop products and processes at the request of industry. There would also be manpower exchange between IITs and industry.

Regional Colleges of Engineering

There are 17 Regional Engineering Colleges in the country which are joint ventures between Government of India and State Governments. They are expected to be pace-setting institutions in their regions. They need academic autonomy and their funding should be from one source, preferably Central Government. The ultimate aim should be to make them deemed universities. A proposal involving assistance of 6 million pound sterling to develop collaboration between RECs and some British Universities in the emerging areas such as design, materials, energy, informatics etc. is being worked out.

The IIMs

The four Indian institutes of Management set up as pace setting and premier centres of excellence in management education and research have been instrumental in producing highly qualified managerial manpower. Their activities need to be revamped, particularly keeping in view the changing scenario both at the national and international level. A consultation held by Planning Commission led to the suggestion that there should be links between management institutes and training institutes in specific sectors like health, rural development, agricultural extension etc. It was also suggested that there should be an integrated view of management education and there should be resource mobilisation, corpus fund, mutual sharing of facilities and division of labour in the matter of thrust areas etc. A plan of action is being prepared in this regard.

Polytechnics for All

It is proposed to cover all the remaining polytechnics under the scheme of CPs by suitably reorganising and strengthening them in the light of the recommendations of the National Expert Committee set up to appraise them. The Community Polytechnics are expected to play a major role in rural manpower development and their outreach should be expanded by resorting to distance education methods.

Provision of Finances

The actual expenditure on technical education in the Seventh Plan was Rs. 1083.34 crores of which Rs. 610.96 crores was in the Central Sector and Rs. 472.38 crores in the State Sector. The Eighth Plan outlays in the State Sector are required to be higher to reflect the implementation of the World Bank-assisted Technician Education Project.

11

Provision of Training

Teachers' Training

In olden times, there was no systematic provision for the education of teachers but it was assumed that, he alone had a right to teach who had acquired complete mastery over knowledge and could also translate it into practical life. In general, an individual won the right to teach when he had arrived at the stage of Vaanprastha ashram. By the time an individual had reached this age, he had acquired complete experience of life, and this was, in essence, the real training. In India, the imparting of education has always been regarded as a noble task, and the teachers of this country had so much renown and prestige that students from Tibet, China and Japan came here to study under them. In foreign countries, too, Indian teachers imparted education with a unique devotion. Society gave these teachers the highest respect because they were committed to bringing about the comprehensive and harmonious development of the student's personality. This sentiment is succinctly expressed in the statement '*aacharya devobhava*' which occurs in the paitriya Upanishad.

Even during the Buddhist and Jain periods, a teacher occupied a very respected place in society. It was presumed that he gave the student real self-knowledge. Respect was shown to him by saying *"Na devah shri guroh"*.

During the Middle Ages, *maktabs* and madrassas came into existence when the Arabic and Persian language won state patronage. A person well versed in religious rituals and performances was regarded as a good teacher. Some evidence of the monitorial system is found in each one of these three ages. The brilliant students guided their juniors in their studies and thus assisted their teachers.

The need for systematic education of teachers was felt during the British period. Its growth can be divided conveniently into three parts.

Monitorial System. Teachers used to give informal training in the art of teaching to their favourite students. The method was referred to as the class monitor method, in which each class or the whole school was divided into groups, and each group was placed under the charge of a brilliant student. This student taught his own group, and in this way he learnt the art of teaching by actual practice.

Teachers' Training. It was in 1881-82 that the Indian Education Commission, for the first time, put forward a suggestion for the training of teachers. First of all, the missionaries from Denmark set up the normal School at Serampur. Later on, similar schools came to be set up at Bombay, Calcutta and Madras also. The Commission offered the following suggestions for the training of teachers at the primary and secondary levels :

1. Training schools should be established at place from which they can conveniently fulfil the demand for teachers in all primary schools. At least one training school should be set up within the area administered by one inspector of schools.

2. Proper arrangements should be made for the setting up of normal schools and training of school inspectors from the funds made available by the regional governments for primary education.

3. Training schools should be spread over the entire country.

4. There should be separate curricula for graduate and pre-graduate teachers, and the programmes for their training should also be different.

5. Training should be an essential pre-requisite for teaching. A training school was set up at Madras in 1826, and between 1849 and 1859, the government established four Model Schools. Similar training institutions were set up in Uttar Pradesh (the erstwhile United Provinces) also. In 1904, the Indian Education Policy laid special stress upon the appointment of able and highly trained individuals to the Indian Education Service. A training period of one year was fixed for graduate teachers, and, in this training, importance was given to theory as well as practice. As a result of this recommendation, teacher training institutions began to grow in number. Different curricula were prepared for pre-graduate and graduate teachers and, in addition, model schools were attached to each teacher training centre. In 1913, the government took the definite step of declaring the policy that no individual should be allowed to teach, in the modern educational system as long as he did not possess a certificate providing his ability as a teacher. In 1910, the Calcutta University Commission introduced education as a subject at the intermediate and graduate levels. In 1929, the Hertog Committee suggested the introduction of refresher courses, and the idea was again stressed later by the Mudaliar and Radhakrishnan Committee. The Kothari Commission gave great importance to the establishment of intensive education colleges for the

training of teachers. Many suggestions were also given to eradicate the alienation which had crept into teacher education.

Various Types

Today, the educational process is divided into a number of levels or stages and for each stage, different kinds of teachers are required. Consequently, we have five distinct levels of teacher training.

Normal School. In these institutions, teachers are trained for imparting education to primary classes, and their training comprehends both basic training and general training.

Secondary Training School. In these schools, teachers are trained for giving education to students of middle schools.

Training Colleges. Teachers in these institutions are trained to teach high school students.

M.Ed. In these institutions, the emphasis is upon imparting training for research in the curricula of education after the candidate has obtained his B.Ed. degree.

Specialised Training. In these institutions, teachers are trained for imparting education in home science, art, industry, physical education and the pre-primary level, or in other specialised subjects.

Basic Problems

Absence of synchronisation between Training Establishments. According to K.G. Saiyidain, the candidate's knowledge of theory and actual conduct in the class-room remain two discrete elements, instead of blending with and strengthening or reinforcing each other. Hence, it is necessary that there should be a balance between theory and practice, so that the gulf between the schools and the training establishments is effectively bridged.

Imbalance between Theory and Practice. Training schools normally lay too much stress upon the principles or theory of teaching, whereas equal importance should be given to practice teaching and theory.

Lack of Suitable Curriculum. The curriculum of training is defective. The student is compelled to study subjects which bear no relationship whatsoever to actual teaching.

Neglect of Human Values. During training, the entire focus is upon objectives , goals, etc., while human values are completely neglected. In the opinion of K.G. Sayidain, the candidates are unable to visualise the fact that education is a specific social and cultural process. Because of lack of foresight and undue emphasis upon minor details or technical necessities, the close relationship of the school with society, the living problems of schools, and other important issues are lost sight of.

Absence of a Free, Untramelled Atmosphere. In training schools, the atmosphere of freedom is noticeably lacking, and because of the oppressive atmosphere, students are often seen indulging in flattery so that they may obtain good divisions.

Problem of Selection for Training. At present, training colleges are facing the problem of granting admissions, and undoubtedly, the choice of able and suitable individuals for training as teachers is a major problem.

In-service Training. In-service training takes within its ambit such activities as refresher courses, short term intensive curricula, practical knowledge of workshops, seminars, professional conferences, etc. However, even those suffer from numerous problems.

Traditional Influence. Even today, the curriculum is an ancient and traditional one, the ideal lessons are patently unpsychological, teaching aids are not used effectively and intelligently, considerable indifference and neglect are often displayed. In addition, the opportunities for frutiful discussion are few and far between, hostel facilities are often lacking, and opportunities for mutual contact and co-operation are negligible. S.N. Mukerjee has pointed out that in order to raise the standard of teacher training, attention should be paid to a proper management and organisation of the teachers' education programme, administration,' finance educational institutions, election for admission, pre-service education, practical training, in-service training, research into and publication of teacher training research work, preparation of college teachers and lack of concourse.

Prof. K.G. Sayidain has put forward the following suggestions for overcoming the shortcomings and problems of teacher's education:-

1. Each state should, with the assistance of its training colleges and department of education, carry out a survey at least once in every five years to ascertain the need for male and female teachers in all the schools of the state. Admissions to teacher training establishments should be based exclusively upon this estimate.
2. Short-term curricula should be prepared for the old and experienced teachers, who, for one reason or the other, could not take admission to training colleges. On receiving systematic training, these teachers will add to their efficiency, win promotions to higher ranks and feel more secure in their jobs.
3. Having made arrangements for the training of old and experienced teachers in the manner outlined above, the question now remains of those individuals who, having completed their college or university admission, wish to secure admission to a teacher's training institution. From among these candidates, only those individuals, who really possess the potential for becoming able and successful teachers, should be chosen.

4. The rough and ready, stereotyped methods in use for the selection of new candidates should be replaced by more effective, adequate and scientific techniques of selection. These techniques should be capable of accurate evaluation of the aspiring candidate's moral and mental qualities.
5. Individuals interested in adopting the teaching profession should keep in mind the needs of their future profession so that they do not acquire piecemeal knowledge and then seek admission to a training establishment. Such individuals should shun all knowledge which bears no relationship to teaching, which is to be their future profession.
6. As is the case in some universities, the science of education should be made one of the alternative or optional subjects.

The view of the Kothari Commission and the Secondary Education Commission is that in order to make professional education more effective, it is necessary to link it, on the one hand with universities, and on the other, with schools. Only then can the development of both aspects take place conveniently.

The following are the views of the Commission:-

1. Education should be introduced as an elective subject for the first as well as the second degree.
2. Universities should set up education colleges which may provide assistance in training teachers and research.
3. In order to bridge the gulf between training institutions and schools, there should be extension service departments at the pre-primary, primary and secondary levels in each training establishment. There should also be an organisation of old students, and it should offer its suggestions regarding the curriculum of training. Candidates receiving training should be sent to recognised

schools. The supervisory staff should be transferred from one school to another at regular intervals.

4. The distance and barriers between particular subjects such as arts, physical education, etc., should be done away with.
5. Training colleges should be raised to the same status and level as that of the colleges of universities.
6. State boards of education should be established at the state level.
7. The period of training for those who have received secondary education should be two years, while graduates should receive training for one year.
8. Proper arrangements should be made for part-time education.

Dr. Sampurnananda has stated that the nation should be conscious of the sentiments and needs of its teachers. On the other hand, it is expected of the teachers that they will provide able and devoted leaders in every sphere of life, despite the fact that the teachers themselves are compelled to live in circumstances which are not conducive to efficiency, skill or even self-respect.

In the context of teacher's education, Dr. Radhakrishnan has observed truthfully that the teacher occupies a very important place in society because he brings about the transfer of the intellectual tradition from one generation to the next. At the same time, he maintains the level of technological skill and keeps the light of civilisation burning bright. He not only guides the individual, he shows the whole nation the right direction. The Kothari Commission, too, has been constrained to observe that the most important thing is to create satisfactory conditions of work for the teachers of our country.

Prevailing Conditions

At the present time, the conditions of service and working conditions of teachers are truly pitiable. Today, we have two kinds of schools- (1) government administered, and (2) privately administered. Both kinds influence the conditions of service and work in their own respective ways.

Service and Working Conditions in Government-managed Schools. In schools managed by the government or local administrative bodies, the conditions of service are generally acceptable and tolerable. The teacher has no fear of losing his job, but when an educational plan is set into motion by administrators ignorant of the process of education, disorganisation is created. Teachers are often transferred to unsuitable places, and often, the transfers are the result of political influence, vested interests or individual influence. Only those teachers are able to derive any advantage who have contacts with officials in the administration. As a consequence, teachers feel constrained to seek the protection of some political pressure group or the other.

Privately Managed Schools. Private management of educational institutions has proved a curse at every level of education, in the context of service and working conditions of teachers. In fact, some schools and colleges have been turned into proftable business organisations. In these institutions, teachers are treated as no better than menials and slaves, and thus, the teachers are compelled to lick the boots of the managers. In other schools, the in-fighting between teachers themselves poses a danger to their very existence. The situation is so grave that even universities have fallen prey to such influences. And, there is no dearth of schools in which the teachers who work devotedly and seek to raise the standard of teaching and education through writing and authorship are served notices and subjected to pressures which render them intellectually impotent.

The Mudaliar Commission noted the sad state of teachers. It said that during its survey, it was sadly compelled to take note of the fact that the social level, salaries and other working conditions of teachers were very far from satisfactory. It was the committee's general view that the teacher's conditions had gradually deteriorated instead of improving.

The suggestions of the Mudaliar Commission with regard to service and working conditions of teachers are as follows:-

1. There should be a uniform policy throughout the country for the selection and appointment of teachers.
2. There should be a committee for the selection of teachers in all privately managed schools as well as those managed by local bodies, and the principal should be a member of this committee.
3. The period of probation should be one year.
4. The Triple Benefit Scheme should be implemented.
5. The principle of equal pay for equal work and equal ability should be applied.
6. Difficulties should be sorted out through the panchayat system, which should include the education director or his representative also.
7. At every stage of education, the children of teachers should be provided free education.
8. In order to improve the social position of teachers, their profession should get respect from all other classes of society.

The foregoing suggestions were put forward for improving the service conditions of teachers, but all that they did was to add to the grandeur of the report of the commission. No noticeable improvement, in the working and service conditions of teachers materialised.

Kothari Commission

The Kothari Commission felt that in such creative activities as research and teaching, stimulating opportunities are absolutely essential for professional development and improvement. They are no less important for attracting talented individuals to this profession, and for ensuring that they remain in the profession. The working conditions in schools should be such that they aid the teacher in achieving the highest levels of efficiency and skill. For this, they should receive certain facilities, such as : (1) facilities in the classroom, (2) necessary teaching materials, (3) facilities of libraries and laboratories, and (4) a proper ratio between students and teachers.

In addition, teachers should also possess adequate freedom to make experiments' in creative activities. They should be free to structure the curriculum according to the conditions existing in the classroom and to make modifications in the method of teaching. Hours of work should be similar to those of administrative officials, and these should include the time consumed in actual classroom teaching in preparing lessons, correction work, evaluation, organisation of teaching materials and extra-curricular activities, tutorials, seminars, guidance of students, student welfare activities, etc.

If the professional abilities and skills of teachers are to be improved, other facilities such as providing liberal leave facilities for attending seminars, for self-study and other intellectual activities, and giving opportunities for promotions to higher levels, are also essential. Reflecting on the rational of such facilities, the Kothari Commission opined that teachers should be given a concessional railway ticket for travel throughout India at least once in five years.

Working Conditions

Teachers can be expected to provide satisfactory results only when the working conditions created for them are suitable and satisfactory. In governmental institutions, service conditions are relatively satisfactory, but the real problem exists in privately managed institutions. In the latter, the administration does not hesitate to neglect or violate the rules laid down by the government. Managers and secretaries work according to their own sweet will. Rules pertaining to educational services should be different from those prevailing in administrative activities because the teachers cannot be tied down by such rules and procedures. For this reason, the Kothari Commission has forcefully suggested the framing of separate rules for the educational service. These rules should be conducive to the professional and individual growth of the teacher. The problems existing in privately managed institutions are : (1) private management boards have not laid down suitable conditions of service for the teachers, (2) the managements can, and do, terminate the services of teachers without due cause.

In order to overcome this difficulty, it is essential that the working and service conditions of teachers should be uniform. As far as termination of service is concerned, there should be a necessary condition that the teacher should be given a fair opportunity to present his case before a group of arbitrators (panchayat). This group should also contain at least one representative of the department of education.

The problem of housing is a very serious one for teachers. In rural areas, this problem is even more grievous. Because of it, the teacher's efficiency is undermined, and he has difficulty in establishing fruitful relations with the community. The following suggestions have been offered for overcoming these difficulties : (1) Every possible effort should be made to increase the housing facilities for teachers in rural areas. (2) The problem should be recognised and accepted as the responsibility of the local community. (3) Wherever possible, the state government should extend all possible aid. (4) Even in urban areas, the problem becomes very acute at certain times, though at others it may be less grave. Hence, programmes for housing construction should be taken up, and teachers should also be given a house rent allowance. (5) Teachers should be given a place in official housing schemes and also loans for constructing their own houses.

Facilities should also be provided to teachers in universities and affiliated colleges. Experience has shown that the universities which do offer housing facilities take advantage of renowned scholars by offering housing accommodation as a major inducement.

One major source of additional income for the teacher is tuition. Private tuitions have increased to such horrifying extent that only students from well-to-do families are able to take advantage of them, and hence, other students do not get equal opportunities of education. The education department of Rajasthan has issued an order to put an end to this malpractice. Other states should take similar steps.

Private coaching or tuition is an evil of the education system. Efforts should be made to ensure that the need for private coaching does not arise at all. It has often been observed that this practice flourishes either because the number of students is too large or because teachers do not perceive their responsibility correctly. The department (Education Department, Rajasthan) believes that the practice cannot be completely eradicated, but if all persons concerned with the problem become aware of it, its evil effects can certainly be mitigated. For this purpose both creative and administrative action is necessary.

At the school level, additional income is generated through guidance and the work of evaluating examination papers. Till the present, it was an established practice that the teacher was required to deposit a part of this income in the school. The Kothari Commission is of the view that a teacher should not be required to part with a percentage of his additional income as long as such additional income is less than 50 per cent of his salary.

Norms for Promotion

It is essential that the profession of teaching possesses avenues and prospects of promotion, because this is an important factor for attracting capable individuals to the profession. For this purpose, the following steps can be taken.

At the School Level. Trained teachers should get opportunities for progress in the future. These opportunities can take the following forms :

1. In primary schools, able and trained teachers should be promoted to the ranks of headmasters or inspectors.
2. The trained graduate teacher, who is doing praiseworthy work in his field, should be given the grades of post-graduate teachers.
3. Teachers of secondary schools possessing the requisite qualifications and ability should be given an opportunity to become teachers in colleges or universities. They should also be given research fellowships for further studies.
4. Teachers doing commendable work in the sphere of teaching can be given advance increments. In general, the teacher's pay scale stretches over 20 years. For 5% teachers at least, opportunities can be provided for reaching the maximum of the scale within ten years.

At the University Level. Though there is no provision for formal training of teachers at the university level, and neither has the need for this been felt, the following suggestions have been given to ensure their progress :

1. In universities, general temporary posts can be created for those honoured and devoted teachers of a scholarly nature who could not get promotion because of the lack of general permanent posts.
2. In post-graduate departments, posts of teachers should be created according to the actual needs of the department.

3. In consultation with the UGC, the pay scale of 1600-1800 can be given to teachers of proved ability.

4. The pay-scales and dearness allowances should be re-assessed every five years, and the dearness allowance should be equal to the allowance paid by the government to its other employees.

Welfare-promoting Activities. Now, some thought is being given to the question of welfare of teachers, but much remains to be done in this direction. The following steps can be considered:

1. A welfare fund for teachers should be established in the states as well as union territories. Teachers should contribute 1.5% of their salaries to this fund. It should be administered by a committee consisting of representatives of teachers and government officials. At a suitable time, the government should establish its own fund for this purpose and amalgamate the teacher's fund with it.

2. New pay-scales should immediately be given to teachers, and the central government should help the state governments in doing so.

Post-retirement Facilities. The facilities available to teachers after their retirement are almost non-existent. Consequently, no ambitious and able person feels attracted towards this profession. Some suggestions in this regard are :

1. Facilities of this nature should first be made available to teachers retiring from government schools, though later on they should be extended to teachers in private schools also.

2. For internal management, the Triple Benefit Scheme (pension, provident fund, insurance) should also be implemented.

3. The age of retirement should, in general, be 60 years, in schools as well as in colleges. Under special circumstances, this age limit may be raised to 65.

4. Teachers should get adequate interest on their provident fund. Their money should be invested responsibly and profitably.

Other General Facilities. Teachers are deprived even of the common facilities that are available as a matter of course to other ordinary citizens. These facilities, outlined below, should be made available to teachers also:-

1. Teachers should have the right to make the best use of their civic rights, such as contesting local, district, state or national level elections or work on any social position, though while engaged in such activities, they must take leave from their institutions.
2. There should be an increase in women teachers at every level. Besides, provisions must also be made for part-time employment.
3. In rural areas, housing facilities must be made available for women teachers.
4. The central social welfare department should introduce and propagate a condensed course for adult ladies.
5. Facilities for postal or correspondence education should be extended.
6. In rural areas, additional allowances may also be given to lady teachers, wherever such allowances are needed.
7. Teachers working in tribal areas should be given special allowances. Arrangements should be made for their housing as well as the education of their children.
8. Teachers working in tribal areas should be given special training also.

Teacher Organisations. Teachers will have to build up their own professional organisations to safeguard their own interests, as other professions have done. Events of the past have proved that teachers have been able to get their rights only through the medium of such organisations. The Kothari Commission has offered the following suggestions on the subject-

1. State and Central governments should recognise those unions of teachers which aim at the growth and development of education and the profession of teaching.
2. At the state level, joint teacher councils should be organised, and it should be entrusted with the task of reflecting on the problems of teachers.

National Awards. The Education Ministry should consider the following suggestions relating to national awards for teachers : (1) the number of national awards should be increased, (2) the selection for the awards should be objective, (3) the person selected for the award be given a travelling allowance equivalent to that of a Class I officer.

The development and growth of skill and efficiency in teaching means national development, but this becomes possible only when teachers possess a high social and moral status. And, respect for the teachers in the other classes of society will be generated only when their economic and social standards are improved. By making provision for the full use of civic rights by teachers, the Commission has taken a definite step towards winning for them a more respected place in society. It has suggested that teachers can contest local, district, state or national elections and also hold social positions.

The powerful vision of the Kothari Commission has fallen not only upon the other problems of education but also upon the real status and conditions of teachers. As a result, the Commission has sought to win for the teachers same social, economic and cultural position which was responsible for teachers being called gods, teachers and fathers in every preceding age. The truth is that, in the process of social struggle, the teacher had lost his position. Now, the Commission has made the government aware of this fact, and sought to restore to the teacher his pristine glory and importance.

The standards and criteria of teacher's education have changed. Today, it has become a powerful and inalienable aspect of national development. Its progress has taken place in the manner outlined below :

Training Facilities. In the last few years, facilities for training of teachers have grown manifold, and, as a consequence, the number of trained teachers has risen from 5% in 1951 to 38% in 1971. The following table reflects this growth for each level of education.

Progress in Teachers' Training

Schools	***% of Trained Teachers***	
	1951	***1971***
Primary	58.8	82.9
Middle	53.3	84.9
Secondary	53.8	81.2

This percentage had gone up even further by the end of the Fourth Plan period. The number of trained teachers has risen because of an expansion in facilities and the fact that training has become a compulsory prerequisite for teaching profession.

In spite of this, the facilities available for such training vary from state to state. When it has been accepted that training is essential for teaching, each state should make arrangements for training every teacher at the primary, middle and secondary levels. Thus, in Himachal Pradesh, Haryana, Punjab, Rajasthan (with the Exception of the Middle level), Andhra Pradesh, Kerala, Tamil Nadu, Gujarat, and the Union Territories (Chandigarh and Delhi) almost every teacher is a trained one. In the five year plans, further arrangements are being made for training of teachers.

It has been envisaged in the sixth plan that for the trained teachers who are unemployed special schemes have been prepared.

In-Service Training. Because of the expansion in training facilities, it has become possible to bring about an increase in the number of trained teachers. Despite this, there are teachers who are untrained or those who have to develop their abilities, and for this in-service training facilities have been provided. Surveys have revealed that at the primary and secondary levels, two-thirds of the untrained teachers are below 30 years of age while 80% of such teachers are less than 35 years. Obviously, these teachers are going to teach for many long years, arid hence it is essential that special arrangements should be made for their education. The following table throws light on the statistical findings of the second educational survey:-

Experienced Untrained Teachers

Experience (Years)	*Primary*	*Percentage Middle*	*Secondary*
4 years	58.24	59.21	62.55
5-8	19.03	19.61	17.87
9-12	9.36	9.44	8.36
13-16	5.36	5.59	4.87
17-20	4.05	3.22	2.94
20 & above	3.67	2.85	3.38

It has been noticed that the untrained teachers are not only young, they also possess a few years of teaching experience. Most of them need formal training. State governments must give fiscal as well as other incentives so that they may willingly obtain formal training. Special training programmes will also have to be introduced. Such teachers must be given knowledge of educational psychology, educational sociology, educational principles and school organisations, etc. Correspondence courses introduced by extension service centres can fulfil this need, while teachers already possessing formal training may supervise the practical aspect of this training.

Educational Qualifications. In order to make school education effective, it is essential to keep in view the educational qualifications of teachers. With the recent expansion in primary, secondary and graduate education, schools have now begun to employ only qualified teachers, but, in spite of this, there is no dearth of teachers in our schools even now who do not have the requisite academic qualifications. The following table provides the statistical details:-

Qualification of Teachers

Edn. Qualification	*Primary*	*Middle*	*Secondary*
Below Middle	1.92	13.09	0.31
Middle Pass	49.65		
Matric	41.27	49.65	8.75
Inter	4.64	11.83	5.25
Graduate	1.39	14.91	54.72
Post-Graduate	0.11	2.55	20.70
Others	0.98	7.92	10.70

The above statistical details have been taken from the second educational survey. From 1965 onwards, the situation has improved further, and yet, there are not a few teachers whose qualifications must be improved. Training establishments provide condensed courses for such teachers to fill the gap in their education.

It has also been observed that the dearth of educational facilities still exists, and that it has a negative impact. Hence, expansion of training facilities is essential. Besides, it is also noteworthy that many training establishments that do exist suffer from lack of laboratories, buildings, resources and other essentials.

Affiliation of Institutions. Many states do not have adequate training institutions and hence they fail to fulfil their demands for trained teachers. Secondly, the standard of training must also be improved. Efforts should be made to ensure that institutions lacking the requisite standards should not come into existence at all. And therefore, affiliation should be offered to them only when they fulfil all the necessary conditions and requirements. Consequently, the responsibility of the State Teacher Training Councils becomes even more onerous. Universities should offer affiliation to training schools only on the recommendation of this council, and in addition, these institutions should be subject to periodical and regular inspections and surveys.

Curriculum Reforms. There are many areas of the training curriculum which are crying out for suitable reforms, for which there are many programmes which do not involve substantial financial outlays. Reform of the curriculum is an important step in this direction. A critical evaluation of the curricula of training schools and colleges is essential, and its objective should be to eliminate unnecessary elements and to utilise the time thus saved for more important elements. The objectives of education should be clearly defined and programmes should be designed for achieving them. The teachers should have knowledge of teaching methods, not only content knowledge. The curriculum should be so designed that the teacher has context knowledge, he is trained through corrective teaching, he should have the cooperation and assistance of institutions and schools, and his vacations should be utilised creatively. Practice Teaching should be initiated at two distinct levels- (1) training should initially be given for one or two weeks to acquaint him with actual classroom conditions, (2) the Internship should be of a long duration, during which the trainee should remain in the school for his entire time and seek solutions to the problems he has faced.

Since the requirements of primary schools are different, the curriculum for this stage is in urgent need of reform. And, since the curriculum differs in nature in the tribal areas, this fact should also be kept in view. Special training will have to be given for teachers of single teacher schools as well as tribal schools. The teacher must remain in contact with the latest methods of imparting knowledge in reading, writing, arithmetic and other subjects. The teacher, teaching class first should develop his knowledge of health education, citizenship, community relations as well as aid to his work experience.

Criteria for Admission. Clearly specified criteria for admission to training institutions should be designed and laid down, the basis for which should be general mental ability as well as educational achievement. What is most important is a natural inclination towards teaching. The most able and interested individuals should be attracted towards teaching. In addition, training programme should also keep in view the needs of the teachers. There is almost invariably a shortage of teachers for certain subjects, such as science and mathematics. In many states, teaching of these subjects is being done by unqualified teachers. The imbalance between demand and supply, in this sphere. is due to the fact that sufficient caution is not exercised at the time of giving admissions to training schools. State governments, in order to make plans for long-term educational development, should keep in view the demand and the supply, as well as the available manpower.

In-service Training. Pre-service training is not the end of a teacher's professional preparation because it is essential for the teacher to remain in constant touch with the latest methods of teaching as well as the changes in content knowledge. Provisions should be made in service rules so that the teacher is compelled to receive in-service training. Similarly, the education code should also lay down rules compelling private schools to send their teachers for in-service training and refresher courses at regular intervals. The education departments should also be aware that such regulations are in fact being followed or not.

In-service training should be compulsory for every school and college, and wherever necessary, additional staff should be made available to these institutions. In addition, adequate financial aid should also be available to them. The purpose of refresher courses is two-fold : to increase the teacher's knowledge, and also to increase his content knowledge. For this purpose, summer courses (or courses during vacations) must be organised. for this, the teachers of colleges can be asked to extend their cooperation. In addition, it is equally necessary that extension service centres be set up in each training establishment, with adequate funds. Initially; the financial aid can be provided by the Union Government, while the NCERT can provide the necessary technical aid.

Training of Untrained Teachers. Even today, almost one-fourth of the teachers in primary and secondary schools are untrained, and in the eastern regions, the situation is even more deplorable because their percentage is even higher. During the fifth Five year plan, the following courses were introduced- (1) a training, course of one to two years for teachers with less than 8 years experience and below 35 years of age, and (2) correspondence courses along with the necessary practical training for the teachers with more than 8 years of experience and above 35 years of age.

Pace Setting Institutions. The qualitative objective or aim of teaching cannot be fulfilled. Training schools are prevented from carrying out experiment because of lack of material as well as faculty-related necessities. Hence, the activities of these institutions are stereotyped. Because of this, revolutionary changes are required in their role, mode of working and facilities. There is a need to increase the number of trained teachers, but for this,an unmanageable load cannot be thrust upon education. However, some selected institutions can be used for this purpose. Hence, it becomes necessary to establish a certain minimum standard for each training school and college, to establish a few institutions of this kind in each state, and to develop them accordingly. These institutions should be able to experiment with new ideas and methods and also help to guide other institutions.

Organisation of Teachers Education. In each state, the teachers' training programme should be organised in the best possible way. for this, an autonomous state teachers training council should be brought into existence, and the following functions entrusted to it:-

1. Making a long-term (five year) plan for the welfare of teachers.
2. Establishing teacher's training schools in accordance with the demand for teachers.
3. Providing advice regarding affiliation to universities and the state government.
4. Maintaining the standards of the state's training institutions.
5. Distributing aid to these training establishments.
6. Preparing the curriculum for training schools and colleges.
7. Making arrangements for in-service training.
8. Creating the necessary teaching materials and literature.

Teachers' Welfare. For the welfare of teachers (1) there should be a teacher training centre in each district (tehsil) where arrangements should exist both for entertainment as well as professional development, (2) on a co-operative basis, there should be provision for house construction as well as medical facilities and services. For this, the fifth plan has made a provision of Rs. 6.36 crores. In addition, a sum of Rs. one crore has been provided by the NCERT for research. Rs. 4.24 crores have been set aside for teacher training.

The teaching community, today, is divided into a number of classes or sub-classes, among which there is little or no interchange or intercourse. The primary teacher regards himself as inferior to the secondary, college or university teacher, just as the university teacher regards himself as far superior to all these other teachers and remains proudly alienated from them.

This alienation can be seen at three levels—

Isolation from University Life. The professional education of the primary teacher is not seen from the view-point which applies to university education. The professional education of the teacher at the secondary level is related to universities, but even that is little relationship with the other subjects taught in the university.

Distant from School Life. Teacher's education at the primary and secondary levels is distinct and distant from the modern development of colleges and college education.

Alienation from Each Other. In various ways, the various teacher training institutions are also alienated from each other, with the result that they have failed to create a cohesive community even among themselves.

Now, we will reflect upon the factors which may help alleviate the alienation pervading the sphere of teacher's education.

The Kothari Commission has felt that the nature of 'education' is different from that of other academic subjects, but despite this, it should be available to the common masses. In its view, education should be included in the main flow of the academic life of the university. In India, education is mainly associated with pedagogy, i.e., it is taught almost exclusively in training institutions, and only to those who have decided to enter the teaching profession. From the educational view-point, in the advanced countries, education is regarded as a separate, specific subject, comparable to any other social science. After assuming that education is a process of social, political and economic change, it is regarded as far removed from implementability or practicality like other philosophies or subjects. It is also worth mentioning that philosophers as well as social scientists, of recent years, have begun to pay special attention to education in their respective fields of specialised reflection. Having considered these factors, the Education Commission has. put forth the following suggestions for putting an end to this distance from the universities.

In order to make education significant and to increase its scope, it is essential that education be recognised as a social science, as an independent subject of academic study. In addition, education as a subject for study at the graduate and post-graduate levels, i.e., as an optional subject, should be offered on the basis of the following arguments:-

1. At the graduate level, the curriculum laid down should be oriented into three spheres - the sociological, philosophical, and psychological bases of education. The contributions of the great educationists, comparative education and some modern educational problems should form parts of the curriculum.

2. At the post-graduate level, there should be provisions for an M.Ed. degree. After the conclusion of the first degree, the time period of this latter degree should be two years. Besides, at this level, it should also be possible to combine the various subjects of the sciences and the humanities with education. Initially, it should be kept as an additional option also, and in order to encourage its study, scholarships can be offered to those who study it in order to become teachers.

3. In each of these curricula-the graduate and the post-graduate—there must be a certain minimum of teaching practice as compulsory, just as laboratory work is a compulsory part of science. The student may be required

to go through a period of internship or compulsory in-service summer course teaching so that he may become a fully qualified teacher.

The Kothari Commission has also recommended that, to bring about the desired result, the foregoing programme should be implemented by the University Grants Commission. In addition, it has also recommended the setting up of 'schools of education' in certain selected universities. In these, in addition to the normal teaching of various subjects, there should be provisions and facilities for training and research in education. Their functions should be as follows :

1. Laying down the curriculum for the graduate and post-graduate levels.
2. Making arrangements for the vocational training and education of teachers of various grades at the pre-primary, primary and secondary levels.
3. Arranging for the setting up of Extension Services in some training institutions at every level.
4. Organising summer courses and in-service courses in professional and other courses of study.
5. Conducting research into the curricula as well as methods of teaching with the help of students of all kinds.
6. Encouraging and developing research in education and considering the potential for interdisciplinary approach and research into it.
7. It has also been the considered view of the Commission that reputed scholars in various subjects should be attached to these institutions for short periods of time. These scholars should create acquaintance with the progress that has taken place in their various disciplines. Such programme will have two advantages (1) The study of education will

take place without teacher training or combined subjects; (2) Many talented students, after studying these subject, will be attracted towards teaching.

The distance from schools emanates from various causes, the main ones being the notion of standard and the idea of being superior or inferior. Training colleges can offer their cooperation for putting an end to this alienation, by offering their advice, at least to neighbouring schools, on such matters as planning of work, modes of teaching, etc. This extension work will benefit the training institutions as well as the schools. The Education Commission has recommended that at every level of training-pre-primary as well as secondary-there should be extension service centres, and their creation should be an integral part of the programme of training establishments. Members of the staff should participate in it regularly.

In this context, it is also worth mentioning that the NCERT has done commendable work in this direction. It has spread extension services to 50% institutions. Similarly, the National Institute of Basic Education, the State Institute of Education, etc., have also done some satisfactory work in this field.

In addition to the steps outlined above, there is another way in which training establishments can eradicate this distance, and that is through maintaining contact with their old students. These institutions should have old students associations through which, from time to time, there should be contact between old and new students, during which immediate educational problems can be discussed, along with new experiments, the implementation of new curricula and new methods and the possible problems that may arise in doing so.

In addition, the Education Commission has also suggested that this alienation may be ended by introducing internship programmes in training institutions. Under these, the teacher-students should spend their entire time in schools and participate in every activity of the school. But for the success of any such internship programme, close co-operation between schools as well as training institutions is of the essence. Obviously, teaching experience through actual practice can only be the consequence of a partnership between the producers (the training colleges) and the consumers (the schools). The educational department should give special recognition to schools selected for practice teaching, and as assisting schools, these should be given a special maintenance grant. In these spheres, the regional colleges have done pioneering work.

Apart from the internship programme, other schemes can be devised for eradicating this harmful alienation. These are, for instance-(1) Progressive teachers working in schools may be appointed on deputation to training colleges ; (2) teachers working in schools may be invited, from time to time, to participate in programmes organised in the training colleges; (3) teachers from the training colleges should go to the assisting schools for teaching work at regular intervals.

Programmes of this kind will produce the following advantages:-

1. Teachers of the training colleges will teach at least one unit of a subject to the students of a school for at least one month ; the effect of this can then be accurately evaluated.
2. Teachers will implement new methods of teaching and the principles of training and thus benefit the student teachers directly.
3. Schools will also come gradually to offer their cooperation in professional studies and educational research, and thus become active partners in a process intended, ultimately, for their own benefit.

At various levels, there is complete absence of harmony of exchange between the teachers themselves. Teachers working at the pre-primary and primary level have secondary level qualifications. Besides, there is a difference in their pay scales also. the distance between them is evinced thus :

1. Training institutions at the primary and pre-primary levels differ from those meant for the secondary level.
2. The pay-scales in these Institutions differ from each other.

Having reflected on both these factors, the Kothari Commission declared that an important reform in this direction is to develop the training establishments for the pre-primary and primary levels to the level of training colleges. Thus, the distance in teacher's training will come to an end.

The actual objective of this programme is- every kind of teacher's training should come within the jurisdiction of a university. It should be so organised that the co-operation of the educational unions and teachers' unions in the states may be advantageously exploited. Some universities have made considerable efforts for the education of teachers at the secondary level, but so far their attention has not turned to the pre-primary and primary levels. Hence, it is essential that this, too, should come within the jurisdiction of the university so as to ensure both the necessary freedom and autonomy as well as intellectual and educational efficiency at every level.

Considering this problem, the Education Commission has recommended that this programme should take three forms -

(i) Establishment of Comprehensive Colleges.
(ii) A programme for raising all training establishments to the college level.
(iii) Establishment of a State Board of Education which may become a link in the organisation of every such programme.

We will now reflect on each of these three situations.

The concept of a Comprehensive Education College implies an institution which provides education at every level of teaching :

primary, secondary, post-graduate, research, domestic science, arts and crafts. Such institutions will improve the standard of teaching. In Chandigarh, Allahabad, Kurukshetra, Trivandrum, and other universities, there are provisions only for M.Ed. and research. But, in fact, no obstacle really exists for dedicated and determined individuals.

Comprehensive Colleges. With reference to the Comprehensive Colleges, the Kothari Commission has opined that such colleges should be located at places where teachers for every level can be trained and prepared. Already, there are a few such institutions and they have produced good results. Now, the thing that is needed is that other institutions must be organised in a planned manner so that they may provide curricula and courses of study intended to produce pre primary, primary and secondary teachers through suitable education. So far, such schools produce teachers for the secondary level alone.

Improvement of Pre-primary and Primary Training Institutions. These institutions comprehend those establishments which train successful secondary or high school students for appointment as teachers at the primary level. For the improvement of these institutions, there is a dire need for a dynamic programme. The responsibility for devising a suitable curriculum and laying down the standards for admission should be taken by universities, and for this purpose, the Education Commission has suggested a period of 15 to 20 years.

State Board of Teacher Education. Today, teacher training is going on through the education departments and universities. A state board of teacher education can function as a bridge or link between the two. It should be constituted from among teachers of universities, representatives of the education departments, principals of teacher training colleges and representatives of teachers' unions, and it should be completely responsible for every conceivable kind of teacher's education at the state level. Its functions should be—

(i) Determining the standards in the teachers' training establishments.

(ii) Developing the curriculum, framing programmes, improving the examination system, arranging for and producing books as well as instructional materials for teachers' education.

(iii) Determining the essential conditions for training establishments and subjecting them to periodical inspections.

(iv) Giving advice to the institutions.

(v) Obtaining a commitment that the student in such institutions will be working in the state's schools after receiving training.

(vi) Making short as well as long-term programmes for the qualitative as well as quantitative improvement of teacher's education.

In this context, the Kothari Commission has suggested that, in each state, such a council should be set up by the state itself. It should also have a full-time secretary. The State's Institute of Education should be affiliated to it. Such a council should take upon itself all the functions of the institutions of pre-primary training, and also advise the training establishments producing teachers for the secondary levels, though such institutions may actually be affiliated to the universities.

The Reforms

The responsibility for the growth and development of the nation is thrust upon the shoulders of teachers, and, to a certain, extent, this is an undeniable fact. The training of the future generation is undoubtedly in the teacher's hands. It is, therefore, obvious that if the education of teachers does not improve qualitatively, the results for the future generations may well prove to be disastrous. When we speak of a qualitative improvement in this context, we mean an increase in the teacher's ability, skill and a broadening of his mental horizon.

What is urgently needed for a qualitative improvement in teacher's education at every level is Reorganisation, a reorganisation which must take place in the following spheres:-

Reorientation of Subject Knowledge. The purpose of such a scheme is that, during training at the primary and secondary level, the trainees should be imparted knowledge of the subject apart from information upon the modalities of teaching. The Kothari Commission's caution is that such a programme should be carefully planned. In it, the use of the given information in the light of basic facts and school subjects should be made sharply explicit. In addition, text books and other teaching materials should be presented at the level of the school as a measure of aid and help. At least 20% of the entire training time should be given over to a study of the subject itself.

In the context of any training there is the eternal question regarding the period of training essential for a specific level. In this context, the Kothari Commission has given two kinds of suggestions-

(i) At the primary level, the training period should be of two years. Where the period is at present of one year, it can conveniently be extended to two years:

(ii) At the secondary level, where the existing curriculum extends over one year, it should be extended to two years, as justice is never done to the curriculum in the short period prescribed at present.

However, the biggest obstacle in this context is that this task is not desirable from either the economic viewpoint or the practical. Consequently, the Education Commission has most wisely suggested that the working days in a year should be increased, from the present 180 or 190 days to at least 230 days. Since such an experiment has proved eminently successful in some training institutions, the Commission suggests that the change should immediately be implemented elsewhere also.

At the secondary level, the cooperation of teachers of the other departments of universities should also be sought for improving content knowledge. The Commission suggests that any such reorientation programme should be composed of the teaching method relevant to the subject as well as special techniques. The traditional ways of preparing lessons should be abandoned.

In this connection, another. suggestion of the Commission is the introduction of integrated curricula. A curriculum combining general as well as vocational elements should be evolved. Some experiments have been conducted in the USA in this direction. In India, too, the Education College of the Kurukshetra University prepared a four-year curriculum for post-high school studies, and five-year course was initiated in the regional college of education. But the departments of education and universities have, as yet not given recognition to these integrated curricula. Doubt has been expressed regarding the validity and success of such courses on the following grounds:-

1. After passing matriculation, the student is unable to decide whether he should become a teacher or not.
2. Students studying under the integrated curricula have not shown better than, or even comparable results, as those studying under the one-year curriculum.

With reference to the success of such. integrated curricula, the Commission has opined that if these integrated curricula are completely integrated, then, in its opinion, they will have a definite place in a new, varied and flexible system.

Vitalising Professional Studies. Many of the topics forming a part of professional or vocational studies at present lack real utility, and hence they should be eliminated. Professional studies should consist exclusively of topics which are useful for student teachers. It has been suggested that the real need is for the synthesizing and harmonising various curricula according to Indian conditions. The Commission's view is that these curricula suffer from the following two defects -

(i) In Indian conditions, because of the total absence or a minimum of research, the teacher educators generally take only theory, and their elaboration is replete with examples taken from foreign countries.

(ii) Teacher education is unfortunately replete with platitudes. The reason for this lies in the absence of a tendency to read the best books on the science of education. At the primary level, there is a distinct tendency to read cheap 'guides' or 'notes'. Another major obstacle is the lack of knowledge of a foreign language.

Improving Methods of Teaching and Evaluation. In training institutions, the methods for evaluating the performance of students, teachers are the traditional ones. Students adopt the following methods for getting the highest possible grades in the practical examinations - (1) pleading with the principals, doing domestic chores to please them, or indulging in back-biting against other teachers, (2) offering unnecessary gifts to the principals.

In the same manner, the principals either neglect or actually hinder the student teachers so that the latter may feel pressed to offer them gifts, work for them without charge, offer them refreshments, etc. At the time of examination, this neglect reaches its peak, and thus leads to a marked increase in gifts to the principals in the form of cash. It has also been noticed that such principals accept very expensive and numerous gifts from the aspiring candidates, with the result that first divisions are scattered broadly , while students too indigent to indulge in such gifts have to suffer loss of career. Obviously, there is urgent and dire need for a change in the modes of evaluating and testing-teacher's education. For this purpose, the Commission has offered the following suggestions:-

(i) Student-teachers should be brought to the required level of maturity through contact, experience, study and debates, for which independent 'study and the cooperation of students is essential. Unfortunately, they do not come with the pre-formed habits of self-study and independent thinking. Training institutions must try to overcome this handicap and accustom students to thinking, Belt-study and discussion. Individual work in the library, preparation of reports and analyses, case studies, project work, seminars, debates, conferences, etc., should be an integral part of the curriculum of training schools.

(ii) The attitudes of the students should be developed and made mature on the basis of human relations, and stress should be laid upon the importance of social values in the development of education.

(iii) In the developed countries, methods of teaching are constantly changing and developing. Such tools as radio, television, film-strips, programme instruction, language laboratories etc., have come into common use there. In India, too, radio and television have begun to broadcast lessons for schools.

Besides, an equally necessary improvement is the change in the system of examination. As in schools, so too in training schools, arrangements are made for external examinations. As long as examinations are not modified and improved, teachers will not adopt the modern methods of evaluation, and hence, there will be no improvement in evaluation through examinations at the school level. Hence, internal assessment must necessarily be recognised as an essential part of evaluation. Training schools should maintain cumulative records of the performance of their students, and the trainees must also be trained in the proper analysis of such records.

Improvement of Student-Teaching. The lessons imparted to student-teachers for training are not suitably planned, examined or evaluated. Most of the lessons are not examined at all, and, in addition, the period of practical teaching work is almost never more than 2 to 6 weeks.

In view of this, the Commission has suggested that student-training should be split into two stages:-

(i) The student-teacher should be made fully aware of the conditions in the schools as well as the actual conditions prevailing in the classroom during teaching.

(ii) The student-teacher should, at the second stage, be made to teach for a continuous period of at least eight weeks. Such teachers must be made to work as integral parts of the teaching staff, not as appendages.

Development of Special Programmes and Courses. As already pointed out above, it is essential for the development of education that new curricula and courses be developed. The Education Commission has spoken in terms of introducing 'education' as a subject at the graduate and post-graduate levels. There should be special courses for principals, and short-term courses for those about to assume the charge of a principal. Short courses should also be devised for educational trainers at the primary and secondary levels. There should be other programmes after the completion of which they can teach higher classes. At the primary and secondary levels, there should be composite courses. The Commission stresses that the devising of such programmes should be the combined responsibility of the NCERT, the department of education, and the National Association of Teacher Education.

Revision and Improvement of Curriculum. The Commission has expressed the hope that the curriculum be revaluated in the light of the suggestions of the Teacher Education

Commission. This revaluation should be oriented primarily towards utility. Its suggestions in this regard are:-

(i) The curriculum of teacher training is divided into two parts. In the theoretical part are the principles of education, child development and the psychology, modalities of teaching, organisation of schools and health education. In the practical aspect are such activities as practice teaching, craft, community life, etc. These subjects should be so reoriented as to create insight in the teacher regarding the school.

(ii) At the primary level, general education should be coextensive with training. They need a curriculum which can evolve a suitable social and cultural attitude to life.

(iii) For the purpose of practical teaching, conditions which are in consonance with the needs of modern society should be created. Fundamental facts should be kept in view while seeking solutions to problems.

What is noteworthy in this connection is that the general and vocational curriculum outlined above should prepare students to recognise and understand the role and importance of education in social, religious, political, economic change and development. As far as the question of initiating the study of 'education' at the M.A. level is concerned, the Commission has laid special stress on it. In its view, the prevailing curriculum fails to develop the requisite insight in the students.

The Commission has suggested some of the following points as the. basis for the curriculum of education at the M.A. level:-

(a) A core curriculum which affords the students opportunities to study the problems of education on a scientific basis.

(b) There should be specialised courses such as educational planning and administration, guidance and counselling, evaluation of teaching, or the psychological foundations of teaching, etc.

(c) Methods of research.

(d) Preparation of Dissertation.

Experience indicates that the standard of M.Ed. students is unsatisfactory because the qualification for admission is B.Ed. If M.A. (Education) is introduced, students will have developed a suitable attitude towards education by the time they arrive at this level, and the- time period for this course of study may it necessary be increased from two to three, or even more, years.

Various Institutions

The standard of teacher's education depends, to a large extent, upon the qualities, work and prestige of the training institutions. In general, such institutions are of two levels- (1) secondary, (2) primary.

The qualitative improvement of these institutions requires thinking in terms of teachers, students and facilities.

Teachers. According to a survey, 40% of the teachers at the secondary level institutions are only graduates, 55% teachers possess post-graduate degrees while 20% of them have Doctorate degrees. Their pay scales are almost equivalent to those of principals of other colleges. Hence, the teaching community of training colleges should be constituted thus- (i) In order to teach the secondary training course, post-graduate qualifications in two subjects should be necessary. Some of them should also have Doctorate degrees. They should also have experience of teaching and training teachers. (ii) They should not have specialised professional training in special subjects such as science, sociology, psychology and mathematics. In order to develop such a programme, the summer institutions should be well planned and organised.

Students. Students coming for teachers training do not possess sufficient content knowledge. In many states, teachers are required to teach even those subjects which they have not studied even at the graduate level. There are some subjects which the student studies only at the graduate level. At the secondary level, it is often difficult to get teachers with post-graduate qualifications in certain subjects. There is a serious dearth of good and qualified teachers for mathematics, science and english. For this, the Commission has suggested that - (i) No student should be allowed to specialise in any subject which he has not studied at the B.A. Level. (ii) Teachers should be required to teach at school only those subjects which they have actually studied at the graduate level. If they are given other subjects, it must be necessary for them to obtain the requisite qualifications in those subjects. (iii) Only first and second class students should be selected for teachers training, and they should also be given necessary scholarships.

Facilities. Many of the training establishments are lacking in hostel facilities. The Commission has laid stress on the creation, use and improvement of libraries, reading rooms, laboratories, teaching aids, etc.

Training establishments responsible for preparing primary teachers are in an even worse plight. Their development should encompass the improvement of teachers, students and facilities.

Teachers. The teachers in such institutions come from secondary schools, though completely lacking the ability to train their wards. Their pay scales are also low. Good teachers do not prefer to go to training institutions. The following are the suggestions of the Commission for bringing about the desired improvements- (a) Teachers imparting training to primary teachers should have post-graduate qualifications, apart from possessing B.Ed. degrees. Primary teachers should possess special training. (b) Only those individuals should be employed as teachers in primary schools who have themselves completed a minimum of 10 years in school, though a little flexibility in this rule may be observed with respect to women and tribal areas.

Students. Another problem in these establishments is the advent of students, because most of the applicants have not received even general education. The following suggestions have been preferred- (a) Liberality must be exercised for education through posts as well as granting leave for studies. (b) Students who have passed their B.A. and wish to teach in primary schools should be required to pass special courses. (c) The period of training should be two years.

Facilities. The following facilities should be made available for a qualitative improvement of training establishments for primary teachers- (i) Tuition fees should be eliminated, and instead, loans and scholarships should be made available. (ii) Every training establishment should have an experimental or demonstration school. (iii) There should be adequate housing facilities for the staff as well as the students. (iv) Libraries, laboratories, workshops, etc, should be available. (v) Similar improvements on the same basis should be made for the other teachers also.

The Education Commission has suggested that the following general conditions for the qualitative improvement of training institutions should also be considered:—

Facilities Available

Opportunities for training should be made available on a priority basis. The purpose of this is, that, at the time of appointment, the applicant should be trained. If he is not trained, he should be sent for training. In view of this, the Commission has opined that:-

(i) Each State should expand and enlarge its training colleges according to its needs, and make arrangements for in-service training also.

(ii) Part-time as well as correspondence education should be expanded, but, in doing so, care must be taken to ensure that the standard of full-time institutions does not deteriorate.

(iii) Untrained teachers should be trained at the earliest.

(iv) The size of training colleges should be large, and they should also be properly planned.

Knowledge is expanding and growing at such a rapid pace that if teachers do not keep in touch with it, their existing knowledge will soon lose its utility. Hence—

(i) At every level, every teacher should be compulsorily required to undergo a three-month in-service training course once in five years.

(ii) Summer Institutes should be expanded for the purpose of in-service training.

Professional Aspects

It is generally observed that teachers engaged in higher education apparently do not need training but when they are faced with the actual classroom situation, they get into serious difficulties. Hence -

(i) There should be arrangements for the proper training of junior lecturers.

(ii) Newly appointed teachers should be given an opportunity to assimilate themselves with the institution. They should be given chances to listen to old and experienced teachers with a reputation for scholarship.

(iii) Provisions should be made for orientation courses for new teachers in every college.

(iv) Such orientation courses should be run permanently by the universities.

Different Standards

At present, the standard of teacher's education is determined by traditional knowledge and methodology, but, as time changes, the standard of teacher's education is changing. In view of this—

(i) At the national level, the UGC should take upon itself the responsibility for fixing the standards for teachers. At the state level, the responsibility for improving the standards of teachers should lie with the State Board of Teacher Education.

(ii) The UGC should possess requisite funds under the various plans for, improving teacher education.

It is evident that any improvement in the quality of teacher's education can really be expected only when the above suggestions are seriously considered, and equally seriously implemented.

One question that has perennially been asked is whether teaching is a profession? Is it, like other professions, to be considered exclusively as a means to a livelihood? A glance at the pages of history dispels this notion. It tells us that it has never been an ideal vocation. Speaking about Brahmanic education, Lord William said that these places of teaching were constructed out of ordinary mud. Generally it was the teacher who made these huts at his own expense, and the teacher begged, not merely. to create the hut, but even to feed his students. This shows that teaching has always been a profession which makes human beings, a profession with its own unique traditions. In this connection, the regional service/extension department of the National Educational Organisation has put forward the following eight points:-

1. A profession should be necessarily equipped with intellectual tendencies.

2. A profession should have opportunities for various kinds of specialised skills and abilities.

3. A profession should also possess opportunities for regular and systematic promotion during the period of service.
4. A profession should possess opportunities for the necessary special training and preparation of those engaged in it.
5. A profession provides an occupation and a permanent membership for the entire life of the participant.
6. A profession generates its own standards.
7. A profession generates the desire for service even more than for personal gain.
8. A profession possesses strong professional organisations associated with it.

On the basis of these eight points or elements, T.M. Stinnet and Albert J. Huggett have established that education is not merely one of the professions, but the creative source or mother of all professions. Having accepted that education is a profession, it is essential to realise the programmes that are essential for making it a success. The Education Commission has offered numerous suggestions for making this profession attractive and interesting, the important ones being the following:-

1. Each State should formulate plans for creating facilities for training teachers on the basis of demand and supply.
2. Correspondence course and part-time curricula should be introduced on a large and extensive scale.
3. The size of training institutions should be enlarged and more facilities should be provided.
4. Teachers should be given opportunities for improving their professional skill during their period of service.
5. If a teacher lacks training at the time of appointment, he should be required to obtain training within three years.

6. At the level of higher education, junior lecturers should be given suitable opportunities for professional training and education.
7. New lecturers should be given a chance to listen to the lectures of old, experienced and scholarly teachers.
8. There should be orientation courses for new teachers.

The following are the suggestions of the Commission for improving the standards of teacher's education:-

1. The UGC should assume the responsibility for improving standards of teacher's education throughout the country, at the national level.
2. At the state level, this responsibility should be borne by the Teacher Education Council. It should also specify the acceptable standards.
3. Funds should be allocated for this purpose in the five year plans.
4. A permanent committee or council should be set up with the help of the UGC and the NCERT.

Education is a profession which, keeping itself completely away from black-marketing, corruption and other evil practices, gives rise to healthy traditions and thus helps to make concrete the dream of national development. When we accept that education is a profession, we must also accept its responsibilities and its burden. Dr. Carr's view is that an analysis of the existing circumstances and the potential for the future makes it evident that there is a universal tendency towards changing the new power and energy of the teacher- (a) people think that education and school are synonymous with each other, (b) seeking education means becoming a victim of the fad prevailing in education, (c) the greatest fear is that the public loses faith in the teacher.

Charles Lamb's view of the teacher is that he is aware, but he has no place of his own in the society of his own level. Amongst his young pupils, he comes as a Gulliver, but he cannot communicate his awareness to you. He cannot meet you at the crossing. He is so busily engaged in his teaching that he would like to teach even you. Lamb's statement reflects the devotion, the majesty but also the neglect of teaching. Prof. Vernan points out that the low level at which the teacher is compelled to work is the gift of those adults who, during their own student days, suffered from an inferiority complex.

Today, conditions have changed. The teacher will have to win to his own cause all those who believe him to be the maker of the nation. How can the teacher be the architect of his country? In the absence of a national educational policy, who will make the nation? The low salaries of the teacher are dispensed by the administration, the exploitation is done by the administration, the conditions of work are made insufferable by the administration, and yet it is claimed that it is the teacher who will build the nation. For this, the reason is that the teacher's objections make no dent upon the mind of the legislators. In view of this, it is necessary that the administration and the community must change its attitude towards the teacher who is being grounded to dust between the two grinding stones of the administration and the management.

The first duty of the administration is to nationalize education. The greatest advantage of such a move would be to put an end to the innumerable problems created by the community, and also generate a sense of equality. It should also modify the declared national educational policy to bring it into consonance with national requirements. It must also make every effort to isolate education from parochial politics so that education may devote itself to the building of a future society instead of seeking immediate and personal gains.

The following suggestions are taken from the 21st Conference of the Universal Teachers Council, for the improvement of teaching profession:-

1. Teachers should be given professional training and the latest knowledge.
2. Teachers at all levels should be treated as equals.
3. Teacher trainees should be kept in contact with actual conditions.
4. All teachers should be given equal opportunities for developing and improving themselves.
5. Unions of teachers should be established to safeguard the interests of the teachers.
6. The Administration should seek the cooperation of teachers in its work.
7. Educational programmes should be planned properly.

The profession of teaching should be developed as a technical profession. Teachers should get equality in such matters as scales of pay and facilities. They should also be remembered when posts with social status and awards are being distributed. If these steps are not taken, the poor teacher, who is living in an atmosphere of distrust and neglect, will once again have to take to revolutionary means to win for himself what society owes him.

12

FINANCIAL FACTORS

Fiscal Provisions

The biggest drawback of India's educational system has been that it has failed to fulfil its obligations towards the country's needs, and development. The main cause of this failure is the lack of proper planning of education. Whatever the government has been spending on education has been given as a kind of donation or charity, with the result that the education given as donation fails to develop either a national character or the individual's personality. It appears that the government is spending on education simply because it is levying taxes from the people and it feels obliged to spend something on education to forestall general criticism. The consequences of this approach are therefore for all of us to see, and we wonder what hell will soon be created as a result. If we want to develop the national structure and a national character in our people, the only alternative before us is to examine the problem of educational finance in the light of the investments made upon education and the benefits derived from this investment.

The important questions that stare us in the face when thinking about the problem of educational finance are the following:-

1. What is the total financial aid desirable for all levels of education if we wish to attain national objectives and bring about rapid development of our national economy, our national strength and security.

2. Which criteria and guiding principles can be accepted while distributing financial aid among the various levels of education, including research, as well as the various spheres at each particular level of education? Secondly, how dependable are these guiding principles?

3. Although quality and quantity cannot be completely divorced from each other, how much of the available resources should be invested upon improving the quality of education and what proportion should be spent upon the spread of education?

In considering these three questions, we should not overlook the fact that in 1846-47, the British government of India spent Rs. 57.7 crores upon education, which worked out to Rs. 1.8 per person, in view of the population then existing. The estimated expenditure during the third five year plan was Rs. 600 crores, which worked out to a per capita expenditure of Rs.12.

Five Year Plans

1. In 1951, the expenditure on education was 114 crores, which rose to Rs 600 crores by 1966, an average annual growth rate of 11.7 per cent. In the first plan, the growth rate was 10.6%, in the second 12.7%, and in the third 11.8%.

2. In the first plan, the per capita expenditure on education was Rs. 3.2 ; it rose to Rs. 4.8 by the end of the plan, while at the end of the second it was Rs. 7.8 and at the

end of third Rs.12.1. Taken together, this rise amounts to 278%.

3. In 1851, the total expenditure upon education was 2.2% of the national income, while in the first plan this percentage rose to 1.9, to 2.4 in the second and to 2.9% in the third, a total growth of 142%.

4. In the first three plans, the rate of expenditure upon education was 11.7% at prevailing prices. This amounted to 2.2 times of the growth rate of national income, which was 5.4%. It was 1.6 times the growth rate of enrolment and 2.7 times the growth rate in the number of teachers.

An analysis of these facts leads us to the following conclusions:-

1. Unfortunately, no attempt was made to covert the expenditure upon education in the country into fixed prices, though the price index of wholesale prices has risen by 53%.

2. Secondly, as compared to the situation in other countries, the percentage of national income spent upon education in India is very low.

3. The increase in the rate of educational expenditure is much faster than the growth rate of the economy.

Expenditure Pattern

It is evident that the expenditure in education can be split into two categories - (1) Direct expenditure, (2) Indirect expenditure. Direct expenditure includes the expenditure upon the three levels of education- primary, secondary and higher education. Indirect expenditure takes the form of expenditure upon buildings, hostels, scholarships. etc. This comprehends the entire field of education, and consequently we must direct our vision to every aspect of education to ensure that no aspect is neglected or rendered unbalanced.

The total expenditure on introductory education is quite low. The major share is spent on school education, and with the industrialization of society the expenditure upon education has risen. Secondly, expenditure is also rising because education is being made compulsory and universal.

Sources of Income

The money spent upon education in India does not come from any one single source. Because of a variety of social factors, many sources have evolved. The central, state or regional and local governments bear the burden of this expenditure. However, included in this are voluntary donations as well as donations from religious institutions, and this, fortunately, has made up for the dearth of resources.

The Education Commission has given deep thought to the sources of finance for education up to 1985-86. Because of the spread of education, the Central and State Governments will have to arrange for about 90 per cent of the total expenditure upon education. Accepting the importance of local agencies and voluntary donations, the Education Commission has said that although it is true that the major share of responsibility for supporting education should fall upon the government, it does not appear reasonable to put the entire financial burden for education upon the central government, since this will eliminate all incentive in financial matters among schools and local agencies. Though the finance thus made available may not amount to much, the fact remains that the administrative system under which this initiative functions or finds encouragement have great importance from the educational view-point. These initiatives or enterprises encourage guardians and local elements to take interest in education and bring about improvements in the standards education.

In view of the above, we now outline the sources of expenditure upon education in the following manners:-

Grants from the Central and State Governments. The central and state governments make investments for the spread of education and management of numerous institutions. They should be in harmony with the needs of the local community.

Donations from Local Autonomous Bodies. This category includes municipal boards and district boards, but the question is : how should these agencies make arrangements for financing the spread of education? Stress has been laid upon modifying the method of giving grants in order to assist the local agencies. We will now clarify the financial role played by municipal boards and district boards.

District School Boards. District councils can levy a cess upon the taxes on land. The grant given should be in proportion to this cess. The grants participating to salaries and allowances of teachers and educational employees should cover the entire expenditure. Finance for extracurricular expenditure should be provided according to the number of students. Two third of the non-recurring expenditure can be provided as a grant.

Municipalities. As the sources of income in cities are more then in rural areas, more money is collected by municipalities. Municipalities should levy a cess of all buildings and landed property, though attention must be paid to the nature of the municipality, the size of population, means available, etc. It would be best to classify 411 municipalities on the basis of their income.

New Sources

The achievement of the ambitions of the country comprehends within itself the knowledge, skill, interests and change in values of all its citizens. This fact is fundamental to every programme of social and economic change, of which India has dire need. This statement of the Education Commission clearly implies that the money spent upon education is an investment, and the future generation provides the return upon this investment to the nation. From this viewpoint, we feel that by 1985-86, we will be able to spend only Rs. 54 per person upon education, and if we compare this expenditure with that of other countries, our position is obviously and truly inglorious because the per capita expenditure upon education in other countries is as follows- Rs. 224 in Japan, Rs. 295 in France, Rs. 378 in Russia, Rs. 515 in England, and Rs.1175 in the U.S.A. In order to reduce this gap, we will have to take the following two steps:-

1. We must make every effort to reserve for education as large a share of the national production as possible.
2. If we want to bring into existence a single system of education which can satisfy individual as well as national needs, it is essential to put a stop to traditional methods of work, shortsighted use of resources and wastage.

If both these points are kept in mind, the following programmes for the proper use of educational finance can be implemented:-

1. The expenditure upon buildings should be curtailed as far as possible.
2. The equipment should be better designed, kept in working order and used for as long as possible.
3. Those techniques should be adopted and implemented on a large scale by means of which many schools can simultaneously take advantage of existing facilities.
4. Expensive equipment should be based on the basis of sharing.
5. School buildings should be utilised for as long a period as possible
6. Curtailment in the wastage of money in the educational sphere should be considered a national goal.

Studies conducted in a few other countries indicate that education has the greatest importance for economic development, but such studies have not been conducted in India. Considering the importance of this issue, the University Grants Commission should encourage studies of this nature in a few selected universities.

Major Hindrances

The third five year plan adheres to the view that for achieving social justice and equal opportunities and establishing the values of independence, education is the most important single factor which imparts dynamism to industrial progress, as well as to the social structure as a whole. It is evident from this that education is an important instrument of revolutionary change. People consider the government's expenditure upon education as a costly luxury but they forget that an important aspect of the people's welfare is the availability of educational opportunities. Hall and Lawrence have expressed the view that education, in each one of its forms, is an important means to national development. This means that education is a production activity. This concept has four aspects—

1. Education is production as well as consumption.
2. It gives indirect and imperceptible benefits.
3. The benefit derived from education depends upon the social and economic development.
4. It is the combination or product of the entire culture, and an important mode of expression for cultural values.

In view of its importance, our opinion is that the following steps must be taken to give educational finance an organised and systematic form:-

1. The structure of education should be completely overhauled, by which we mean that education should be nationalised The central government should take upon its own shoulders the burden of education. Regional factors lead to differences in the investment upon education and consequently differences in standards are also found.

2. It is often seen that the government does not take adequate interest in the development of education. State governments as well as the central government have had considerable experience of teacher movements. These governments measure their own efficiency in terms of the cuts they can make in the budget for education. This approach should be abandoned.

3. Parochial politics have come to dominate education, and it is only natural that this should have an impact upon educational finance. This influence must be prevented.

Clarifying the intimate relationship between educational planning and educational administration, Dr. V. K. R. V. Rao has laid stress upon (1) technical efficiency, (2) motivation, (3) organisation, (4) planning for the unemployed and partly employed manpower, and (5) planning technique. It is essential that education should be purposeful, it should have clearly defined goals. It should bring about the development of the individual's personality, intellect and character. For this goal to be achieved, it is essential that education should be properly planned, within the framework of the finance available for it. Planning implies science, rational thought and utilisation of natural resources. Hence, it is essential that the science known as educational management should undergo development. The basis for the development of the system of knowledge consists of a strong desire for economic development, a strong desire to take risks and show enterprise and initiative in economic activities, and to invest the desired amount from the increased income resulting from economic development upon education. This comprehends education in agriculture, industry, public administration and the professions.

Dr. Rao views education as an investment. He says that the money spent upon education assumes the form of a cost incurred for the purpose of economic development. The criterion of cost applies most suitably to the volume and content of education. In order to achieve the goal of economic development, education should aim not merely at productivity, but even its methodology and technique should be conducive to the achievement of the goal.

In the same context, J.P Naik has expressed the view that it was unfortunate that the Chinese aggression had an adverse impact upon our national resources because our resources, in the context of education, have become restricted. Secondly, during the British period, there was no correlation between national progress and education. The same situation continued to exist in the fourth plan. Hence, it can be said that, in the last few decades, an important feature of our planning was that, in the fourth plan, education and economic development were brought into direct relationship with each other.

Thus, it is evident that the roots of educational finance and its problematic nature lie in faulty educational planning. We can link our education, with economic growth only through proper planning of education, and this alone can bring about the welfare of the individual as well as the nation.

13

CONSTITUTIONAL GUARANTEE

Prior to 1947, education in India was conducted according to the educational system introduced by the British government. At this time, India was centrally administered, and the Centre and State governments worked in their own respective spheres. By the enactment of 1935, autonomous administration had come into existence in the states, as a result of which in 1937, Congress governments were established in 7 out of 11 states, while in the remaining, rule by the majority was introduced. It was at this time that education was given certain constitutional provisions. In 1937, the Wardha Scheme was accorded recognition for the purpose of creating universal, free education. Attention was given to every aspect of education.

The time was not auspicious for India. As a result of the World War II of 1939 and the bitter, cruel and malicious attitude of the British towards the people of India, Indians felt compelled to give up the self-government which had been granted to them by the British rulers. In 1944, after the victory of the Allies in World War II, the British administration once again turned its attention to the development of education in the post-war-period.

In consequence, the Sergeant Plan came into being. The last foreign government came into existence in India, which continued to function till August 15, 1947. After winning independence, the problem of developing education confronted us. The education ministries of the states and the centre devoted their best thought to facing this problem.

On January 26,1950, the People of India faithfully dedicated their Constitution to themselves, with the words-"We, the people of India, having solemnly resolved to constitute India, into a Sovereign Democratic Republic and to secure to all its citizens-Justice, social, economic and political, Liberty of thought, expression, belief, faith and worship; Equality of status and opportunity; and to promote among them all Fraternity assuring the dignity of the individual and the unity of the Nation in our Constituent Assembly do hereby adopt, enact and give to ourselves this Constitution. "The Constitution lays particular stress upon adult franchise, liberty, equality and social justice. For this reason, various provisions have been made for education in the Constitution itself."

Constitutional Provisions

The following provisions have been made in our Constitution regarding the rights pertaining to culture and education:-

Article 39 : Protection of the Interests on Minorities. (1) The constitution states that the citizens residing in any part of the country, but having their own language, script or culture, will have the right to maintain them.

1. Any educational institution supported by the government receiving aid from the government's funds will not have the right or deny the right of admission to any individual on the basis of religion, caste, creed or language, or any one of these bases.

Article 30 : The Right of Minorities to set up and administer educational institutions. (1) All Minorities based on religion or language will have the right to set up and administer institutions in their own interest.

2. In giving aid to educational institutions, the government will not discriminate against any institution on the basis of its being set up and administered by the particular religious or linguistic minority.

These two constitutional provisions can be analysed in the following manner. It is clear from the provisions that the government will not foist any language of its own choice on any minority. The minority status of a group will be determined on the basis of its population in the state. Every institution receiving aid from the government will have to keep in mind and secure the interests of the minorities. The rights of minorities will be secured against exploitation through corrupt political practices.

The same article also speaks of religion, caste, language and creed. These factors will not be taken into consideration in providing educational facilities. The reservation of some seats for particular groups will not be considered as a violation of the Constitution. At the same time, no educational institution will be entitled to refuse admission to any child on the basis of religion, caste, creed or language.

Article 45 : Provision of free and compulsory education for children. It is provided that the state shall endeavour to provide free and compulsory education to all children upto the age of 14 years, within ten years from the date of the adoption of the Constitution,.

This Article expresses the resolve of the people of India to make provisions for free and universal education. This Article does not violate the Constitution. Instead, it lays down guidelines for schools for obtaining aid from the government. Under Article 30 (1), the government can seek to achieve its objective of universal education through its own schools as well as schools receiving aid from the government.

Article 46 : Promoting the educational and economic interests of the Scheduled Castes, Tribal groups and other Weaker sections. The Constitution states that the State will protect and promote, with special care, the educational and economic interests of the weaker sections, particularly the Scheduled Castes and Scheduled Tribes, and also protect them against social injustices and exploitation of all kinds.

The objectives outlined in the above section do not enjoy any constitutional validity, which means that if backward classes do not get educational facilities, the law cannot help them. According to this Article, educational and economic development depends upon the will of the state. In 1951, a constitutional amendment was made to provide that efforts should necessarily be made for the backward and weaker sections of society.

Statutory Factors

In the Indian Constitution, education is specifically a state subject. The second paragraph in the Seventh Scheduled of the Constitution state's that notwithstanding the conditions stated in articles 63, 64, 65 and 66 of Schedule I and Article 25 of Schedule 3, the responsibility for education, including university education, will rest with the states.

The following provisions regarding education are contained in our Constitution—

Free and Compulsory Education. The framers of our Constitution foresaw that the widespread illiteracy in our country could not be eradicated without making education free and compulsory, and hence provision to this effect was made in Article 45 of the Constitution. It is provided that the state will provide for the free and compulsory education of all children upto the age of 14, within ten years from the date of adoption of the Constitution.

The Constitution clarifies the concept of state by stating that the term comprehends the government of India and Parliament, and the government of each state and legislative assembly, and local and other offices within the union territories, as well as other offices under its control.

Education of the Backward Classes. The Constitution has paid particular attention to the education of the backward classes. Constitution clarifies that the state will not be hindered, either by this Article or by para (2) of Article 29, from taking any steps for the progress of educationally and socially backward citizens or for making any special provisions for the Scheduled Tribes and Scheduled Castes.

Education of Women. Keeping in mind the basic right of equality, it has been stated in Article 15 (3), with reference to the education of women and children, that anything contained in this Article does not prevent the state from making special provisions for the education of women and children.

Religious Education. There are many religions in India, with very substantial numbers of followers. Though our country is itself a Secular state, the Constitution of our country has shown great awareness of that religious susceptibilities of the people. In Article 28, the following ideas have been expressed on the subject of religious education- (1) Any educational institution drawing its total financial assistance from the government's funds must not impart education of any religion. (2) The conditions in part (1) shall not apply to any educational institution administered by the state, but in the case of an institution established by a trust or a religious body, religious education may be carried on. (3) Any educational institution which receives aid from the government funds shall not compel any individual admitted to that institution to take part in any religious activities conducted in the institution or any place of worship attached to it, as long as Permission to do so has not been obtained from that individual, or, if he is a minor, from his guardians.

Religious education is the life-stream of Indian life, but having declared itself a secular state, the country cannot make arrangements for providing religious education of any kind. The Constitution has stated this condition very clearly. The Article cited back clarifies that in institutions of the first kind no religious education of any kind can be imparted while in institutions of the latter two kinds, it cannot be imparted by compulsion. And, the truth of the matter is, that religious belief is an individual and private matter, which cannot be turned into a social question. For this reason, religious education has been placed on an individual basis.

Protection of Language and Teaching of Language. The most controversial part of the Constitution is the part dealing with the teaching of languages. Article 29 (1) states that the citizens in any part of the country having their own specific language, script and culture, will have the right to maintain these languages, scripts and cultures. The Article clearly grants to the individual the right to choose his own culture and language, and it also clarifies that each state and its citizens will be free to choose their own language and culture.

Article 350 states that every individual has the right to give representation to an officer in state or central language.

Similarly, Article 350 (a) advises that education be imparted in the mother tongue, stating that it will be the endeavour of every state, and of every local official within the state, to provide suitable facilities for providing education to the children of linguistic minorities in their mother tongue at the primary stage. The President will have the right to direct a state to provide such facilities.

For the proper performance of this article, it has been stated in Article 350 (b) that—(1) there will be a special officer appointed by the President for linguistic minorities, (2) it will be the duty of this special officer to conduct research or studies into all subjects related to the notion of linguistic minorities, as defined in this Constitution, and to send suggestions to the President regarding these subjects. The President will place all such recommendations before each House of Parliament and also send them to the governments of the concerned states.

Hindi Language. On the question of Hindi, Article 351 of the Constitution states that it will be the duty of the Union to bring about the spread and progress of Hindi so that it can become the medium for the expression of all elements of the social culture of India but it is to do so by adopting words primarily from Sanskrit and secondarily from the other languages, by integrating into it the style, form and terminology of the languages mentioned in Schedule 8 of the Constitution, without however doing violence to the originality of Hindi itself.

Regional Languages. Articles 345, 346 and 347 express the views of the framers of the Constitution on the regional languages.

345 : State languages. While remaining within the bounds of the conditions of Articles 345 and 347, the Legislative Assembly of a state will by law, be able to accept any one, or all, or alternatively Hindi, of the languages used for any one or all of the state's purposes. However, it is also provided that as long as the State Legislative Assembly does not by law exercise this option, or if it does not make any other provision, English will be continued for all the purposes of the State, within the state, for which it was being used immediately prior to the introduction of the Constitution.

346: The State language for Communication between one state and another or between a state and the Union. The authorised language being used in the Union for official purposes will, for the time being, continue to be the official language for all communications between one state and another, or between a state and the union. However, if two or more states declare that the official language for communication between them will be Hindi, it may be so used.

347 : Special Provisions relating to a language spoken by a section of the population of a state. In the event of a supplementary demand being raised, if the President is convinced that an adequate proportion of the population of a state wants that the language spoken by it should be commonly known, the President may direct that an ordinance may be issued for the use of such a language in the state, or any part of it, for all or some specified purposes.

343: Official Language of the Union. It is stated herein that the official language of the Union will be Hindi,. in the Devnagri script. For official purposes, the Union will make use of international numerals.

Equal Opportunities for Education. India's democratic constitution provides for the creation of equal opportunities in education for all individuals, without any kind of discrimination whatsoever. Articles 29 and 30 contain this declaration. It is clarified therein that any educational institution receiving aid from the government, or recognised by the government; will not deny admission to any person on the basis of religion, caste, creed or race, or on any other basis. Article 30 provides that linguistic and religious minorities will have the right to set up and administer educational institutions of their own choice.

Protection of Monuments. The Constitution provides for the protection of monuments of national importance as a part of education. Article 49 states that every monument or place declared by the Parliament to be of national importance or artistic or cultural interest will be protected by the state.

The Three Lists

The Constitution contains three lists, dividing legislative powers between the States and the Union. These are—

The Union List. The Parliament can enact laws on the subjects contained in the Union list, of which Articles 13, 62, 63, 64, 65 and 66 pertain to education. The Union may keep these subjects under its own jurisdiction. These subjects are

1. Participating in international conferences, institutions or other agencies and implementing the decisions taken therein.
2. Protection and maintenance of the National Library, Indian Museum, Imperial War Museum, Victoria Memorial, India War Museum, and any other institution given partial or complete financial aid by the government of India, or any other institution lawfully declared by the Parliament to be of national importance.
3. At the commencement of this Constitution, the maintenance of institutions known by the name of Kashi Hindu University, Aligarh Muslim University, and Delhi University, as well as any other institution lawfully declared by Parliament to be of national importance.
4. Institutions receiving financial aid from the government of India, either partially or fully, or any institution lawfully declared to be of national importance by the Parliament, or technical education institutions.
5. Union agencies and institutions which (a) are meant for vocational, (*vratika*) or handicraft training, inclusive of institutions for the training of police officials, or (b) are meant for the development of special studies or researches, (c) are meant for providing scientific or technical assistance in the study of crime.
6. Determination of standards and bringing of uniformity into higher education, research institutions, scientific and technical institutions.
7. Merchant Navy and Navy include tide transportation and other related training and education.

The State List. States are authorised to enact legislation on the 66 subjects contained in this list.

1. This is inclusive of entries 63 to 66 of the Union List and Article 25 of the Concurrent list while remaining within the constraints of Article 25 of education, which also comprehends university education.
2. In entry 12, there are the libraries, museums or other similar institutions financed or managed by the state, and ancient and historical buildings and monuments (those not under the jurisdiction of parliament or declared by it to be of national importance).

The Concurrent List. In this list, there are 47 subjects on which laws can be enacted. Of these, the following two entries relate to education—

1. Economic and Social Planning.
2. Vocational and Craft training of workers.
3. J.P Naik has divided these activities into two parts—

Preventing Functions. These include (1) educational and cultural activation, (2) obtaining ideas and information about education, (3) creating co-ordination between the educational activities of states and the Union, and (4) education in the, sphere of states.

Concurrent Functions. These include (1) scientific research, (2) technical training, (3) developing and ensuring the spread of Hindi, (4) protecting national art and culture, (5) protection of language, (6) education of the handicapped, (7) educational research and co-operation, (8) protection of the cultural interests of the minorities, (9) protection of the interests of the Scheduled Castes and Tribes, (10) national unity, (11) providing scholarships to able students, (12) higher vocational training, (13) administering the central educational institutions, (14) making arrangements for providing free and compulsory education for children upto the age of 14.

Other Options

Many ideas have been expressed upon the constitutional provisions relating to education. Being a state subject, education has been the cause of considerable controversy and difference of opinion. The fact is that it was the British who had placed education in the state list, and the same tradition continues till the present.

The erstwhile parliamentarian, Dr. L.M. Singhvi had proposed that education be placed in the concurrent list. Welcoming the suggestion, Mr. M.C. Chagla said that in making the Constitution, it was a mistake to place education in the state list. However, education could now be put in the concurrent list only if the majority of the states favoured the change.

The Kothari Commission has voiced the view that after examining the issue in depth, it felt that education should not be divided into two, with one element in the state list and the other in the concurrent list. It felt that education must always be considered a single entity. In our opinion, the organisation expressed in our Constitution is the correct one for such a large country as India, because under the leadership of the centre, it will be able to develop unobstructed. Putting education into the concurrent list will bring into it the evils of centralisation, thus putting an end to the freedom of research, which is so essential for the growth and development of education. Although the Union and the States have not so far combined together to do the maximum for education, it is our confidence that the constitutional provisions provide adequate scope for the Union and the states to work satisfactorily in the field of education. After considering the matter in its entirety, it is our view that we have the opportunity to evolve a national policy on education by taking advantage of the constitutional provisions. The issue should be considered in depth after another ten years.

According to Dr. B.P Lulla the most important indication is to be found in the Preamble to the Constitution, according to which the citizens of the country will enjoy every kind of justice, freedom of thought and action, equality and brotherhood. The question is: what have schools and institutions of higher learning done in this regard? What changes have they made for the spread of the idea expressed above or for the organisation of students on these bases?

In reality, what has happened is that practical politics has turned to ridicule the educational provisions of the Constitution. We have neither achieved the objective of providing compulsory education nor succeeded in making Hindi the national language.

The governments of the country, too have been playing games with education. One erstwhile government placed education in the concurrent list, while the succeeding government returned it in the state list. It is obvious that the most important question here is: is it not essential, for maintaining the unity of the nation that a single system of education should exist throughout the country and receive its inspiration from the spirit of the Constitution?

Thus, it is essential that our political leaders, educational planners and administrators make their plans according to the instructions explicit and implicit in the Constitution so that the Constitution may get due respect and the country may move towards progress.

Bibliography

Addaval, S.B. (ed.): *The Third India Year Book of Education Educational Research,* NCERT, New Delhi, 1968.

Aggarwal, J.C. : *National Policy on Education,* Arya Book Depot, New Delhi, 1979.

Alva Myrdal : *"The Power of Education"*, Lancer Books, New York, 1965.

Anderson, C.A. and M.J. Bowman : *Education and Economic Development,* Frank Cass, London, 1971.

Aparna Basu : *The Growth of Education and Political Development in India,* Oxford University Press, Delhi, 1970.

Berdie, R.F. : *An Educational Technique*, 1949.

Biswas, Dutt Sunnittee : *The New Educational Pattern in India,* Vikas Publishing House. Delhi, 1916.

Bhatnagar : *Education and Social Change,* The Minerva Associates, Calcutta, 1972.

Brij Raj Chauhan, G. Narayan and T.R. Singh : *Scheduled Castes and Education,* Anu Publications, Meerut, 1975.

Buch, M.B., (ed.) : *Research in Education,* Centre of Advanced Study in Education, M.S. University of Baroda, Baroda, 1974.

Charles Jeffries : *Illiteracy : A World Problem*, Pall Mall Press London, 1967.

Chourasia, G. : *Challenges andInnovations in Education*, Sterling Publishers, New Delhi, 1977.

Denis, Lawton : *Education and Social Justice*, Sage Publications, London, 1977.

Desai, A.R. : "*Social Change and Educational Policy*", NCERT, New Delhi.

Dharni, P. Sinha : *Descriptive-cum-Critical Study of Education System*, Administrative Staff College of India, Hyderabad, 1976.

Don Adams : *Education and Modernisation in Asia*, Addison Wesley Publishing Company, London, 1970.

Ehsanul Haq : *Education and Political Culture in India*, Sterling Publishers, New Delhi, 1981.

Gandhi, M.K. : *My Views on Education*, Bharatiya Vidya Bhavan, Bombay, 1970.

Ganguly, S.N.: *Tradition, Modernity and Development*, MacMillan Company of India, Delhi, 1977.

Ghosh, S.C. (ed.) : *Educational Strategies in Developing Countries*, Sterling Publishers, New Delhi, 1976.

Goel, S.C., *Education and Economic Growth in India*, The MacMillan Company of India Ltd., Delhi, 1975.

Gopinathan Nair, P.R.: *Primary Education, Population Growth and Socio-Economic Change*, Allied Publishers, New Delhi, 1981.

Gore, M.S., and others (ed.) : *Sociology of Education*, NCERT, New Delhi, 1967.

Guilford, J.P. *Fundamental Statistics in Psychology and Education*, McGraw Hill, New York, 1965.

Inamdar, N.R.: *Educational Administration*, Popular Prakashan, Bombay, 1974,

Iqbal Narain : *Educational Administration,* Aalakli Publishers, Jaipur, 1976.

James, A.R. : *Vocation, Education and Guidance*, Charles E. Marril Publishing Co., Columbus, Ohio, 1970.

John W., Hanson and Cole S. Brem Beck: *Education and the Development of Nations,* Holt, Rinehart and Winston, New York, 1966.

John Vaizey : *Education for Tomorrow,* Penguin, London, 1966.

Joshi, R.N.: *Education—Elsewhere and Here,* Bharatiya Vidya Bhavan, Bombay, 1979.

Julian, E. Butter Worth and Howard A. Dawson : *The Modern Rural School,* McGraw Hill, New York, 1952.

Kamat, A.R. : *Educational Situation,* People's Publishing House, New Delhi, 1973.

Kishore Gandhi : *Issues and Choices in Higher Education,* B.R. Publishing Corporation, Delhi, 1977.

Kidd, J.R. : *Education for Perspective,* Indian Education Association, New Delhi, 1969.

Kochhar, S.K. : *Pivotal Issues in Indian Education*, Sterling, New Delhi, 1981.

Lakshmana Swamy Mudaliar A.: *Education in India*, Asia Publishing House, Bombay, 1960.

Louis Malassis : *Education and Development,* Croom Helm, London, 1976.

Mukherji, S.N. (ed.) : *Administration of Education in India.* Acharya Book Depot, Baroda, 1962.

Mukherjee, R.K : *The Social Structure of Values*, S. Chand & Company, New Delhi, 1964.

Naik, J.P. : *Policy and Performance in Indian Education*, Dr. K.G. Saiyidain Memorial Trust, New Delhi, 1955.

— *The Single Teacher School : Studies in Education and Psychology,* Ministry of Education, Government of India, 1953.

— *Educational Planning in India,* Allied Publishers, Bombay, 1965.

— *Education of the Scheduled Castes,* Occasional Monograph, ICSSR, New Delhi.

Niblett, W.R. : *Essential Education,* University of London, London,1955.

Nural Hasan, S. : *Challenges in Education, Culture and Social Welfare,* Allied Publishers, Bombay, 1977.

Oldhan, J.N. : *Village Education in India,* Oxford University Press, London, 1922.

Panchamukhi, P.R.: *"Financing of Primary Education in India",* NCERT, 1970.

Pandey, S.N. : *Education and Social Changes,* Motilal Banerasidas, Delhi, 1976.

Paulo Freire : *Education : The Practice of Freedom,* Writers and Readers Publishing Co-operative, London, 1976.

Prem Kripal : *A Decade of Education in India,* Indian Book Company, Delhi, 1968.

Premi, M.K. : *Educational Planning in India : Implications of Population Trends,* Sterling Publishers, New Delhi, 1972.

Raghunath Safaya : *Innovations and Latest Trends in Education,* The Associated Publishers, Ambala Cantt., 1976.

Rajagopal, M.V. : *Kothari Commission on School Education,* Telugu Vidyardhi Prachuranalu, Machilipatnam, 1967.

Rao, M.S. : *"Education Social Stratification and Mobility,"* NCERT, New Delhi, 1997.

Rao, V.K.R.V. : *Education and Human Resource Development,* Allied Publishers, Bombay, 1966.

Ratna, G. Revankar : *The Indian Constitution,* Associate University Press, Canbury, New Jersey, 1941.

Rudolph & Rudolph (ed.) : *Education and Politics in India,* Harvard University Press, Cambridge, 1972.

Russell, Bertrand : *Education and the Social Order,* Unwin, London, 1977.

— *On Education,* Unwin Books, London, 1971.

Saini, S.K.: *Development of Education in India,* Cosmo Publications, New Delhi, 1980

Sateswari Saxena : *Education Planning in India,* Sterling Publishers, New Delhi, 1974

Sharma, G.S. : *Educational and Cultural Development of the Minorities,* ICSSR, New Delhi, 1973.

Shipman, M.D.: *Education and Modernisation* : Faber and Faber London, 1971.

Shrimali, K.L.: *A Search for Values in Indian Education:* Vikas Publishers, Delhi, 1974

Shri Prakash : *Educational System of India,* Concept Publishing Company, Delhi, 1977.

Shukla, P.D. : *Towards the New Pattern of Education in India,* Sterling Publishers, New Delhi, 1976.

Singla M.M. : *The Constitution of India-Studies in Perspective,* The World Press, Calcutta, 1975,

Siqueira, T.N. : *The Education of India-History and Problems,* Oxford University Press, London, 1952.

Stephen J. Knezevich : *Administration of Public Education:* Harper and Brothers, New York, 1962.

Sundaram, P.S. : *Education or Catastrophe?* Vikas Publishing House, New Delhi, 1976.

Tiwari, D.D. : *Education at the Cross Roads,* Chugh Publications, Allahabad, 1975.

— *Thoughts on Education,* Chugh Publications, 1972.

Venkatasubramanian, K. : *Education and Learning,* N. Vidyaranya Swamy, Secunderabad, 1979.

